I0005072

CONFIGURING HUMAN RESOURCE MANAGEMENT WITHIN DYNAMICS AX 2012

BY MURRAY FIFE

© 2015 Blind Squirrel Publishing, LLC, All Rights
www.dynamicsaxcompanions.com

Copyright © 2015 Blind Squirrel Publishing, LLC

All Rights Reserved

ISBN-10: 1514817527

ISBN-13: 978-1514817520

© 2015 Blind Squirrel Publishing, LLC, All Rights
www.dynamicsaxcompanions.com

Preface

What You Need For This Guide

All the examples shown in this blueprint were done with the Microsoft Dynamics AX 2012 virtual machine image that was downloaded from the Microsoft Customer Source or Partner Source site. If you don't have your own installation of Microsoft Dynamics AX 2012, you can also use the images found on the Microsoft Learning Download Center or deployed through Lifecycle Services. The following list of software from the virtual image was leveraged within this guide:

- Microsoft Dynamics AX 2012 R3

Even though all the preceding software was used during the development and testing of the recipes in this book, they may also work on earlier versions of the software with minor tweaks and adjustments, and should also work on later versions without any changes.

Errata

Although we have taken every care to ensure the accuracy of our content, mistakes do happen. If you find a mistake in one of our books—maybe a mistake in the text or the code—we would be grateful if you would report this to us. By doing so, you can save other readers from frustration and help us improve subsequent versions of this book. If you find any errata, please report them by emailing editor@blindsquirrelpublishing.com.

Piracy

Piracy of copyright material on the Internet is an ongoing problem across all media. If you come across any illegal copies of our works, in any form, on the Internet, please provide us with the location address or website name immediately so that we can pursue a remedy.

Please contact us at legal@blindsquirrelpublishing.com with a link to the suspected pirated material.

We appreciate your help in protecting our authors, and our ability to bring you valuable content.

Questions

You can contact us at help@blindsquirrelpublishing.com if you are having a problem with any aspect of the book, and we will do our best to address it.

© 2015 Blind Squirrel Publishing, LLC, All Rights
www.dynamicsaxcompanions.com

Table Of Contents

© 2015 Blind Squirrel Publishing, LLC, All Rights
www.dynamicsaxcompanions.com

© 2015 Blind Squirrel Publishing, LLC, All Rights
www.dynamicsaxcompanions.com

CONFIGURING RECRUITING PROJECTS (CTD)

© 2015 Blind Squirrel Publishing, LLC, All Rights
www.dynamicsaxcompanions.com

© 2015 Blind Squirrel Publishing, LLC, All Rights
www.dynamicsaxcompanions.com

INTRODUCTION

The Human Resource Management area within Dynamics AX not only allows you to manage all of your employees employment information, but it also allows you to track jobs & positions within the organization, track recruiting projects, and much more. A lot of the core information that you can configure within the Human Resource Management area is also leveraged by other areas of Dynamics AX for approvals, skill matching, and also resource management so even if you are not going to be using all of the Human Resource Management features right away, you will definitely be using some of them.

Setting up the Human Resource Management area is not hard to do either, and this guide is designed to give you step by step instructions on how to configure all of the base codes and controls that you need to make the Human Resource Management area tick correctly and also to give you step by step instructions on how you can quickly load all of the necessary worker, position and job information so that you can speed up the data load process and get you up and running quickly.

© 2015 Blind Squirrel Publishing, LLC, All Rights Reserved
www.dynamicsaxcompanions.com

© 2015 Blind Squirrel Publishing, LLC, All Rights Reserved
www.dynamicsaxcompanions.com

CONFIGURING HUMAN RESOURCE MANAGEMENT CONTROLS

Before we start setting up our **Workers** and **Jobs**, there is a little bit of house-keeping that we need to do by setting up some of the codes and parameters that will be used by the **Human Resource Management** area. This includes the configuration of some of the **Reason Codes** that you will be using, the setup of some of the common **Document Types** and also the configuration of the **Human Resource Management Parameters**.

© 2015 Blind Squirrel Publishing, LLC, All Rights Reserved
www.dynamicsaxcompanions.com

© 2015 Blind Squirrel Publishing, LLC, All Rights Reserved
www.dynamicsaxcompanions.com

Configuring Reason Codes

To start off we will want to load in a handful of **Reason Codes** that we will be able to use within the **Human Resource Management** area to classify you activities.

© 2015 Blind Squirrel Publishing, LLC, All Rights Reserved
www.dynamicsaxcompanions.com

Configuring Reason Codes

Reason code	Description	Type
CAREER	Career Change	Worker
COMPETITOR	Left to work for competitor	Worker
ENTRY LEVEL	Enrty level worker	Payroll
INEXPERIENCED	Lacking minimal qualifications	Application
INTERVIEW	Does not match job profile	Application
INVOLUNTARY	Involuntary termination	Worker
LEAVE	Out on leave	Skill mapping
LOW SALARY	Left due to low salary	Worker
NOT INTERESTED	Not interested in being considered	Skill mapping
PAY EXPECTATION	Low compensation and benefits	Application
PROMOTION	Promotion	Worker
REDUCTION	Reduction in force	Worker
REORGANIZATION	Organization restructuring	Worker
RESIGNATION	Voluntary resignation	Worker
RETIREMENT	Retirement	Worker
TEMP	Temporary worker	Skill mapping
TOP MANAGEMENT	Executives	Payroll

Table 1: Example Reason Codes

© 2015 Blind Squirrel Publishing, LLC, All Rights Reserved
www.dynamicsaxcompanions.com

Configuring Reason Codes

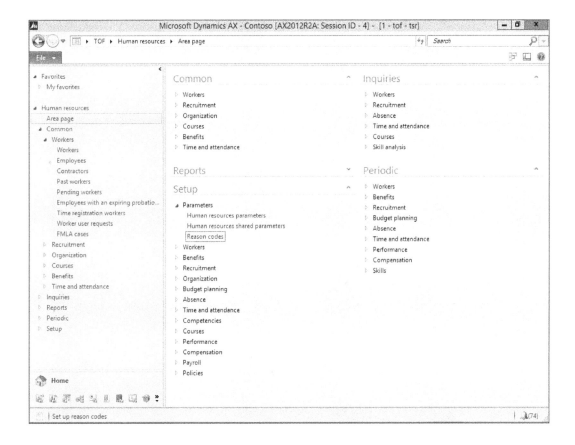

To do this, click on the **Reason Codes** menu item within the **Setup** group of the **Human Resources** area page.

© 2015 Blind Squirrel Publishing, LLC, All Rights Reserved
www.dynamicsaxcompanions.com

Configuring Reason Codes

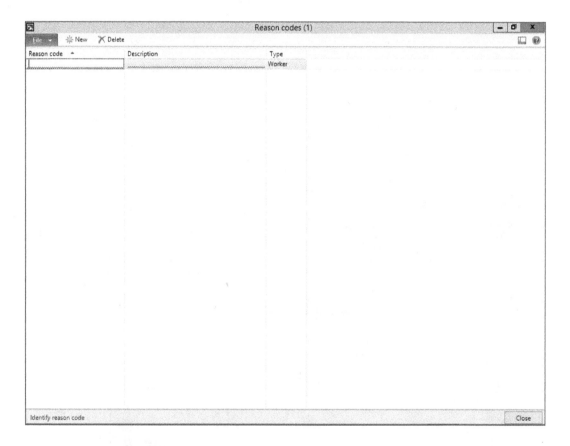

When the **Reason Codes** maintenance form is displayed, click on the **New** button within the menu bar to create a new record.

© 2015 Blind Squirrel Publishing, LLC, All Rights Reserved
www.dynamicsaxcompanions.com

Configuring Reason Codes

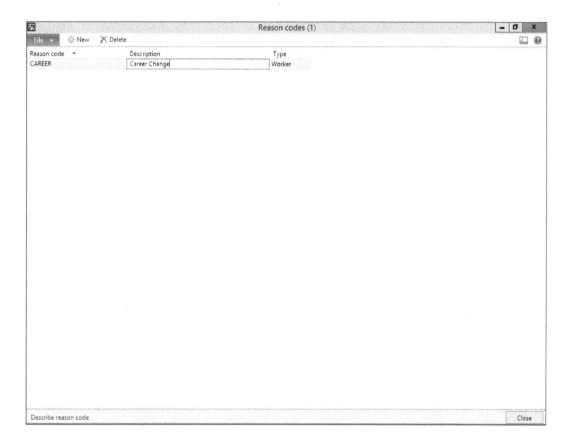

Set the **Reason Code** to **CAREER** and the **Desciption** to **Career Change**.

© 2015 Blind Squirrel Publishing, LLC, All Rights Reserved
www.dynamicsaxcompanions.com

Configuring Reason Codes

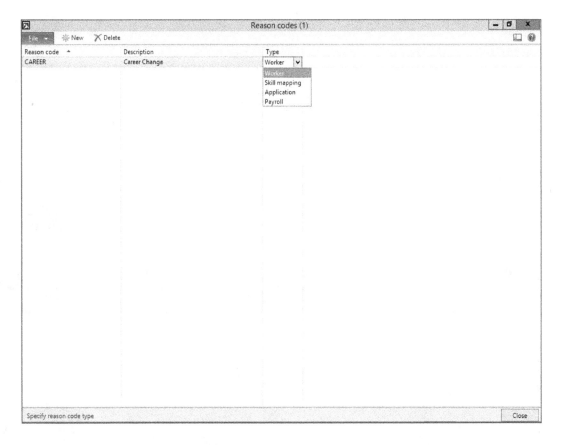

Then click on the **Type** dropdown list and select the **Worker** Type to indicate that this reason code will be used for the **Worker** entity.

You can continue adding additional Reason Codes by hand if you like and when you are done, just click on the **Close** button to exit from the form.

© 2015 Blind Squirrel Publishing, LLC, All Rights Reserved
www.dynamicsaxcompanions.com

© 2015 Blind Squirrel Publishing, LLC, All Rights Reserved
www.dynamicsaxcompanions.com

© 2015 Blind Squirrel Publishing, LLC, All Rights Reserved
www.dynamicsaxcompanions.com

Importing Reason Codes Using Excel

Rather than entering all of the reason codes manually, you can speed up the process by using Excel to import in all of the **Reason Codes** from a template.

© 2015 Blind Squirrel Publishing, LLC, All Rights Reserved
www.dynamicsaxcompanions.com

Importing Reason Codes Using Excel

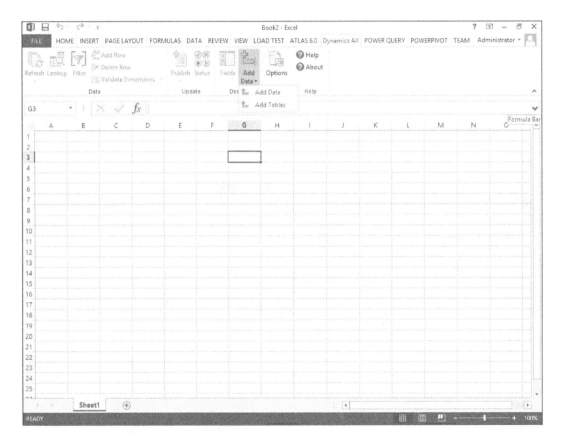

To do this, open up **Excel**, and click on the **Add Data** button within the **Data** group of the **Dynamics AX** ribbon bar, and then select the **Add Tables** menu item.

© 2015 Blind Squirrel Publishing, LLC, All Rights Reserved
www.dynamicsaxcompanions.com

Importing Reason Codes Using Excel

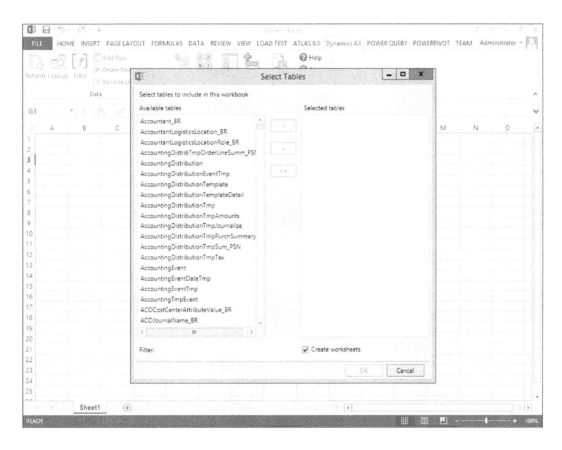

This will open up the **Select Tables** dialog box showing you all of the tables that are within the **Dynamics AX** database.

© 2015 Blind Squirrel Publishing, LLC, All Rights Reserved
www.dynamicsaxcompanions.com

Importing Reason Codes Using Excel

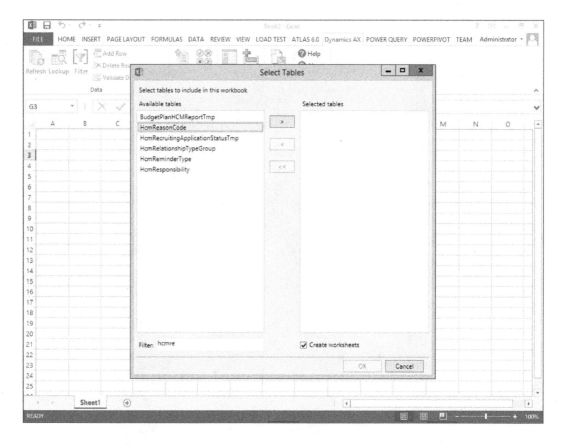

To refine the number of tables that you are searching through, type in **hcmre** into the **Filter** field.

Then click on the **HcmReasonCode** table within the **Available Tables** list box and click on the **>** button.

© 2015 Blind Squirrel Publishing, LLC, All Rights Reserved
www.dynamicsaxcompanions.com

Importing Reason Codes Using Excel

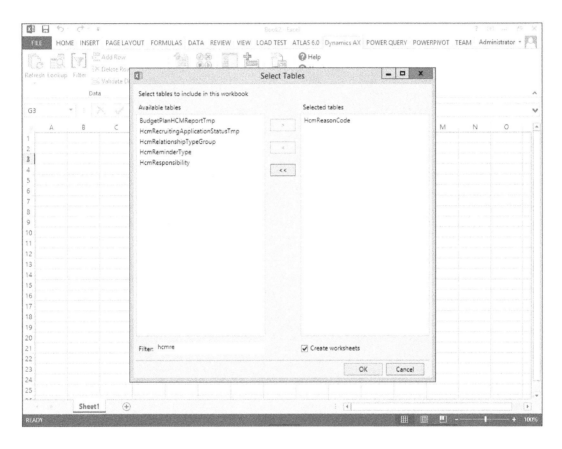

This will add the **HcmReasonCode** table to the **Selected Tables** list and you can now just click on the **OK** button.

© 2015 Blind Squirrel Publishing, LLC, All Rights Reserved
www.dynamicsaxcompanions.com

Importing Reason Codes Using Excel

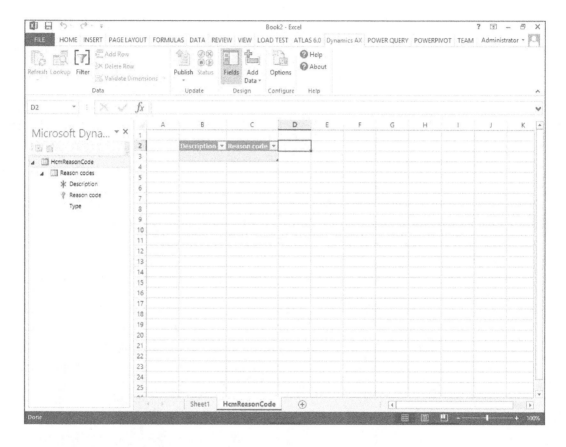

This will create a new Workbook within Excel for you with the key fields for the
HCMReasonCode table.

© 2015 Blind Squirrel Publishing, LLC, All Rights Reserved
www.dynamicsaxcompanions.com

Importing Reason Codes Using Excel

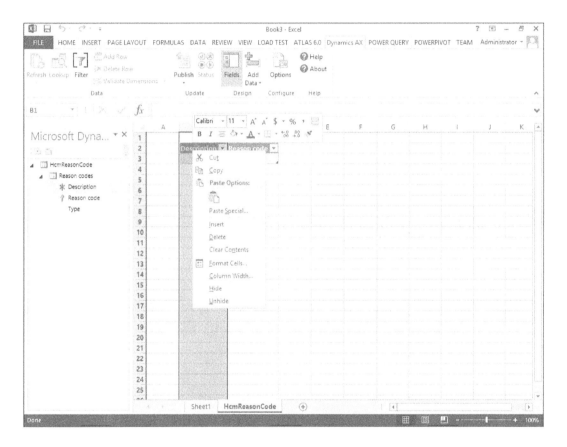

But the order of the fields is not quite right – let's make the **Reason Code** the first column. To do this, select the entire **Description** column and right-mouse-click on it to see the context menu. Then click on the **Delete** menu item.

© 2015 Blind Squirrel Publishing, LLC, All Rights Reserved
www.dynamicsaxcompanions.com

Importing Reason Codes Using Excel

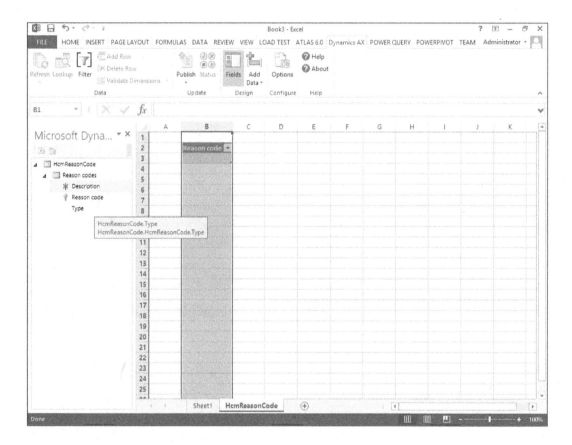

Now you will just see the **Reason Code** column.

© 2015 Blind Squirrel Publishing, LLC, All Rights Reserved
www.dynamicsaxcompanions.com

Importing Reason Codes Using Excel

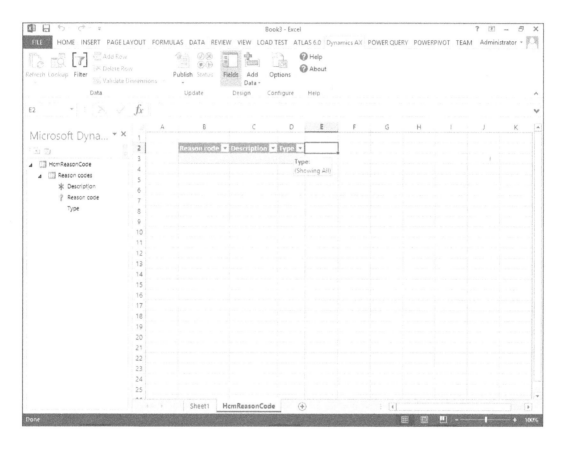

Drag the **Description** and **Type** field from the fields from the selection panel on the left hand side of Excel into the **Workbook** to add it to the worksheets columns.

© 2015 Blind Squirrel Publishing, LLC, All Rights Reserved
www.dynamicsaxcompanions.com

Importing Reason Codes Using Excel

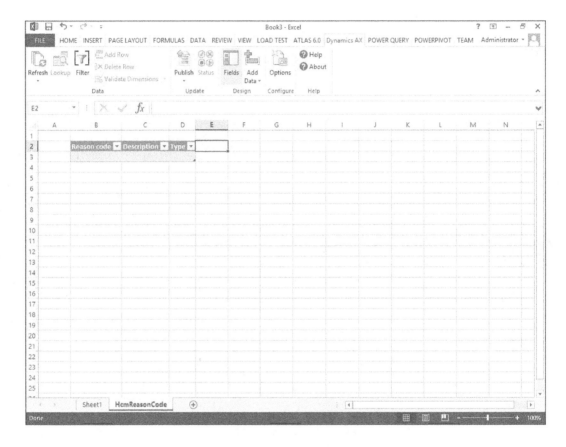

Now click on the **Fields** button to exit from design mode into edit mode.

© 2015 Blind Squirrel Publishing, LLC, All Rights Reserved
www.dynamicsaxcompanions.com

Importing Reason Codes Using Excel

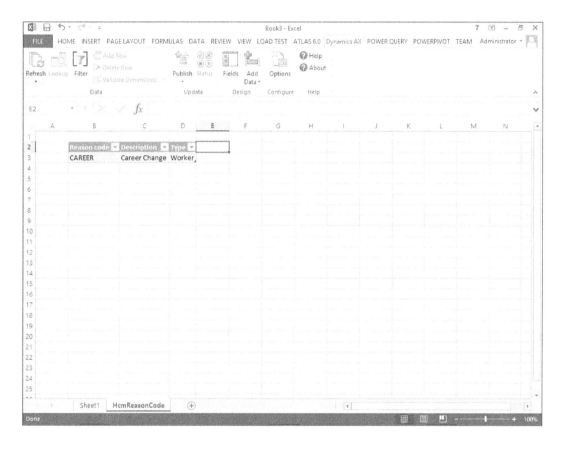

Then click on the **Refresh** button within the **Data** group of the **Dynamics AX** ribbon bar to refresh the data. You should see the **Reason Code** that you just configured within Dynamics AX.

© 2015 Blind Squirrel Publishing, LLC, All Rights Reserved
www.dynamicsaxcompanions.com

Importing Reason Codes Using Excel

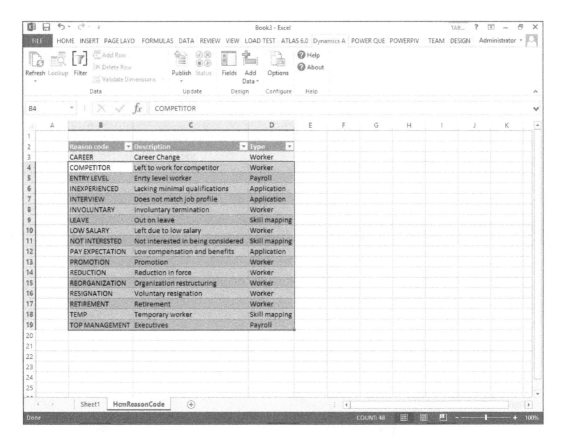

Now just paste in all of the **Reason Codes** that you want to import into Dynamics AX into the worksheet.

© 2015 Blind Squirrel Publishing, LLC, All Rights Reserved
www.dynamicsaxcompanions.com

Importing Reason Codes Using Excel

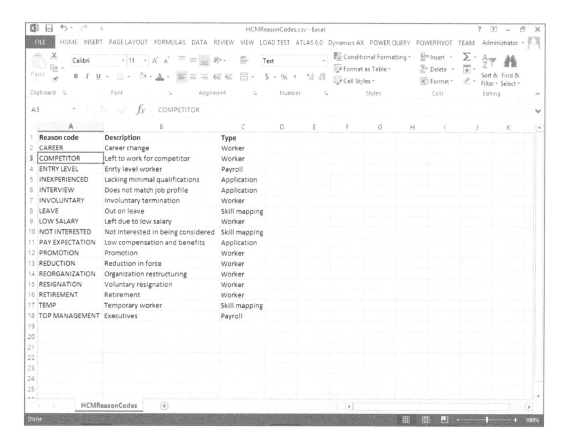

To save time, we have created a **CSV** file that contains all of the suggested **Reason Codes** that you might want to use and they are available for download from the **Dynamics AX Companions** site. Here is the link to the resources page:

http://www.dynamicsaxcompanions.com/Bare-Bones-Configuration-Guides/Configuring-Human-Resources

© 2015 Blind Squirrel Publishing, LLC, All Rights Reserved
www.dynamicsaxcompanions.com

Importing Reason Codes Using Excel

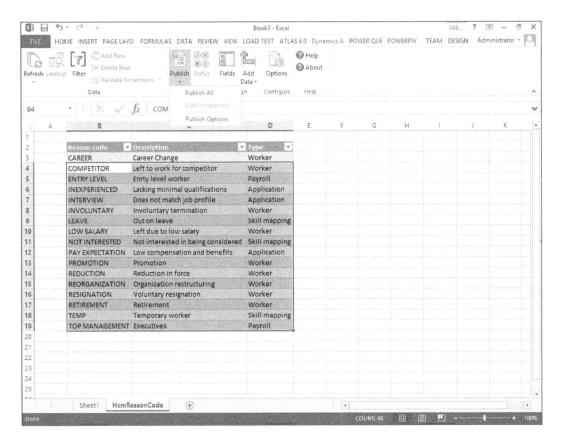

Now click on the **Publish** button within the **Update** group of the **Dynamics AX** ribbon bar and click on the **Publish All** menu item.

© 2015 Blind Squirrel Publishing, LLC, All Rights Reserved
www.dynamicsaxcompanions.com

Importing Reason Codes Using Excel

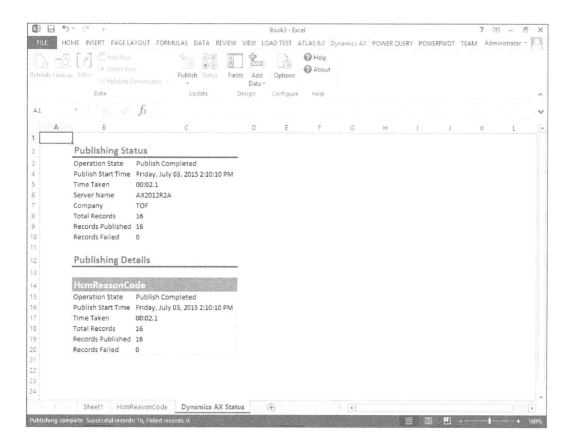

If everything goes well, then you will be able to switch to the new **Dynamics AX Status** worksheet that is created and see that all of the reason codes have been added for you.

Importing Reason Codes Using Excel

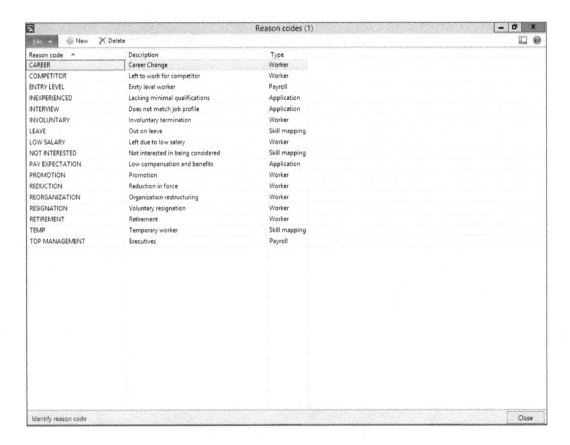

When you return back to the **Reason Codes** maintenance form you will see that all of your **Reason Codes** are available for you.

Now that should save you some time for sure.

© 2015 Blind Squirrel Publishing, LLC, All Rights Reserved
www.dynamicsaxcompanions.com

© 2015 Blind Squirrel Publishing, LLC, All Rights Reserved
www.dynamicsaxcompanions.com

© 2015 Blind Squirrel Publishing, LLC, All Rights Reserved
www.dynamicsaxcompanions.com

Creating HR Document Types

Within the Human Resource Management functions, there is the ability to create **Word** documents from templates. When these are created they are attached to the record as document attachments. In order for this to work, we will need to have a **Document Type** for the system to use for the attachment. So in this step we will create one just for Human Resource Management.

© 2015 Blind Squirrel Publishing, LLC, All Rights Reserved
www.dynamicsaxcompanions.com

Creating HR Document Types

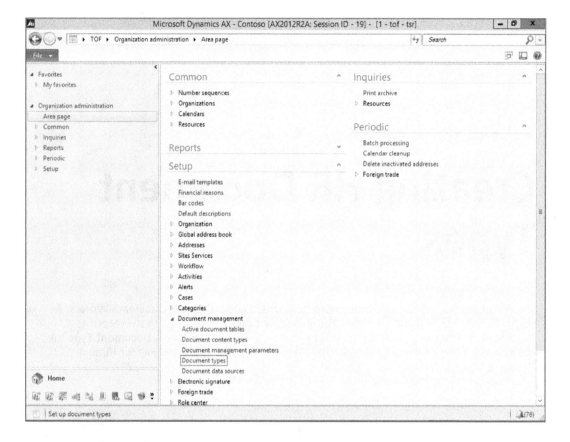

To do this, click on the **Document Types** menu item within the **Document Management** folder of the **Setup** group within the **Organization Administration** area page.

© 2015 Blind Squirrel Publishing, LLC, All Rights Reserved
www.dynamicsaxcompanions.com

Creating HR Document Types

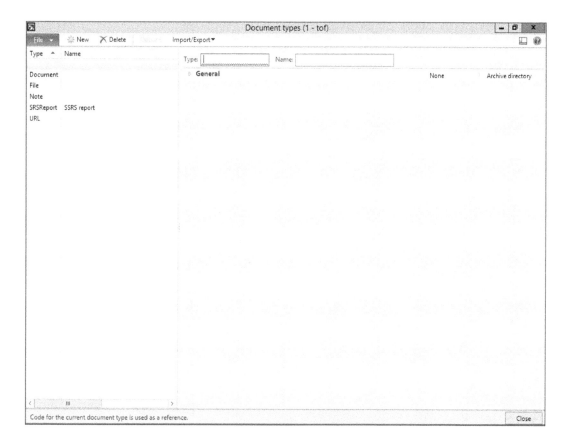

When the **Document Types** maintenance form is displayed, click on the **New** button in the menu bar to create a new record.

© 2015 Blind Squirrel Publishing, LLC, All Rights Reserved
www.dynamicsaxcompanions.com

Creating HR Document Types

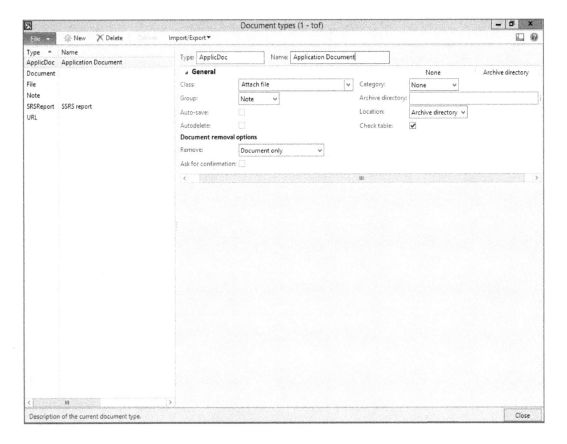

Set the **Type** to **ApplicDoc** and the **Name** to **Application Document**.

Then expand out the **General** fast tab if it is not expanded already.

© 2015 Blind Squirrel Publishing, LLC, All Rights Reserved
www.dynamicsaxcompanions.com

Creating HR Document Types

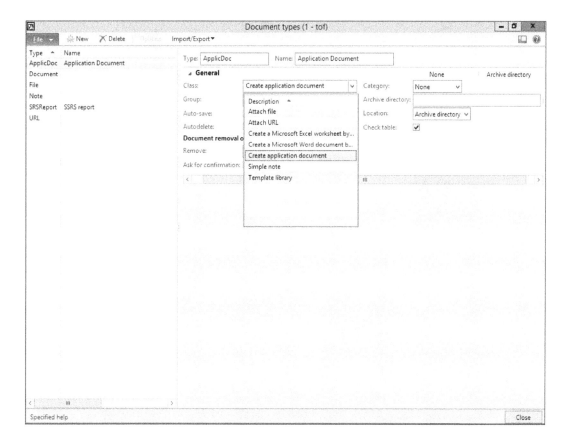

Click on the **Class** dropdown list and select the **Create Application Document**.

© 2015 Blind Squirrel Publishing, LLC, All Rights Reserved
www.dynamicsaxcompanions.com

Creating HR Document Types

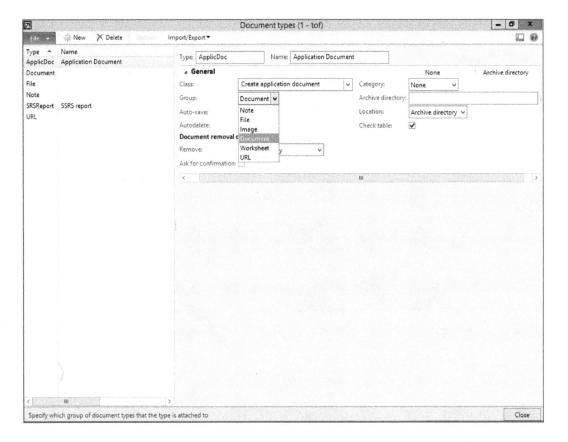

And then click on the **Group** field and select the **Document** value from the dropdown list.

© 2015 Blind Squirrel Publishing, LLC, All Rights Reserved
www.dynamicsaxcompanions.com

Creating HR Document Types

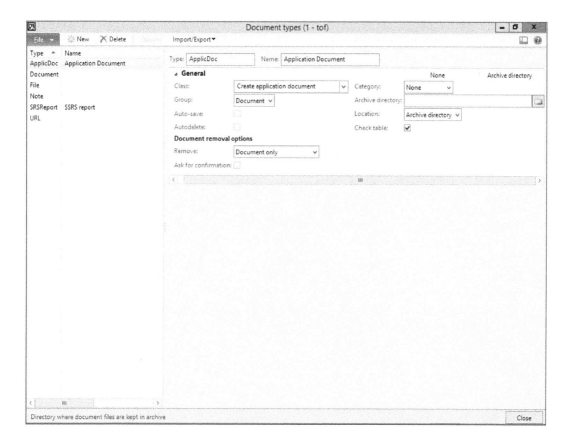

Now click on the **Folder** icon to the right of the **Archive Directory** field.

© 2015 Blind Squirrel Publishing, LLC, All Rights Reserved
www.dynamicsaxcompanions.com

Creating HR Document Types

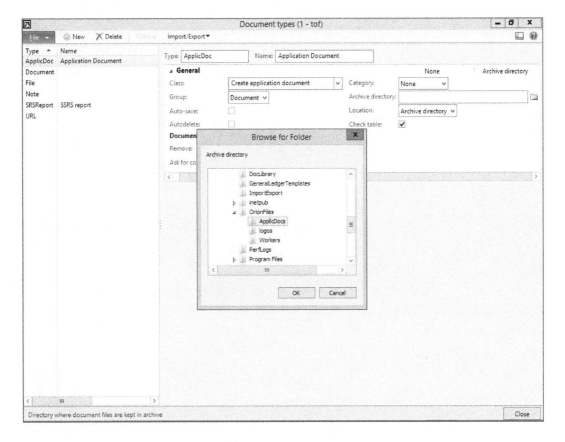

When the **Browser for Folder** dialog box is displayed, navigate to an archive folder where you can store all of the temporary document files and click on the **OK** button.

© 2015 Blind Squirrel Publishing, LLC, All Rights Reserved
www.dynamicsaxcompanions.com

Creating HR Document Types

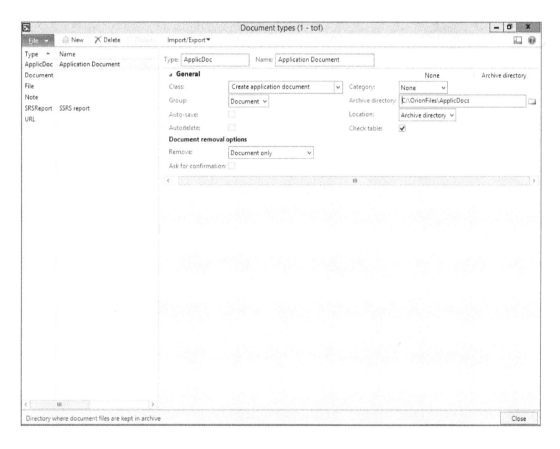

Once you have done that, just click on the **Close** button to exit from the form.

© 2015 Blind Squirrel Publishing, LLC, All Rights Reserved
www.dynamicsaxcompanions.com

© 2015 Blind Squirrel Publishing, LLC, All Rights Reserved
www.dynamicsaxcompanions.com

Configuring The Human Resources Parameters

Now we just want to tweak a few of the parameters within the **Human Resource Management** area and we will be done.

© 2015 Blind Squirrel Publishing, LLC, All Rights Reserved
www.dynamicsaxcompanions.com

Configuring The Human Resources Parameters

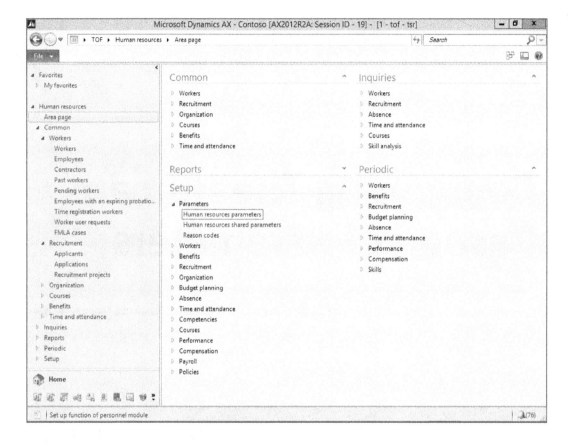

To do this, click on the **Human Resource Parameters** menu item within the **Setup** group of the **Human Resources** area page.

© 2015 Blind Squirrel Publishing, LLC, All Rights Reserved
www.dynamicsaxcompanions.com

Configuring The Human Resources Parameters

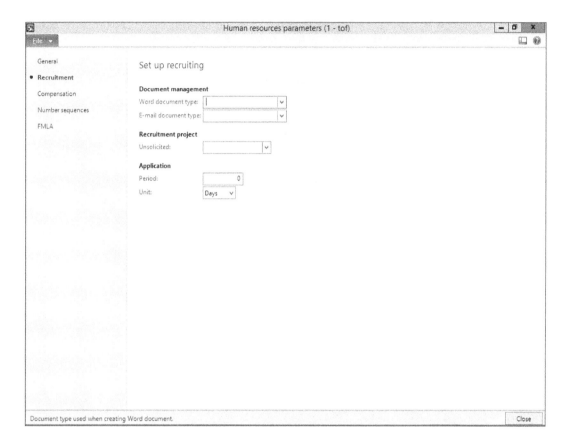

When the **Human Resources Parameters** maintenance form is displayed, click on the **Recruitment** tab on the left hand side of the form.

© 2015 Blind Squirrel Publishing, LLC, All Rights Reserved
www.dynamicsaxcompanions.com

Configuring The Human Resources Parameters

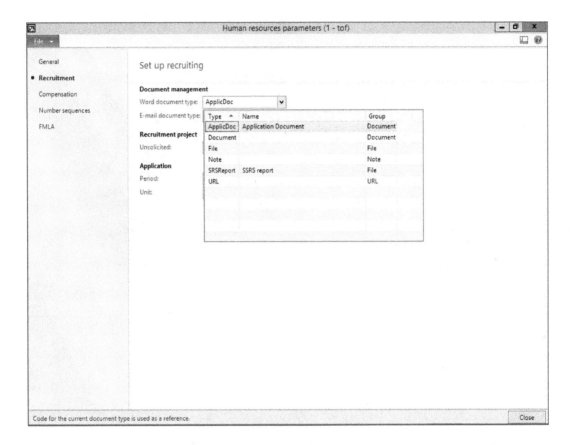

Click on the **Word Document Type** dropdown list and select the **ApplicDoc** document type that you just created.

© 2015 Blind Squirrel Publishing, LLC, All Rights Reserved
www.dynamicsaxcompanions.com

Configuring The Human Resources Parameters

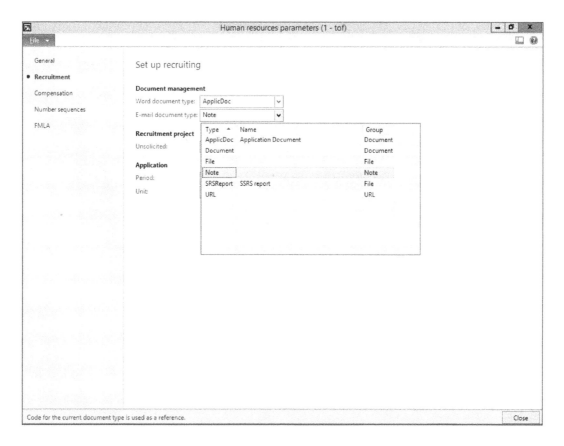

Then click on the **E-mail Document Type** dropdown list and select the **Note** document type to indicate that you want to archive off e-mails as notes.

© 2015 Blind Squirrel Publishing, LLC, All Rights Reserved
www.dynamicsaxcompanions.com

Configuring The Human Resources Parameters

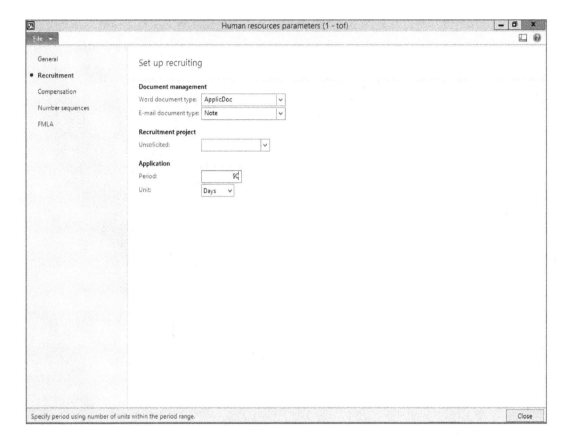

Finally, just to make things tidy, set the **Period** field within the Application group to **90**.

After you have done that, click on the **Close** button to exit from the form.

© 2015 Blind Squirrel Publishing, LLC, All Rights Reserved
www.dynamicsaxcompanions.com

© 2015 Blind Squirrel Publishing, LLC, All Rights Reserved
www.dynamicsaxcompanions.com

© 2015 Blind Squirrel Publishing, LLC, All Rights Reserved
www.dynamicsaxcompanions.com

CONFIGURING WORKERS AND EMPLOYEES

Once the general configuration has been completed we can start setting up some of the more interesting parts of the **Human Resource Management** area. And the first place that we will start is configuring the **Workers** and **Employees**. The **Worker** is the general way to classify people within Dynamics AX, and you will want to load everyone that you want to track within the Human Resources in as **Workers**.

Workers can then be classified as **Employees** or **Contractors** depending on if they are paid by the company or just external parties that you work with. In this section we will just focus on setting up the **Employees** and leave the other worker variations to a later subject.

© 2015 Blind Squirrel Publishing, LLC, All Rights Reserved
www.dynamicsaxcompanions.com

Configuring Ethnic Origins

Before we start creating **Workers** though we will want to set up some additional codes that we will use to segregate out our workers. The first one that we will set up will be the **Ethnic Origins** so that we can track the diversity with the organization.

© 2015 Blind Squirrel Publishing, LLC, All Rights Reserved
www.dynamicsaxcompanions.com

Configuring Ethnic Origins

American Indian	A person having origins American Indian or Alaska Native
Alaska Natives	A person having origins as Alaska Natives
Albanian	A person having origins as Albanian
Algerians	A person having origins as Algerians
American Indian	A person having origins American Indian or Alaska Native
American Jews	A person having origins as American Jews
Angolan	A person having origins as Angolan
Appalachian	A person having origins as Appalachian
Arab	A person having origins as Arab
Armenian	A person having origins as Armenian
Ashkenazi Jews	A person having origins as Ashkenazi Jews
Asian	A person having origins in the Far East, Southeast Asia...
Asian Pacific	A person having origins as Asian Pacific
Assyrians	A person having origins as Assyrians
Bangladeshi	A person having origins as Bangladeshi
Black Dutch	A person having origins as Black Dutch
Black/African	A person having origins in ... Africa
Brazilian	A person having origins as Brazilian
British	A person having origins as British
Cambodian	A person having origins as Cambodian
Canadian	A person having origins as Canadian
Chilean	A person having origins as Chilean
Chinese	A person having origins as Chinese
Cuban	A person having origins as Cuban
Egyptian	A person having origins as Egyptian
European	A person having origins as European
French	A person having origins as French
Frisian	A person having origins as Frisian
German	A person having origins as German
Greek	A person having origins as Greek
Haitian	A person having origins as Haitian
Han Chinese	A person having origins as Han Chinese
Hispanic/Latino	A person of Cuban, Mexican, Puerto Rican, South or Central..
Indonesian	A person having origins as Indonesian
Iranian	A person having origins as Iranian

Table 2: Example Ethnic Origins

© 2015 Blind Squirrel Publishing, LLC, All Rights Reserved
www.dynamicsaxcompanions.com

Configuring Ethnic Origins

American Indian	A person having origins American Indian or Alaska Native
Iraqi	A person having origins as Iraqi
Irish	A person having origins as Irish
Italian	A person having origins as Italian
Jordanian	A person having origins as Jordanian
Mexican	A person having origins as Mexican
Native Hawaiian	A person of native Hawaiian or other Pacific Islander
Pakistani	A person having origins as Pakistani
Palestinian	A person having origins as Palestinian
Portuguese	A person having origins as Portuguese
Romanian	A person having origins as Romanian
Russian	A person having origins as Russian
Two or More	Two or More Races
White	A person having origins Europe, Middle East, or North Africa

Table 2: Example Ethnic Origins

© 2015 Blind Squirrel Publishing, LLC, All Rights Reserved
www.dynamicsaxcompanions.com

Configuring Ethnic Origins

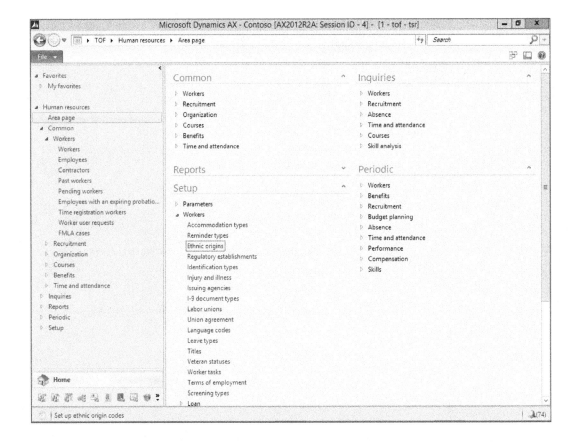

To do this, click on the **Ethnic Origins** menu item within the **Workers** folder of the **Setup** group within the **Human Resources** area page.

© 2015 Blind Squirrel Publishing, LLC, All Rights Reserved
www.dynamicsaxcompanions.com

Configuring Ethnic Origins

When the **Ethnic Origins** maintenance form is displayed, click on the **New** button within the menu bar to create a new record.

© 2015 Blind Squirrel Publishing, LLC, All Rights Reserved
www.dynamicsaxcompanions.com

Configuring Ethnic Origins

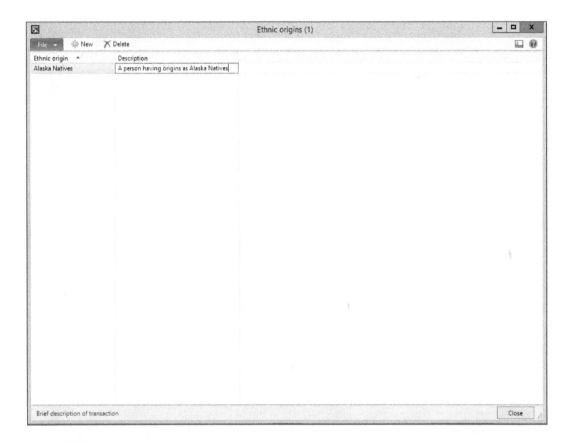

Then set the **Ethnic Origin** to **Alaska Natives** and the **Description** to **A person having origin as Alaska Natives**.

If you want to add another **Ethnic Origin** then just repeat the process and when you are done, just click on the **Close** button to exit from the form.

© 2015 Blind Squirrel Publishing, LLC, All Rights Reserved
www.dynamicsaxcompanions.com

© 2015 Blind Squirrel Publishing, LLC, All Rights Reserved
www.dynamicsaxcompanions.com

© 2015 Blind Squirrel Publishing, LLC, All Rights Reserved
www.dynamicsaxcompanions.com

Importing Ethnic Origins Using Excel

Rather than entering all of the **Ethnic Origins** manually, you can speed up the process by using Excel to import in all of the **Ethnic Origins** from a template.

Importing Ethnic Origins Using Excel

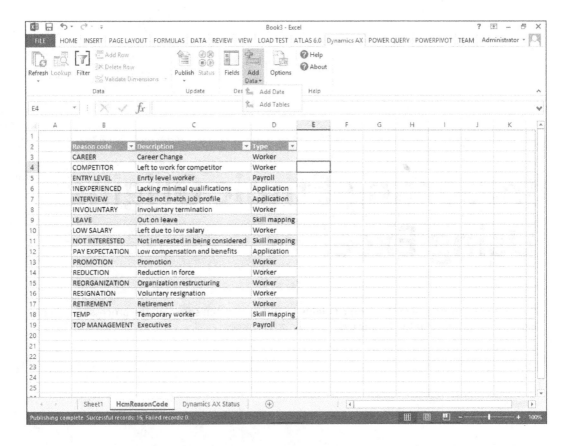

To do this, return to your Excel workbook that you used to import in the **Reason Codes** and click on the **Add Data** button within the **Data** group of the **Dynamics AX** ribbon bar, and click on the **Add Tables** menu item again.

© 2015 Blind Squirrel Publishing, LLC, All Rights Reserved
www.dynamicsaxcompanions.com

Importing Ethnic Origins Using Excel

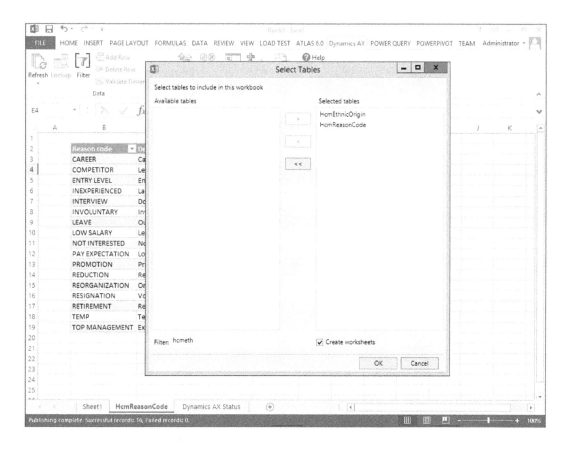

This time when the **Select Tables** dialog box is displayed, filter the table list down to the **HcmEthnicOrigin** table, click on the **>** button to add it to the **Selected Tables** group and then click on the **OK** button.

© 2015 Blind Squirrel Publishing, LLC, All Rights Reserved
www.dynamicsaxcompanions.com

Importing Ethnic Origins Using Excel

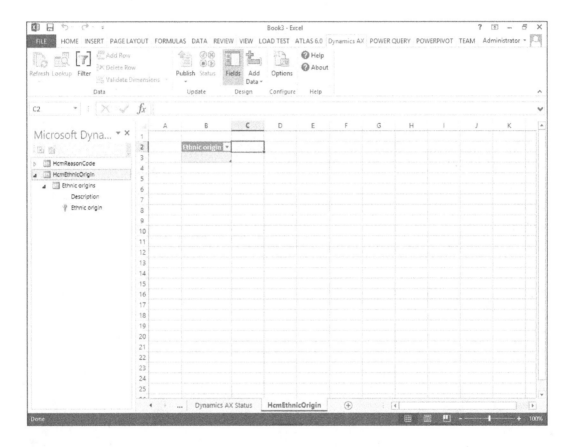

This will create a new worksheet for you linked to the **HcmEthnicOrigin** table.

© 2015 Blind Squirrel Publishing, LLC, All Rights Reserved
www.dynamicsaxcompanions.com

Importing Ethnic Origins Using Excel

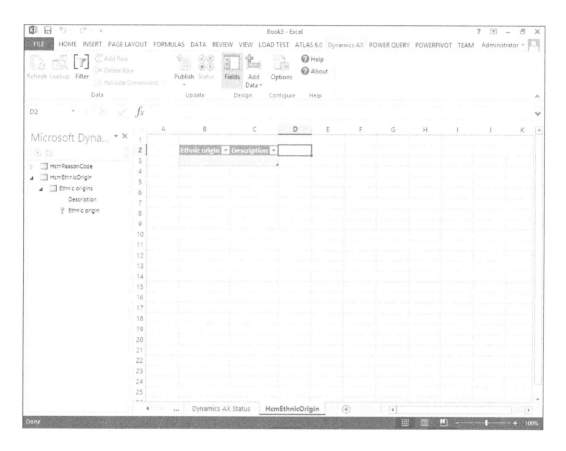

Drag the **Description** field from the field explorer on the left hand side for the workbook and add it to the table within the worksheet.

© 2015 Blind Squirrel Publishing, LLC, All Rights Reserved
www.dynamicsaxcompanions.com

Importing Ethnic Origins Using Excel

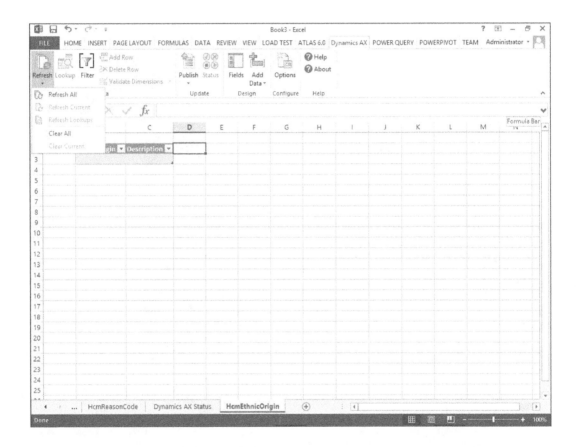

Now click on the **Fields** button within the **Design** group of the **Dynamics AX** ribbon bar to exit from design mode and then click on the **Refresh** button within the **Data** group of the **Dynamics AX** ribbon bar and click on the **Refresh All** menu item.

© 2015 Blind Squirrel Publishing, LLC, All Rights Reserved
www.dynamicsaxcompanions.com

Importing Ethnic Origins Using Excel

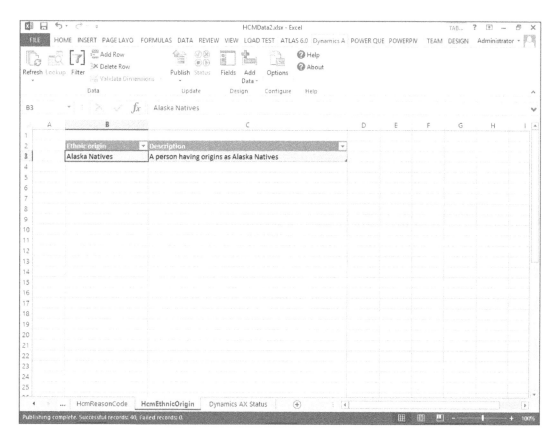

This will refresh the worksheet and you will be able to see all of the **Ethnic Origin** records that you loaded in by hand.

© 2015 Blind Squirrel Publishing, LLC, All Rights Reserved
www.dynamicsaxcompanions.com

Importing Ethnic Origins Using Excel

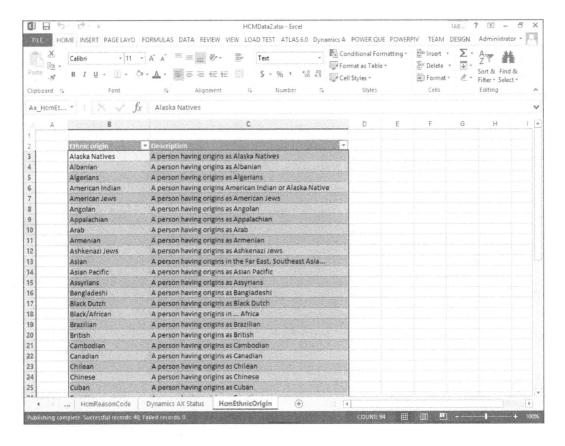

Now just paste in all of the **Ethnic Origins** that you want to import into Dynamics AX into the worksheet.

© 2015 Blind Squirrel Publishing, LLC, All Rights Reserved
www.dynamicsaxcompanions.com

Importing Ethnic Origins Using Excel

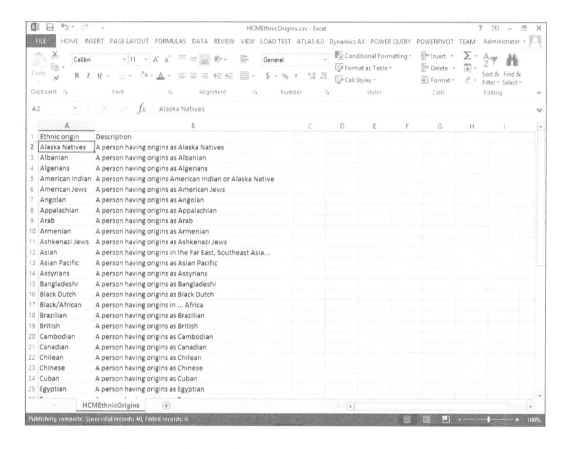

To save time, we have created a **CSV** file that contains all of the suggested **Ethnic Origins** that you might want to use and they are available for download from the **Dynamics AX Companions** site. Here is the link to the resources page:

http://www.dynamicsaxcompanions.com/Bare-Bones-Configuration-Guides/Configuring-Human-Resources

© 2015 Blind Squirrel Publishing, LLC, All Rights Reserved
www.dynamicsaxcompanions.com

Importing Ethnic Origins Using Excel

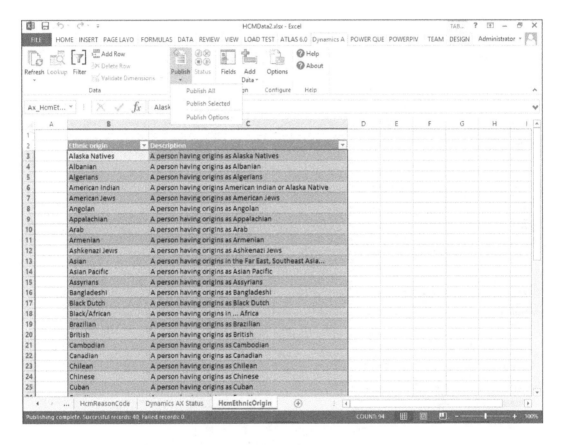

Now click on the **Publish** button within the **Update** group of the **Dynamics AX** ribbon bar and click on the **Publish All** menu item.

© 2015 Blind Squirrel Publishing, LLC, All Rights Reserved
www.dynamicsaxcompanions.com

Importing Ethnic Origins Using Excel

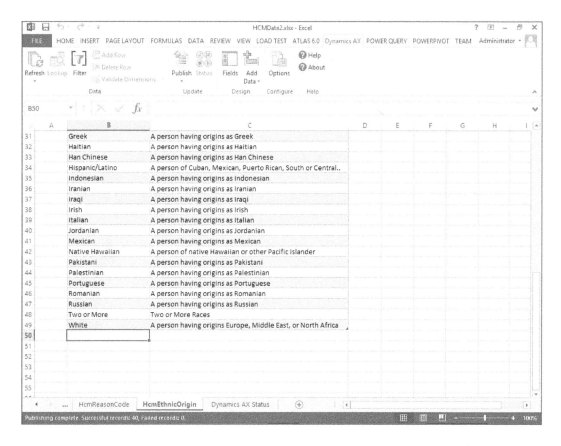

If everything goes well, then the worksheet will refresh and you will see all of the rows that you just added.

© 2015 Blind Squirrel Publishing, LLC, All Rights Reserved
www.dynamicsaxcompanions.com

Importing Ethnic Origins Using Excel

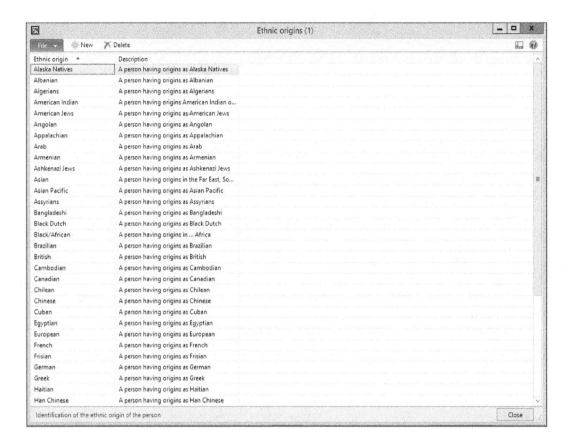

When you return back to the **Ethnic Origin** maintenance form you will see that all of your **Ethnic Origins** are available for you.

That is definitely easier than typing it in by hand.

© 2015 Blind Squirrel Publishing, LLC, All Rights Reserved
www.dynamicsaxcompanions.com

© 2015 Blind Squirrel Publishing, LLC, All Rights Reserved
www.dynamicsaxcompanions.com

© 2015 Blind Squirrel Publishing, LLC, All Rights Reserved
www.dynamicsaxcompanions.com

Configuring Identification Types

Next we will want to configure the **Identification Types** that we want to accept for our workers.

© 2015 Blind Squirrel Publishing, LLC, All Rights Reserved
www.dynamicsaxcompanions.com

Configuring Identification Types

Identification type	Description
Alien/Admission	Alien/Admission no.
CBA	Certificate of birth abroad
Drivers license	Drivers license
INS-N-550	Certificate of Naturalization
INS-N-560	Certificate of United States Citizenship
National ID	National ID card
Passport	Passport
School ID	School identification
SSN	Social Security Number
Visa	Visa

Table 3: Example Identification Types

© 2015 Blind Squirrel Publishing, LLC, All Rights Reserved
www.dynamicsaxcompanions.com

Configuring Identification Types

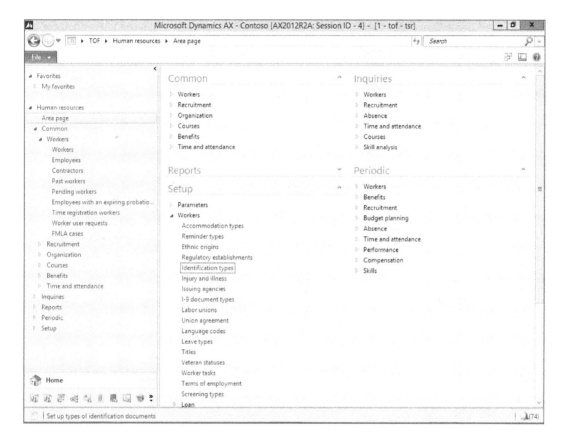

To do this, click on the **Identification Types** menu item within the **Workers** folder of the **Setup** group within the **Human Resources** area page.

© 2015 Blind Squirrel Publishing, LLC, All Rights Reserved
www.dynamicsaxcompanions.com

Configuring Identification Types

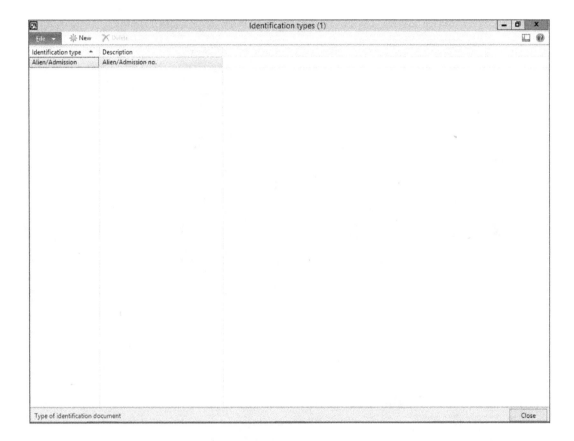

When the **Identification Types** maintenance form is displayed, click on the **New** button in the menu bar to create a new record.

Then set the **Identification Type** to **Alien/Admission** and the **Description** to **Alien/Admission No.**

You can continue adding more Identification Types by repeating the process and when you are done, just click on the **Close** button to exit from the form.

© 2015 Blind Squirrel Publishing, LLC, All Rights Reserved
www.dynamicsaxcompanions.com

© 2015 Blind Squirrel Publishing, LLC, All Rights Reserved
www.dynamicsaxcompanions.com

© 2015 Blind Squirrel Publishing, LLC, All Rights Reserved
www.dynamicsaxcompanions.com

Importing Identification Types Using Excel

Just as with the previous codes, rather than entering all of the **Identification Types** manually, you can speed up the process by using Excel to import them in from a template.

© 2015 Blind Squirrel Publishing, LLC, All Rights Reserved
www.dynamicsaxcompanions.com

Importing Identification Types Using Excel

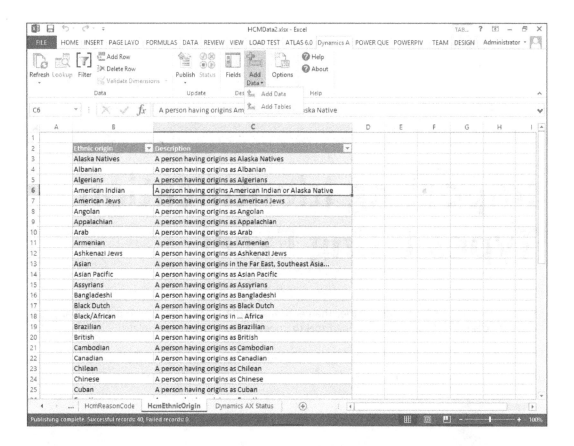

To do this, return to your Excel workbook that you used to import in the **Reason Codes** and click on the **Add Data** button within the **Data** group of the **Dynamics AX** ribbon bar, and click on the **Add Tables** menu item again.

© 2015 Blind Squirrel Publishing, LLC, All Rights Reserved
www.dynamicsaxcompanions.com

Importing Identification Types Using Excel

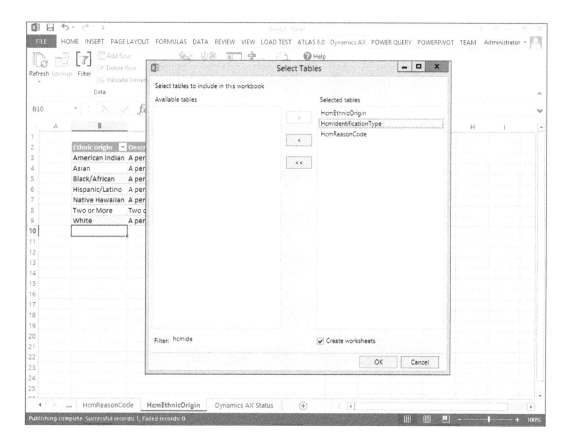

This time when the **Select Tables** dialog box is displayed, filter the table list down to the **HcmIdentificationType** table, click on the **>** button to add it to the **Selected Tables** group and then click on the **OK** button.

© 2015 **Blind Squirrel Publishing, LLC, All Rights Reserved**
www.dynamicsaxcompanions.com

Importing Identification Types Using Excel

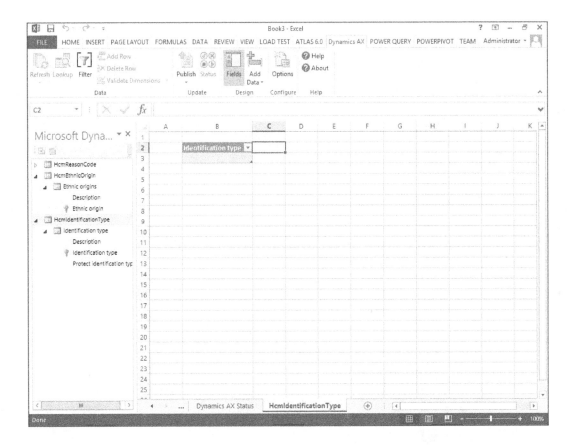

This will create a new worksheet for you linked to the **HcmIdentificationType** table.

© 2015 Blind Squirrel Publishing, LLC, All Rights Reserved
www.dynamicsaxcompanions.com

Importing Identification Types Using Excel

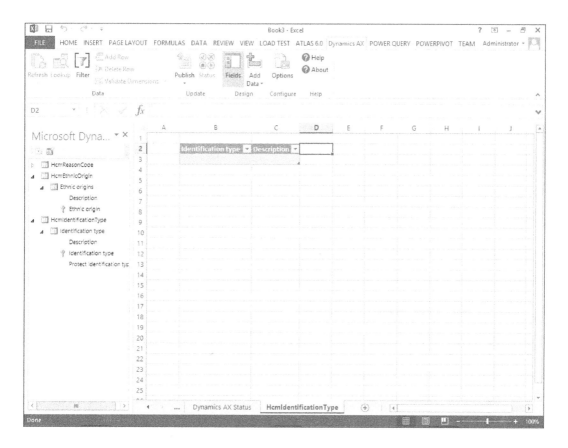

Drag the **Description** field from the field explorer on the left hand side for the workbook and add it to the table within the worksheet.

© 2015 Blind Squirrel Publishing, LLC, All Rights Reserved
www.dynamicsaxcompanions.com

Importing Identification Types Using Excel

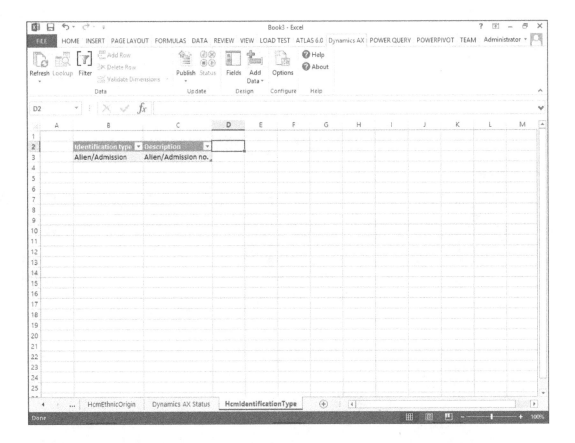

Now click on the **Fields** button within the **Design** group of the **Dynamics AX** ribbon bar to exit from design mode and then click on the **Refresh** button within the **Data** group of the **Dynamics AX** ribbon bar and click on the **Refresh All** menu item.

This will refresh the worksheet and you will be able to see all of the **Identification Type** record(s) that you loaded in by hand.

© 2015 Blind Squirrel Publishing, LLC, All Rights Reserved
www.dynamicsaxcompanions.com

Importing Identification Types Using Excel

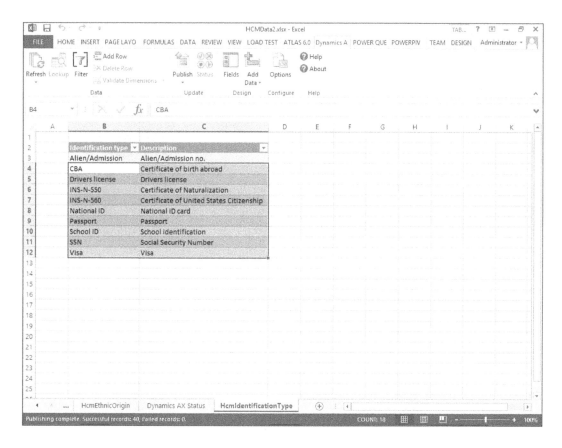

Now just paste in all of the **Identification Types** that you want to import into Dynamics AX into the worksheet.

© 2015 **Blind Squirrel Publishing, LLC, All Rights Reserved**
www.dynamicsaxcompanions.com

Importing Identification Types Using Excel

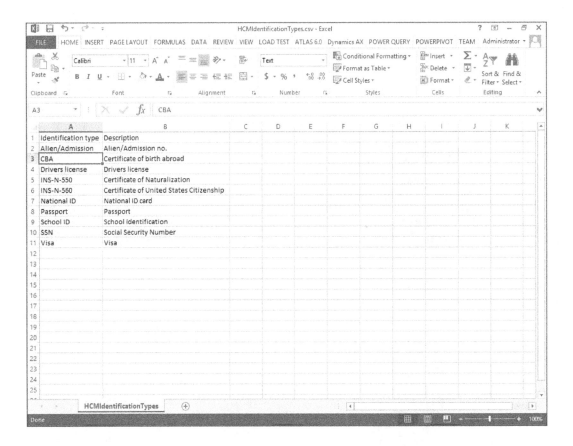

To save time, we have created a **CSV** file that contains all of the suggested **Identification Types** that you might want to use and they are available for download from the **Dynamics AX Companions** site. Here is the link to the resources page:

http://www.dynamicsaxcompanions.com/Bare-Bones-Configuration-Guides/Configuring-Human-Resources

© 2015 Blind Squirrel Publishing, LLC, All Rights Reserved
www.dynamicsaxcompanions.com

Importing Identification Types Using Excel

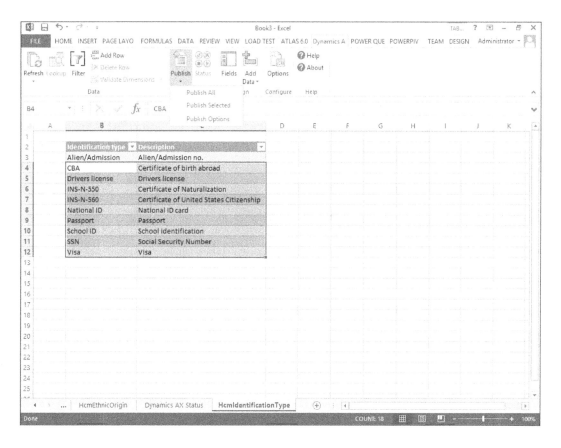

Now click on the **Publish** button within the **Update** group of the **Dynamics AX** ribbon bar and click on the **Publish All** menu item.

© 2015 Blind Squirrel Publishing, LLC, All Rights Reserved
www.dynamicsaxcompanions.com

Importing Identification Types Using Excel

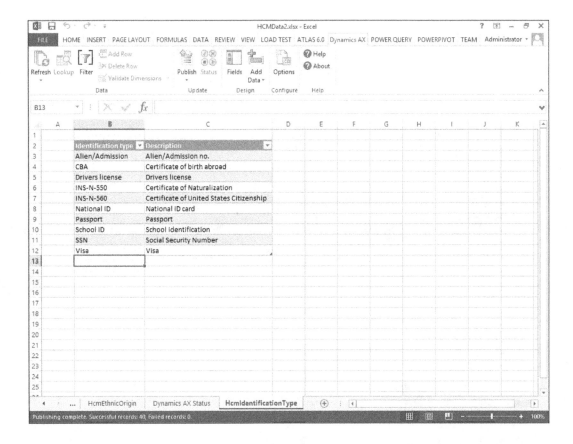

If everything goes well, then the worksheet will refresh and you will see all of the rows that you just added.

© 2015 Blind Squirrel Publishing, LLC, All Rights Reserved
www.dynamicsaxcompanions.com

Importing Identification Types Using Excel

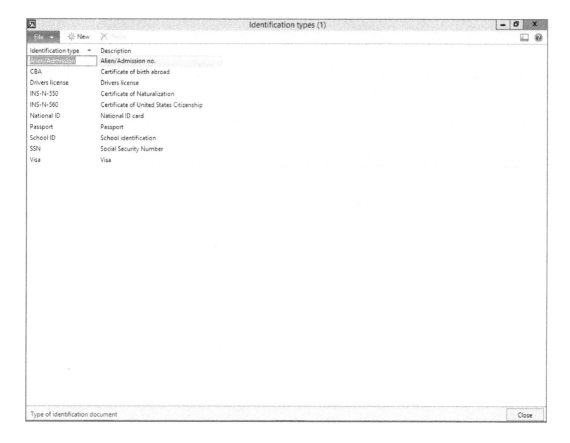

When you return back to the **Identification Types** maintenance form you will see that all of your **Identification Types** are available for you.

How easy is that?

© 2015 Blind Squirrel Publishing, LLC, All Rights Reserved
www.dynamicsaxcompanions.com

© 2015 Blind Squirrel Publishing, LLC, All Rights Reserved
www.dynamicsaxcompanions.com

Configuring Language Codes

Next we will want to load in some **Language Codes** for our workers so that we can record their native language.

© 2015 Blind Squirrel Publishing, LLC, All Rights Reserved
www.dynamicsaxcompanions.com

Configuring Language Codes

Language code	Description	Language code	Description
ABKHAZ	Abkhaz	COMORIAN	Comorian
ADANGME	Adangme	CORNISH	Cornish
ADYGHE	Adyghe	CREE	Cree
AFRIKAANS	Afrikaans	CRIOULO	Crioulo
ALBANIAN	Albanian	CROATIAN	Croatian
ALTAY	Altay	CZECH	Czech
AMHARIC	Amharic	DAGAARE	Dagaare
ARABIC	Arabic	DAGBANI	Dagbani
ARMENIAN	Armenian	DANISH	Danish
ASSAMESE	Assamese	DARI	Dari
AYMARA	Aymara	DGÈRNÉSIAIS	Dgèrnésiais
AZERBAIJANI	Azerbaijani	DHIVEHI	Dhivehi
BALINESE	Balinese	DOGRI	Dogri
BALOCHI	Balochi	DOGRIB	Dogrib
BASHKIR	Bashkir	DOLGAN	Dolgan
BASQUE	Basque	DUTCH	Dutch
BELARUSIAN	Belarusian	DZONGKHA	Dzongkha
BENGALI	Bengali	ENGLISH	English
BIKOL	Bikol	ERZYA	Erzya
BISLAMA	Bislama	ESTONIAN	Estonian
BODO	Bodo	EVENK	Evenk
BOSNIAN	Bosnian	EWE	Ewe
BULGARIAN	Bulgarian	FAROESE	Faroese
BURIAT	Buriat	FIJIAN	Fijian
CANTONESE	Cantonese	FILIPINO	Filipino
CAROLINIAN	Carolinian	FINNISH	Finnish
CATALAN	Catalan	FRENCH	French
CEBUANO	Cebuano	FRISIAN	Frisian
CHAMORRO	Chamorro	FRIULIAN	Friulian
CHECHEN	Chechen	FULA	Fula
CHICHEWA	Chichewa	GA	Ga
CHIPEWYAN	Chipewyan	GAGAUZ	Gagauz
CHUKCHI	Chukchi	GALICIAN	Galician
CHUVASH	Chuvash	GEORGIAN	Georgian

Table 4: Example Language Codes

© 2015 Blind Squirrel Publishing, LLC, All Rights Reserved
www.dynamicsaxcompanions.com

Configuring Language Codes

Language code	Description
GERMAN	German
GONJA	Gonja
GREEK	Greek
GUARANÍ	Guaraní
GUJARATI	Gujarati
GWICH'IN	Gwich'in
HAITIAN CREOLE	Haitian Creole
HAUSA	Hausa
HAWAIIAN	Hawaiian
HEBREW	Hebrew
HILIGAYNON	Hiligaynon
HINDI	Hindi
HINDUSTANI	Hindustani
HIRI MOTU	Hiri Motu
HUNGARIAN	Hungarian
ICELANDIC	Icelandic
IGBO	Igbo
ILOKANO	Ilokano
INDONESIAN	Indonesian
INGUSH	Ingush
INUINNAQTUN	Inuinnaqtun
INUKTITUT	Inuktitut
IRISH	Irish
ITALIAN	Italian
JAPANESE	Japanese
JÈRRIAIS	Jèrriais
JULA	Jula
KABARDIAN	Kabardian
KALAALLISUT	Kalaallisut
KALANGA	Kalanga
KALMYK	Kalmyk
KANNADA	Kannada
KAPAMPANGAN	Kapampangan
KARACHAY-BALKAR	Karachay-Balkar
KASEM	Kasem
KASHMIRI	Kashmiri
KAZAKH	Kazakh
KHAKAS	Khakas
KHANTY	Khanty
KHMER	Khmer
KIKONGO	Kikongo
KINARAY-A	Kinaray-a
KINYARWANDA	Kinyarwanda
KIRGHIZ	Kirghiz
KIRIBATI	Kiribati
KIRUNDI	Kirundi
KOMI-PERMYAK	Komi-Permyak
KOMI-ZYRIAN	Komi-Zyrian
KONKANI	Konkani
KOREAN	Korean
KORYAK	Koryak
KURDISH	Kurdish
LADIN	Ladin
LAO	Lao
LATVIAN	Latvian
LINGALA	Lingala
LITHUANIAN	Lithuanian
LOWER SORBIAN	Lower Sorbian
LUXEMBOURGISH	Luxembourgish
MAGUINDANAO	Maguindanao
MAITHILI	Maithili
MALAGASY	Malagasy
MALAY	Malay
MALAYALAM	Malayalam
MALTESE	Maltese
MANDARIN	Mandarin
MANIPURI	Manipuri
MANSI	Mansi

Table 4: Example Language Codes

© 2015 Blind Squirrel Publishing, LLC, All Rights Reserved
www.dynamicsaxcompanions.com

Configuring Language Codes

Language code	Description	Language code	Description
MAORI	Maori	ROMANI	Romani
MARANAO	Maranao	ROMANIAN	Romanian
MARATHI	Marathi	ROMANSH	Romansh
MARI	Mari	RUSSIAN	Russian
MARSHALLESE	Marshallese	RUTHENIAN	Ruthenian
MEÄNKIELI	Meänkieli	SAMI	Sami
MOKSHA	Moksha	SAMOAN	Samoan
MOLDOVAN	Moldovan	SANGO	Sango
MONGOLIAN	Mongolian	SANSKRIT	Sanskrit
MOORE	Moore	SANTALI	Santali
MUNUKUTUBA	Munukutuba	SARDINIAN	Sardinian
NAURUAN	Nauruan	SCOTS	Scots
NDEBELE	Ndebele	SCOTTISH GAELIC	Scottish Gaelic
NENETS	Nenets	SERBIAN	Serbian
NEPALI	Nepali	SESELWA	Seselwa
NIUEAN	Niuean	SINDHI	Sindhi
NORTHERN SOTHO	Northern Sotho	SINHALA	Sinhala
NORWEGIAN	Norwegian	SLAVEY	Slavey
NURISTANI	Nuristani	SLOVAK	Slovak
NZEMA	Nzema	SLOVENIAN	Slovenian
OCCITAN	Occitan	SOMALI	Somali
ORIYA	Oriya	SONINKE	Soninke
OSSETIC	Ossetic	SOTHO	Sotho
PALAUAN	Palauan	SPANISH	Spanish
PAMIRI	Pamiri	SWAHILI	Swahili
PANGASINAN	Pangasinan	SWAZI	Swazi
PASHAI	Pashai	SWEDISH	Swedish
PASHTO	Pashto	TAHITIAN	Tahitian
PERSIAN	Persian	TAJIK	Tajik
PITCAIRNESE	Pitcairnese	TAMAZIGHT	Tamazight
POLISH	Polish	TAMIL	Tamil
PORTUGUESE	Portuguese	TATAR	Tatar
PUNJABI	Punjabi	TAUSUG	Tausug
QUECHUA	Quechua	TELUGU	Telugu

Table 4: Example Language Codes

© 2015 Blind Squirrel Publishing, LLC, All Rights Reserved
www.dynamicsaxcompanions.com

Configuring Language Codes

Language code	Description
THAI	Thai
TIBETAN	Tibetan
TIGRINYA	Tigrinya
TOK PISIN	Tok Pisin
TOKELAUAN	Tokelauan
TONGAN	Tongan
TSHILUBA	Tshiluba
TSONGA	Tsonga
TSWANA	Tswana
TURKISH	Turkish
TURKMEN	Turkmen
TUVALUAN	Tuvaluan
TUVIN	Tuvin
TWI	Twi
UDMURT	Udmurt
UKRAINIAN	Ukrainian
UPPER SORBIAN	Upper Sorbian
URDU	Urdu
UYGHUR	Uyghur
UZBEK	Uzbek
VENDA	Venda
VIETNAMESE	Vietnamese
WARAY-WARAY	Waray-Waray
WELSH	Welsh
WOLOF	Wolof
XHOSA	Xhosa
YAKUT	Yakut
YIDDISH	Yiddish
YORUBA	Yoruba
ZHUANG	Zhuang
ZULU	Zulu

Table 4: Example Language Codes

© 2015 Blind Squirrel Publishing, LLC, All Rights Reserved
www.dynamicsaxcompanions.com

Configuring Language Codes

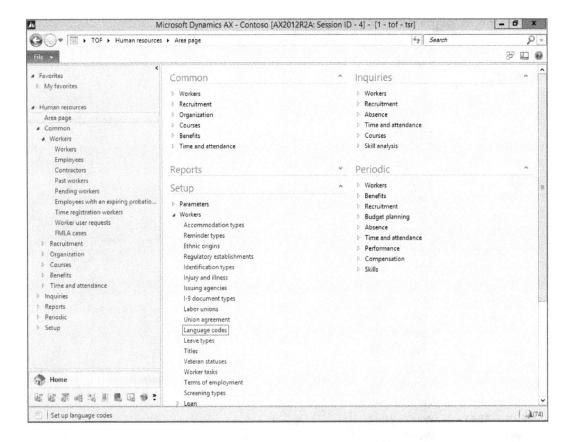

To do this, just click on the **Language Codes** menu item within the **Workers** folder of the **Setup** group within the **Human Resources** area.

© 2015 Blind Squirrel Publishing, LLC, All Rights Reserved
www.dynamicsaxcompanions.com

Configuring Language Codes

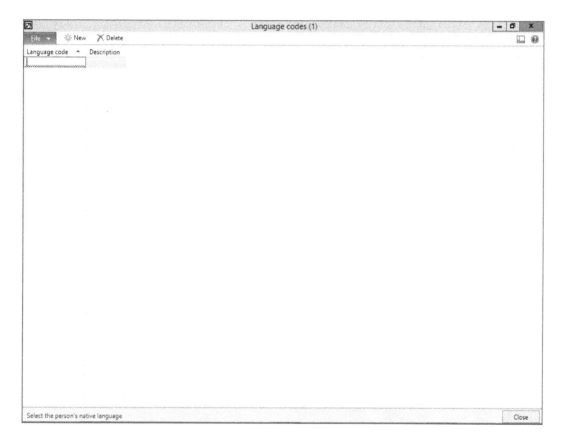

When the **Language Codes** maintenance form is displayed, click on the **New** button in the menu bar to create a new record.

© 2015 Blind Squirrel Publishing, LLC, All Rights Reserved
www.dynamicsaxcompanions.com

Configuring Language Codes

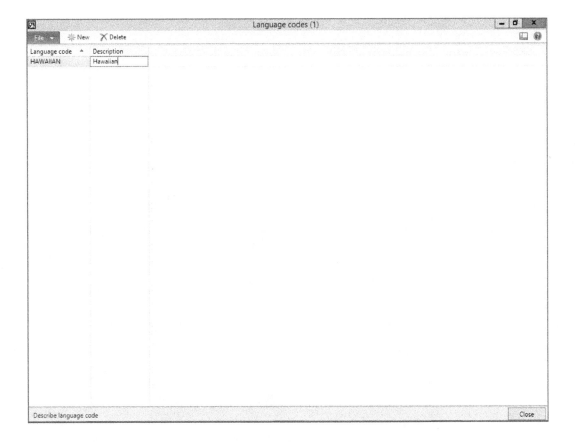

Then enter in the **Language Code** of **HAWAIIAN** and the **Description** of **Hawaiian**.

You can continue adding more Language Codes by repeating the process and when you are done, just click on the **Close** button to exit from the form.

© 2015 Blind Squirrel Publishing, LLC, All Rights Reserved
www.dynamicsaxcompanions.com

© 2015 Blind Squirrel Publishing, LLC, All Rights Reserved
www.dynamicsaxcompanions.com

© 2015 Blind Squirrel Publishing, LLC, All Rights Reserved
www.dynamicsaxcompanions.com

Importing Language Codes Using Excel

If you want to have a comprehensive list of Language Codes within Dynamics AX, then you probably don't want to load them all in by hand. To speed up the process we will show you how to use Excel to import them in from a template file.

© 2015 Blind Squirrel Publishing, LLC, All Rights Reserved
www.dynamicsaxcompanions.com

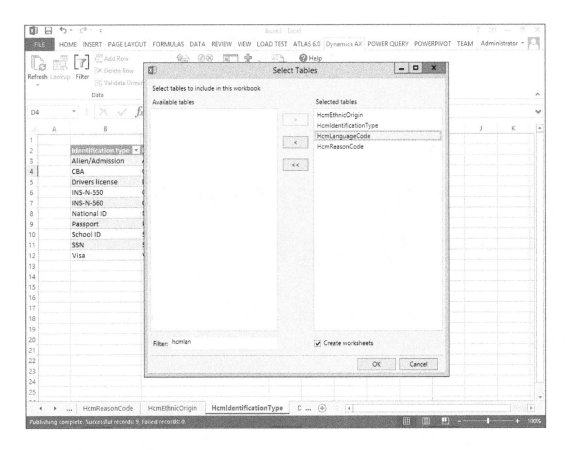

To do this, return to your Excel workbook that you used to import in the other codes and click on the **Add Data** button within the **Data** group of the **Dynamics AX** ribbon bar, and click on the **Add Tables** menu item again.

When the **Select Tables** dialog box is displayed, filter the table list down to the **HcmLanguageCodes** table, click on the **>** button to add it to the **Selected Tables** group and then click on the **OK** button.

© 2015 Blind Squirrel Publishing, LLC, All Rights Reserved
www.dynamicsaxcompanions.com

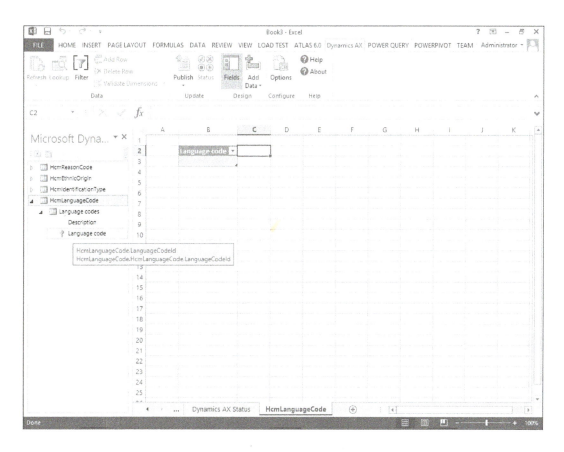

This will create a new worksheet for you linked to the **HcmLanguageCodes** table.

© 2015 Blind Squirrel Publishing, LLC, All Rights Reserved
www.dynamicsaxcompanions.com

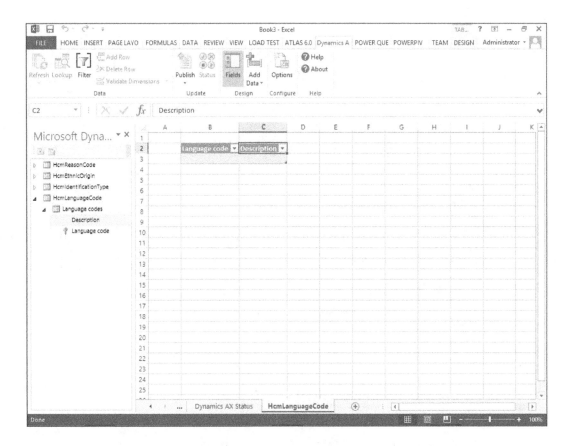

Drag the **Description** field from the field explorer on the left hand side for the workbook and add it to the table within the worksheet.

© 2015 Blind Squirrel Publishing, LLC, All Rights Reserved
www.dynamicsaxcompanions.com

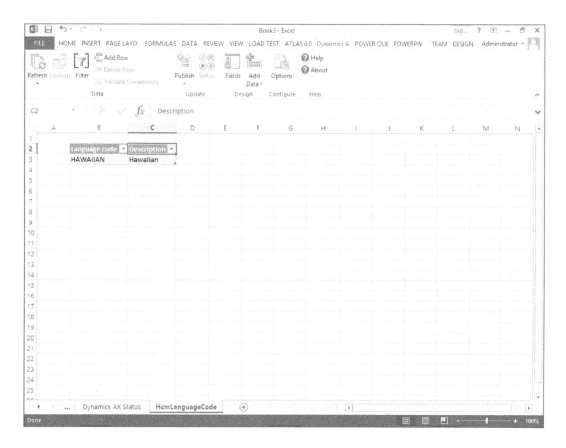

Now click on the **Fields** button within the **Design** group of the **Dynamics AX** ribbon bar to exit from design mode and then click on the **Refresh** button within the **Data** group of the **Dynamics AX** ribbon bar and click on the **Refresh All** menu item.

This will refresh the worksheet and you will be able to see all of the **Language Code** record(s) that you loaded in by hand.

© 2015 Blind Squirrel Publishing, LLC, All Rights Reserved
www.dynamicsaxcompanions.com

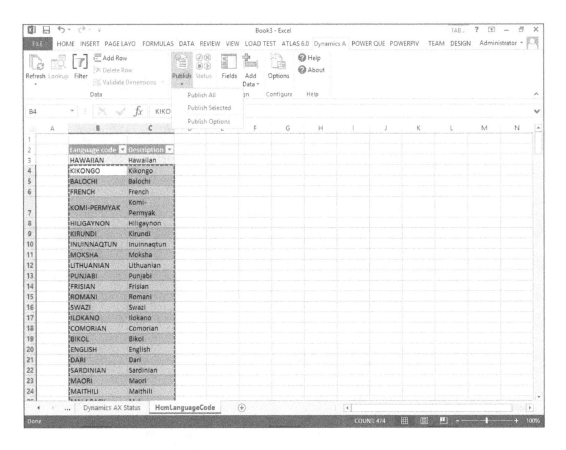

Now just paste in all of the **Language Codes** that you want to import into Dynamics AX into the worksheet.

Then click on the **Publish** button within the **Update** group of the **Dynamics AX** ribbon bar and click on the **Publish All** menu item.

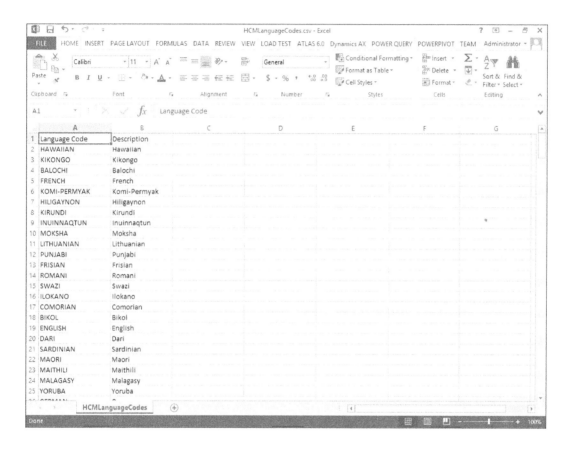

To save time, we have created a **CSV** file that contains all of the suggested **Language Codes** that you might want to use and they are available for download from the **Dynamics AX Companions** site. Here is the link to the resources page:

http://www.dynamicsaxcompanions.com/Bare-Bones-Configuration-Guides/Configuring-Human-Resources

© 2015 Blind Squirrel Publishing, LLC, All Rights Reserved
www.dynamicsaxcompanions.com

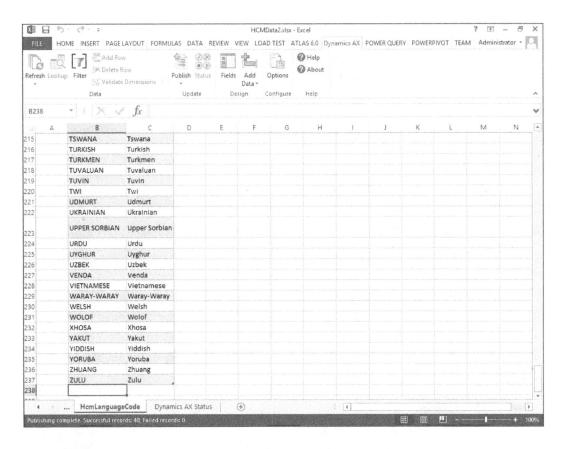

If everything goes well, then the worksheet will refresh and you will see all of the rows that you just added.

© 2015 Blind Squirrel Publishing, LLC, All Rights Reserved
www.dynamicsaxcompanions.com

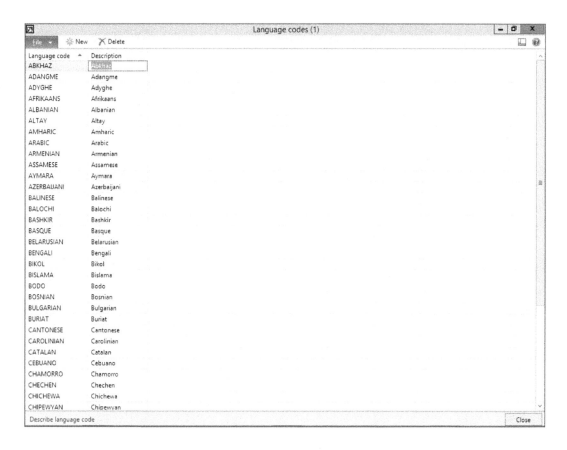

When you return back to the **Language Codes** maintenance form you will see that all of your new records are available for you.

© 2015 Blind Squirrel Publishing, LLC, All Rights Reserved
www.dynamicsaxcompanions.com

© 2015 Blind Squirrel Publishing, LLC, All Rights Reserved
www.dynamicsaxcompanions.com

Configuring Titles

One more set of codes that we will want to define are **Titles**. These are used to identify the business titles of all of the workers, and is important to do, because you cannot actually just enter in miscellaneous titles, they need to be in this list.

© 2015 Blind Squirrel Publishing, LLC, All Rights Reserved
www.dynamicsaxcompanions.com

Configuring Titles

Title	Title
Account Manager	Inventory & Allocation Manager
Accountant	IT Engineer
Accounting Manager	IT Manager
Accounts Payable Coordinator	Lean Officer
Accounts Receivable Coordn.	Lease Administrator
Allocation Specialist	Loss Prevention Manager
AR Administrator	Machine Operator
Attorney	Manager of Client Services
Budget Manager	Manager of Finance
Business Application Developer	Manager of Human Resources
Business Manager	Manager of Legal
Business System Developer	Manager of Sales & Marketing
Caixa de Loja	Managing Partner
Catalog Manager	Marketing Assistant
Category Manager	Marketing Executive
Chief Financial Officer	Marketing Manager
Compensation & Benefits Cons.	Marketing Staff
Consultant	Materials Manager
Controller	Merchandising Director
Credit and Collections Manager	Mgr of Category Mgrs
Customer Service Manager	Operations Manager
Customer Service Rep	Order Processor
Dedicated Sales Rep	Outbound Technician
Dedicated Sales Representative	Payroll Administrator
Design & Construction Manager	Picker
Director	Practice Manager
Director of Human Resources	President
Director of Marketing	Principal Consultant
Dispatcher	Process Engineer
E-Commerce Manager	Procurement Specialist
Fleet Manager	Product Designer
HR Assistant	Production Manager
HR Generalist	Production Planner
In-house Developer	Project Division Mgr

Table 6: Example Titles

© 2015 Blind Squirrel Publishing, LLC, All Rights Reserved
www.dynamicsaxcompanions.com

Configuring Titles

Title
Project Manager
Project Team Member
Purchasing Agent
Purchasing Manager
Quality Controller
Receptionist
Recruiting Specialist
Recruiting&Staffing Consulant
Regional Manager
Resource Manager
Retail Director
Sales Associate
Sales Manager
Senior Consultant
Shipping & Receiving Staff
Shop Supervisor
Store Cashier
Store Designer
Store Manager
Store Merchandiser
Systems Consultant
Training & Development Cons.
Transport Coordinator
Treasurer
Value Stream Manager
Vice President
VP of Finance & Administration
VP of Human Resources
VP of Operations
Warehouse Manager
Warehouse Worker
Waterspider

Table 6: Example Titles

© 2015 Blind Squirrel Publishing, LLC, All Rights Reserved
www.dynamicsaxcompanions.com

Configuring Titles

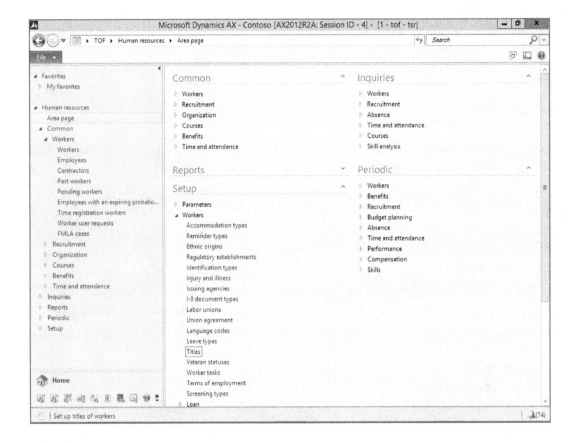

To do this, click on the **Titles** menu item within the **Workers** folder of the **Setup** group within the **Human Resources** area page.

© 2015 Blind Squirrel Publishing, LLC, All Rights Reserved
www.dynamicsaxcompanions.com

Configuring Titles

When the **Titles** list page is displayed, click on the **New** button in the menu bar to create a new record.

© 2015 Blind Squirrel Publishing, LLC, All Rights Reserved
www.dynamicsaxcompanions.com

Configuring Titles

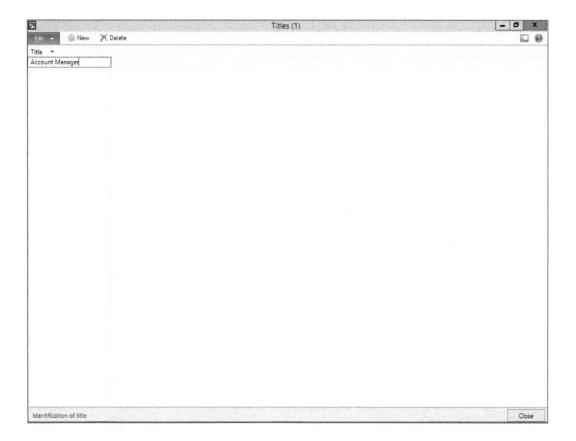

Then set the **Title** to **Account Manager.**

You can continue adding more **Titles** by repeating the process and when you are done, just click on the **Close** button to exit from the form.

© 2015 Blind Squirrel Publishing, LLC, All Rights Reserved
www.dynamicsaxcompanions.com

© 2015 Blind Squirrel Publishing, LLC, All Rights Reserved
www.dynamicsaxcompanions.com

© 2015 Blind Squirrel Publishing, LLC, All Rights Reserved
www.dynamicsaxcompanions.com

Importing Titles Using Excel

To make the loading of the Titles just a little bit easier, let's use Excel to import them in from a template file, and speed up the process a little.

© 2015 Blind Squirrel Publishing, LLC, All Rights Reserved
www.dynamicsaxcompanions.com

Importing Titles Using Excel

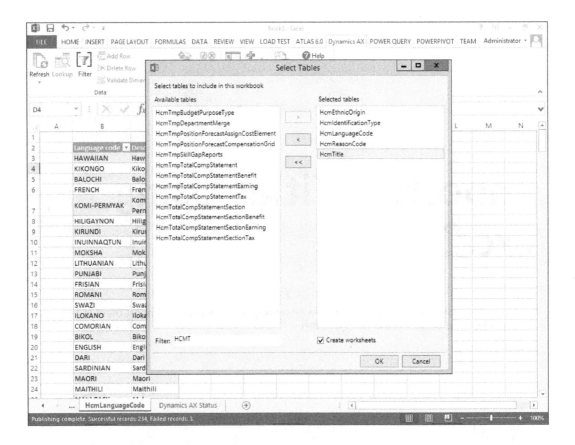

To do this, return to your Excel workbook that you used to import in the other codes and click on the **Add Data** button within the **Data** group of the **Dynamics AX** ribbon bar, and click on the **Add Tables** menu item again.

When the **Select Tables** dialog box is displayed, filter the table list down to the **HcmTitle** table, click on the **>** button to add it to the **Selected Tables** group and then click on the **OK** button.

© 2015 Blind Squirrel Publishing, LLC, All Rights Reserved
www.dynamicsaxcompanions.com

Importing Titles Using Excel

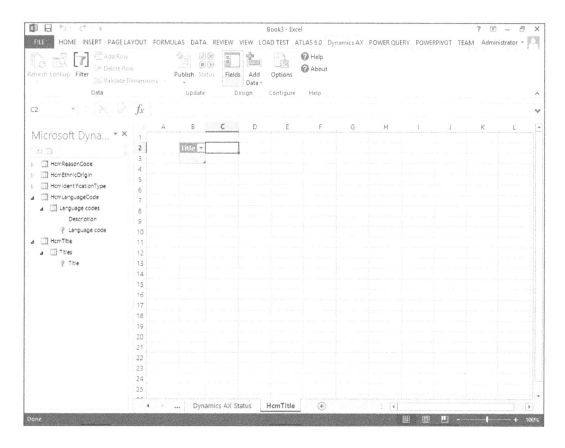

This will create a new worksheet for you linked to the **HcmTitle** table.

© 2015 Blind Squirrel Publishing, LLC, All Rights Reserved
www.dynamicsaxcompanions.com

Importing Titles Using Excel

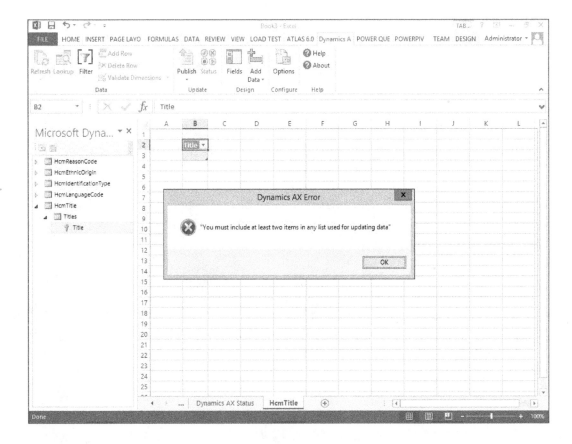

Note: There is a small quirk with this table though – there is only one field in the table, and if you try to exit out of design mode Excel will tell you that you need more than one field in the table before you can continue.

© 2015 Blind Squirrel Publishing, LLC, All Rights Reserved
www.dynamicsaxcompanions.com

Importing Titles Using Excel

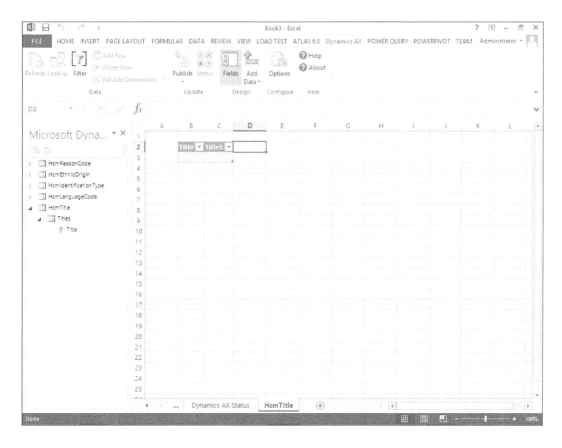

Don't worry – there is a trick – just drag the **Title** field from the field browser on the left over to the fields in the worksheet to create a second **Title** column.

© 2015 Blind Squirrel Publishing, LLC, All Rights Reserved
www.dynamicsaxcompanions.com

Importing Titles Using Excel

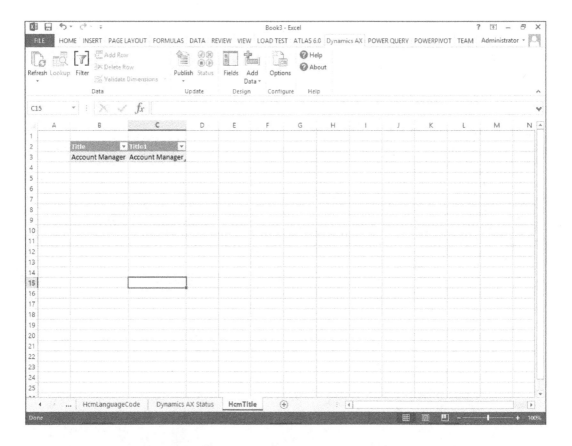

Now click on the **Fields** button within the **Design** group of the **Dynamics AX** ribbon bar to exit from design mode and then click on the **Refresh** button within the **Data** group of the **Dynamics AX** ribbon bar and click on the **Refresh All** menu item.

This will refresh the worksheet and you will be able to see all of the **Title** record(s) that you loaded in by hand, except the title is repeated.

© 2015 Blind Squirrel Publishing, LLC, All Rights Reserved
www.dynamicsaxcompanions.com

Importing Titles Using Excel

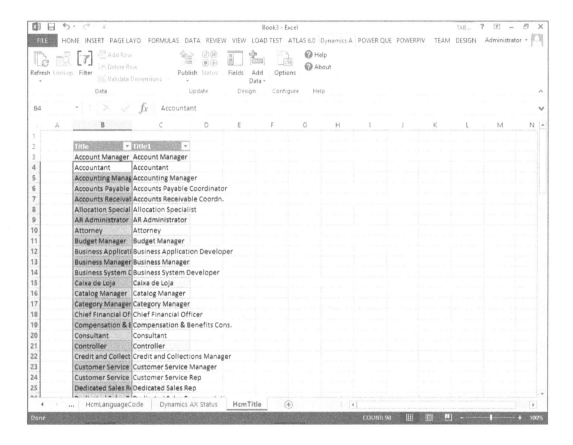

Now just paste in all of the **Titles** that you want to import into Dynamics AX into the worksheet.

Note: You only have to do this in one column, the second dummy column will automatically populate.

Then click on the **Publish** button within the **Update** group of the **Dynamics AX** ribbon bar and click on the **Publish All** menu item.

© 2015 Blind Squirrel Publishing, LLC, All Rights Reserved
www.dynamicsaxcompanions.com

Importing Titles Using Excel

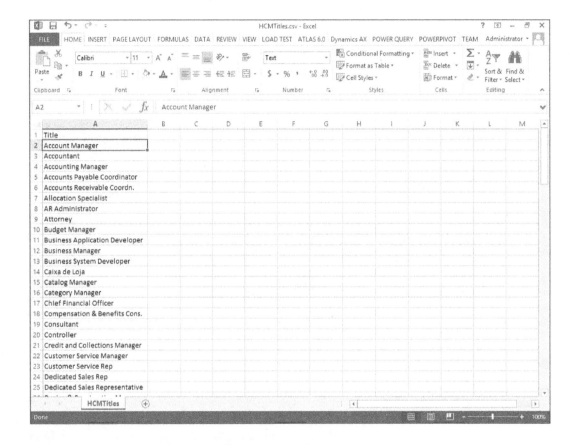

To save time, we have created a **CSV** file that contains all of the suggested **Titles** that you might want to use and they are available for download from the **Dynamics AX Companions** site. Here is the link to the resources page:

http://www.dynamicsaxcompanions.com/Bare-Bones-Configuration-Guides/Configuring-Human-Resources

© 2015 Blind Squirrel Publishing, LLC, All Rights Reserved
www.dynamicsaxcompanions.com

Importing Titles Using Excel

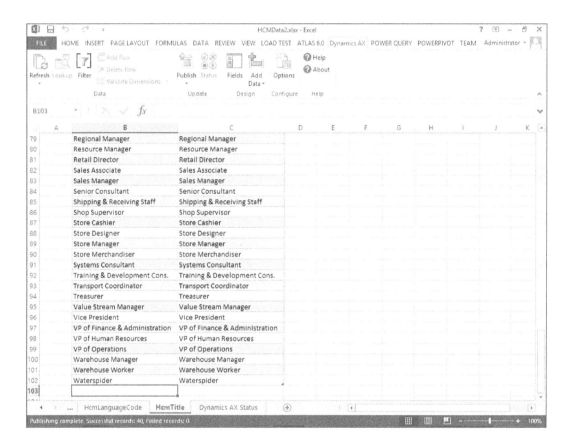

If everything goes well, then the worksheet will refresh and you will see all of the rows that you just added.

© 2015 Blind Squirrel Publishing, LLC, All Rights Reserved
www.dynamicsaxcompanions.com

Importing Titles Using Excel

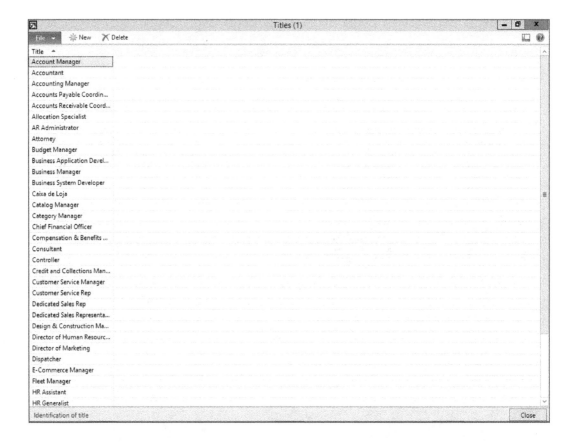

When you return back to the **Titles** maintenance form you will see that all of your new records are available for you.

© 2015 Blind Squirrel Publishing, LLC, All Rights Reserved
www.dynamicsaxcompanions.com

© 2015 Blind Squirrel Publishing, LLC, All Rights Reserved
www.dynamicsaxcompanions.com

© 2015 Blind Squirrel Publishing, LLC, All Rights Reserved
www.dynamicsaxcompanions.com

Creating A New Employee Worker

Now that we have all of our main codes configured we can start creating our **Employees** and **Workers** within the **Human Resources** area.

© 2015 Blind Squirrel Publishing, LLC, All Rights Reserved
www.dynamicsaxcompanions.com

Creating A New Employee Worker

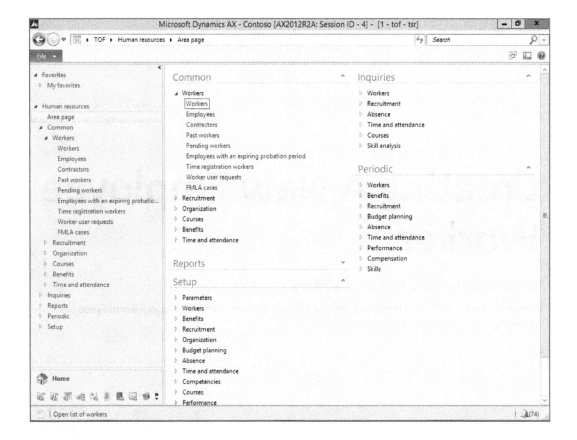

Wo do this, click on the **Workers** menu item within the **Workers** folder of the **Common** group within the **Human Resources** area page.

© 2015 Blind Squirrel Publishing, LLC, All Rights Reserved
www.dynamicsaxcompanions.com

Creating A New Employee Worker

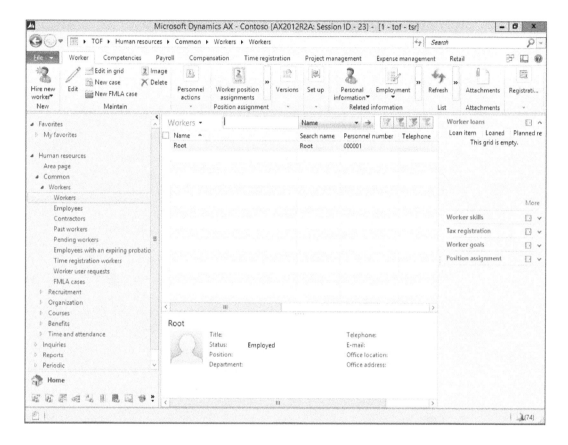

When the **Workers** list page is displayed you will be able to see all of your existing **Workers** that have been loaded.

© 2015 Blind Squirrel Publishing, LLC, All Rights Reserved
www.dynamicsaxcompanions.com

Creating A New Employee Worker

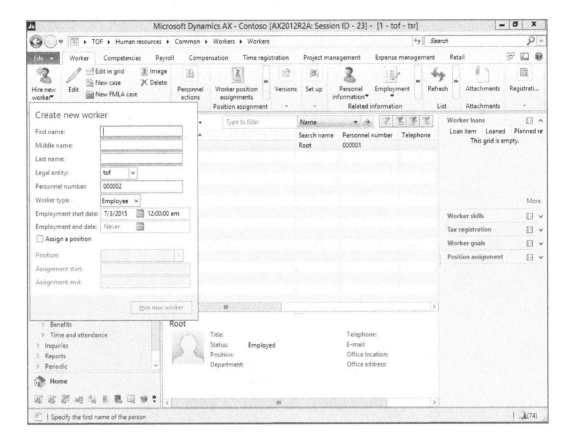

To add a new worker, click on the **Hire New Worker** button within the **New** group of the **Worker** ribbon bar. This will open up a quick entry form with the key **Worker** fields.

© 2015 Blind Squirrel Publishing, LLC, All Rights Reserved
www.dynamicsaxcompanions.com

Creating A New Employee Worker

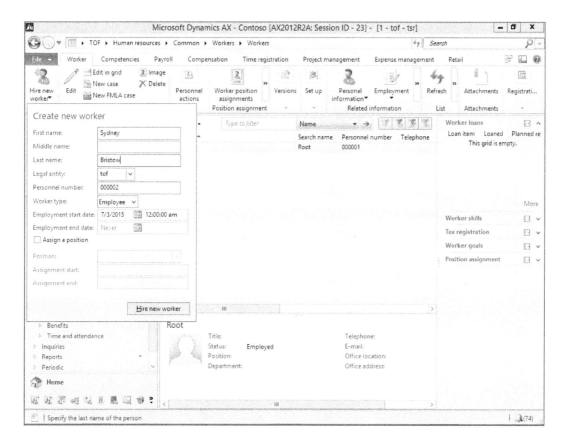

Enter in the **First Name** and **Last Name** of the worker – for example, **Sydney** and **Bristow** respectively,

© 2015 Blind Squirrel Publishing, LLC, All Rights Reserved
www.dynamicsaxcompanions.com

Creating A New Employee Worker

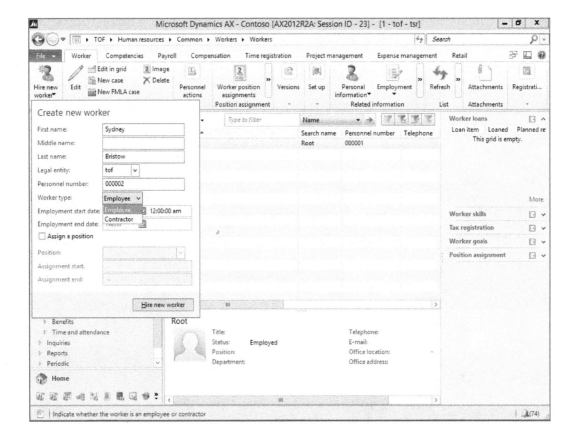

Then click on the **Worker Type** dropdown list and select the **Employee** value.

Note: If you chose the **Contractor** type then you would create a worker but it would be separated out from the full time employees.

Creating A New Employee Worker

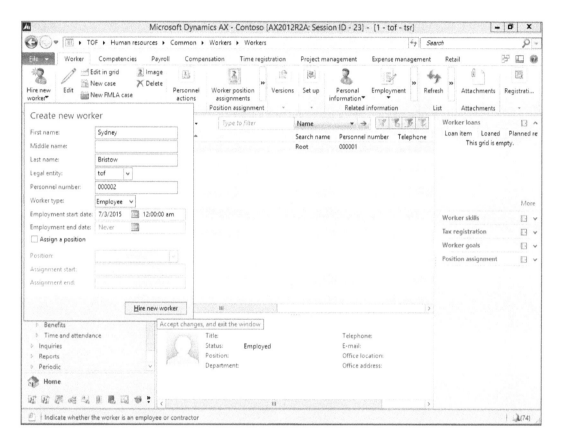

If you want, you can update the **Employment Start Date** and when you are ready, just click on the **Hire New Worker** button.

© 2015 Blind Squirrel Publishing, LLC, All Rights Reserved
www.dynamicsaxcompanions.com

Creating A New Employee Worker

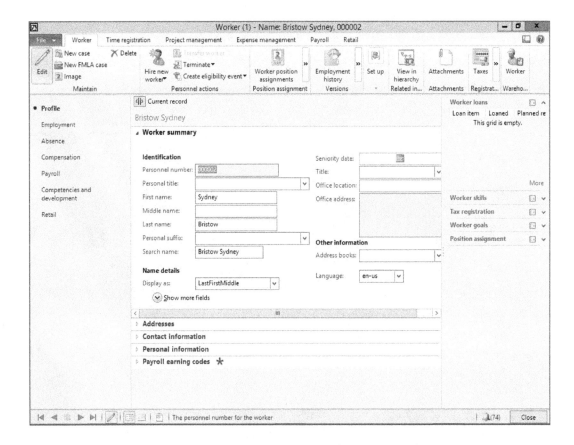

This will take you straight into the **Worker** details form and you are done.

© 2015 Blind Squirrel Publishing, LLC, All Rights Reserved
www.dynamicsaxcompanions.com

© 2015 Blind Squirrel Publishing, LLC, All Rights Reserved
www.dynamicsaxcompanions.com

© 2015 Blind Squirrel Publishing, LLC, All Rights Reserved
www.dynamicsaxcompanions.com

Updating Worker Details

Once you have your **Worker** created you can then start polishing up the data within the record to add more color to the information.

© 2015 Blind Squirrel Publishing, LLC, All Rights Reserved
www.dynamicsaxcompanions.com

Updating Worker Details

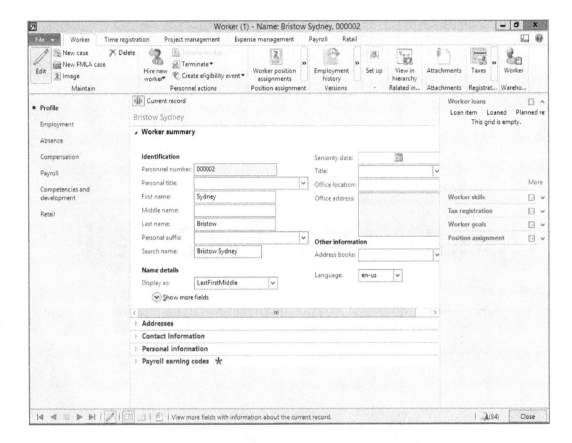

To start off, return to your **Worker** details and you will notice that there is a button at the bottom of the **General** tab group that is labeled **Show More Fields**. Click on it.

© 2015 Blind Squirrel Publishing, LLC, All Rights Reserved
www.dynamicsaxcompanions.com

Updating Worker Details

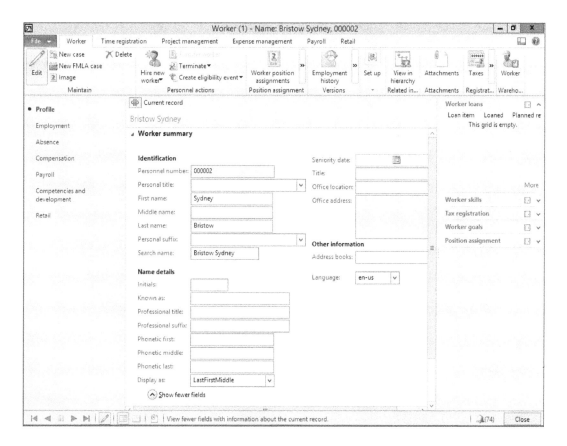

You will now be able to see more of the fields that are contained within the **General** tab group.

© 2015 Blind Squirrel Publishing, LLC, All Rights Reserved
www.dynamicsaxcompanions.com

Updating Worker Details

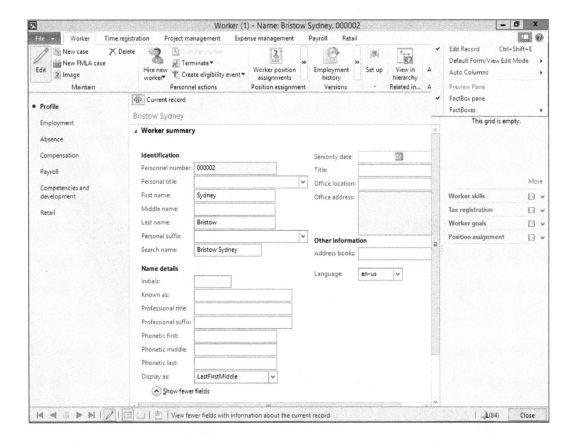

Also, the **Fact Boxes** on the right are hiding some of the information, so just to get more space to view the **Worker** details, click on the **Navigation Options** button in the top right of the form and when the menu is displayed, click on the **Fact Boxes** menu item to turn off the fact boxes.

© 2015 Blind Squirrel Publishing, LLC, All Rights Reserved
www.dynamicsaxcompanions.com

Updating Worker Details

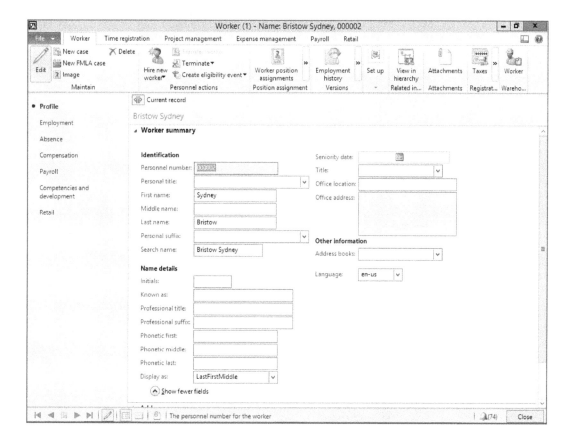

Now you can see just a little more data.

Note: If you want to turn on the Fact Boxes, then just repeat the process.

Updating Worker Details

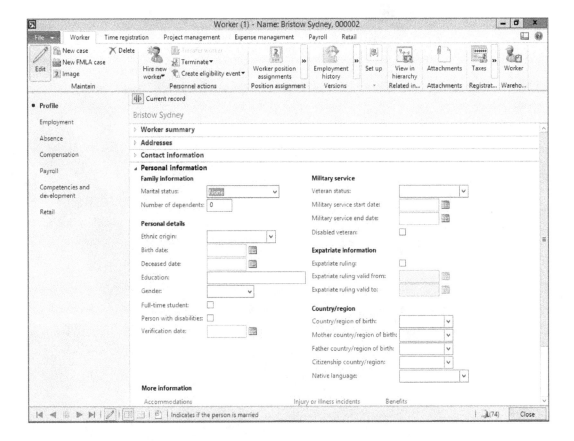

Now expand out the **Personal Information** tab group and you will be able to see some of the codes that we configured earlier.

Updating Worker Details

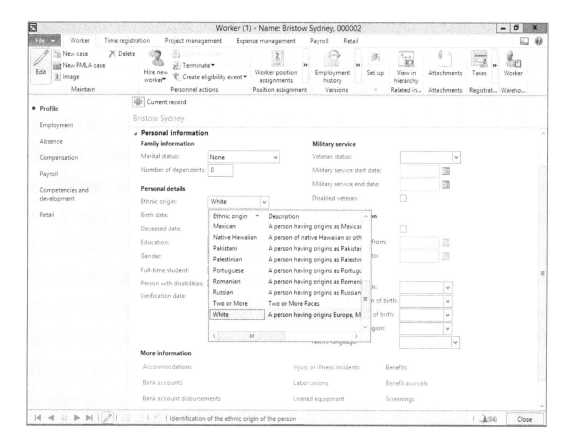

Click on the **Ethnic Group** dropdown list and select the record that the **Worker** is associated with. In this case Sydney Bristow is **White**.

© 2015 Blind Squirrel Publishing, LLC, All Rights Reserved
www.dynamicsaxcompanions.com

Updating Worker Details

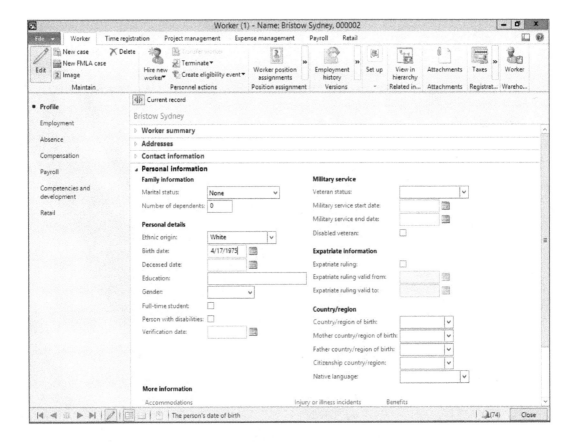

Then enter in the **Birth Date** of the employee. According to Wikipedia this is **April 17 1975**.

© 2015 Blind Squirrel Publishing, LLC, All Rights Reserved
www.dynamicsaxcompanions.com

Updating Worker Details

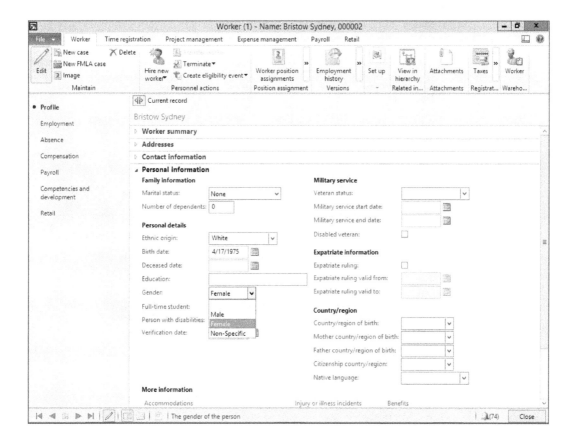

Now click on the **Gender** dropdown list and select the **Workers Gender**. That would be **Female**.

© 2015 Blind Squirrel Publishing, LLC, All Rights Reserved
www.dynamicsaxcompanions.com

Updating Worker Details

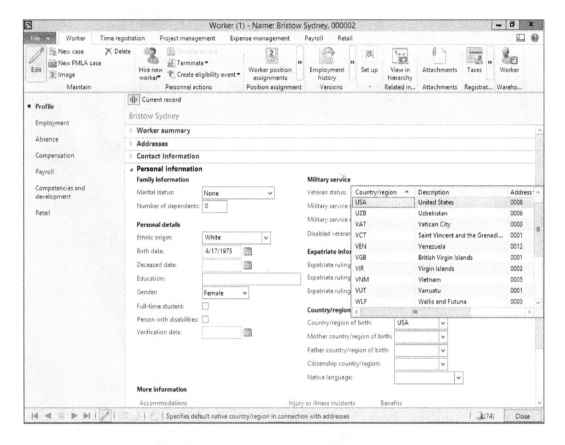

Now we will specify the **Workers** nationality and regional information. Start off by clicking on the **Country/Region of Birth** dropdown list and select **USA**.

Do the same for the **Mother Country/Region of Birth**, the **Father Country/Region of Birth**, and also the **Citizenship Country/Region**.

© 2015 Blind Squirrel Publishing, LLC, All Rights Reserved
www.dynamicsaxcompanions.com

Updating Worker Details

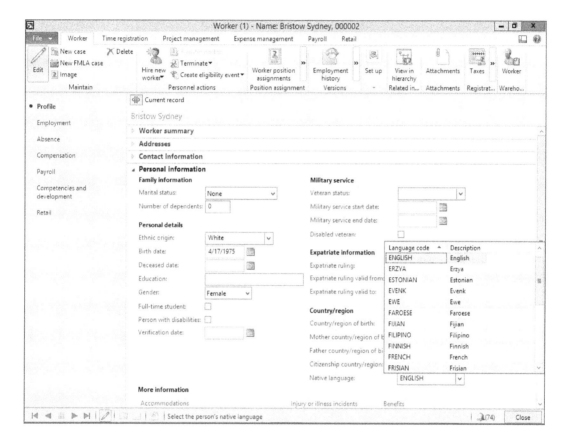

Now click on the **Native Language** dropdown list and select the primary language for the **Worker**. Here we will choose **ENGLISH**.

© 2015 Blind Squirrel Publishing, LLC, All Rights Reserved
www.dynamicsaxcompanions.com

© 2015 Blind Squirrel Publishing, LLC, All Rights Reserved
www.dynamicsaxcompanions.com

Adding An Image To The Employee Record

If you want to be very efficient, you can also assign a photo to the **Workers** record so that they are easier to identify visually.

© 2015 Blind Squirrel Publishing, LLC, All Rights Reserved
www.dynamicsaxcompanions.com

Adding An Image To The Employee Record

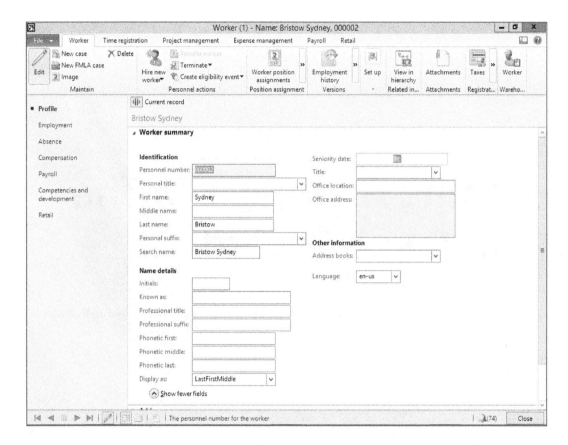

To do this, open up your **Worker** details and click on the **Image** button within the **Maintain** group of the **Worker** ribbon bar.

© 2015 Blind Squirrel Publishing, LLC, All Rights Reserved
www.dynamicsaxcompanions.com

Adding An Image To The Employee Record

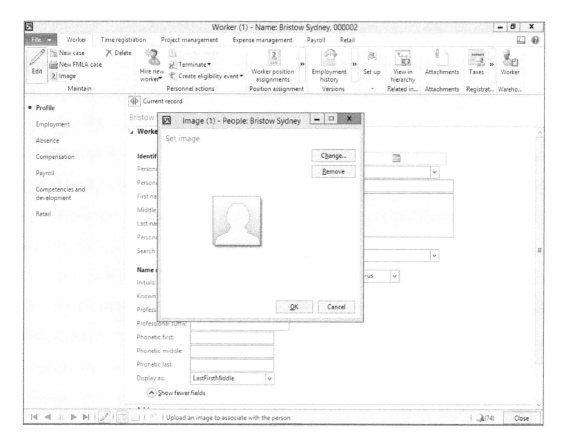

When the **Set Image** dialog box is displayed, click on the **Change Image** button to the right of the form.

© 2015 Blind Squirrel Publishing, LLC, All Rights Reserved
www.dynamicsaxcompanions.com

Adding An Image To The Employee Record

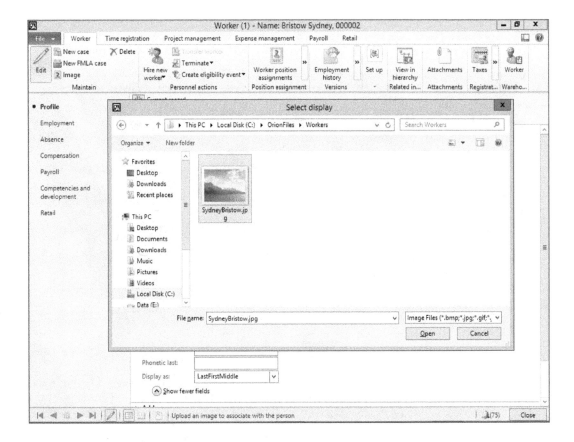

This will allow you to browse to the image file for the worker, and you can then just click the **Open** button to use it on the **Worker** record.

© 2015 Blind Squirrel Publishing, LLC, All Rights Reserved
www.dynamicsaxcompanions.com

Adding An Image To The Employee Record

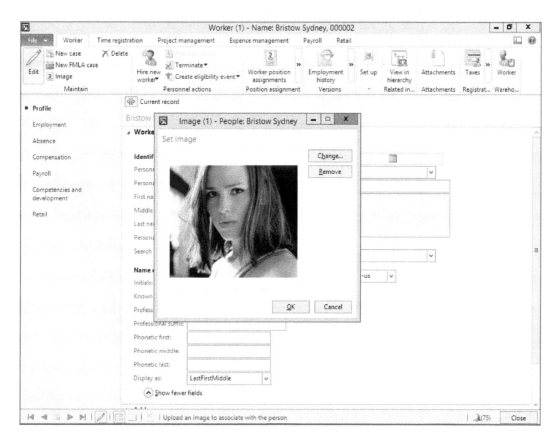

When you return back to the **Set Image** dialog box you will see that the image is now associated with the **Worker** and you can click on the **OK** button to exit from the form.

© 2015 Blind Squirrel Publishing, LLC, All Rights Reserved
www.dynamicsaxcompanions.com

Adding An Image To The Employee Record

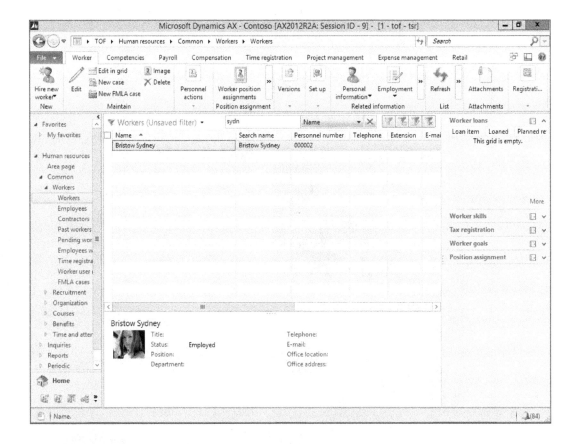

Just as a side note, now when you browse through the **Worker** list page, when you select the **Worker** the image will show in the preview pane at the bottom as well.

© 2015 Blind Squirrel Publishing, LLC, All Rights Reserved
www.dynamicsaxcompanions.com

© 2015 Blind Squirrel Publishing, LLC, All Rights Reserved
www.dynamicsaxcompanions.com

© 2015 Blind Squirrel Publishing, LLC, All Rights Reserved
www.dynamicsaxcompanions.com

Importing In Employees Using The Data Import Export Framework

If you have a handful of employees then adding them by hand is not a big deal, but if you have a lot of employees that you want to load into Dynamics AX, then you will probably want to use the Data Import Export Framework within Dynamics AX to load the data in from a spreadsheet.

© 2015 Blind Squirrel Publishing, LLC, All Rights Reserved
www.dynamicsaxcompanions.com

Importing In Employees Using The Data Import Export Framework

PersonnelNumber	FirstName	LastName	Gender	LegalEntity	EmploymentType
100001	Michael	Vaughn	Male	TOF	Employee
100002	Jack	Bristow	Male	TOF	Employee
100003	Arvin	Sloane	Male	TOF	Employee
100004	Marcus	Dixon	Male	TOF	Employee
100005	Marshall	Flinkman	Male	TOF	Employee
100006	Eric	Weiss	Male	TOF	Employee
100007	Julian	Sark	Male	TOF	Employee
100008	Will	Tippin	Male	TOF	Employee
100009	Francie	Calfo	Male	TOF	Employee
100010	Irina	Derevko	Female	TOF	Employee
100011	Lauren	Reed	Female	TOF	Employee
100012	Nadia	Santos	Female	TOF	Employee
100013	Renée	Rienne	Female	TOF	Employee
100014	Rachel	Gibson	Female	TOF	Employee
100015	Thomas	Grace	Male	TOF	Employee
100016	Kelly	Peyton	Female	TOF	Employee
100017	Anna	Espinosa	Female	TOF	Employee
100018	Katya	Derevko	Female	TOF	Employee
100019	Elena	Derevko	Female	TOF	Employee
100020	Judy	Barnett	Female	TOF	Employee
100021	Emily	Sloane	Female	TOF	Employee
100022	Carrie	Bowman	Female	TOF	Employee
100023	Arthur	Devlin	Male	TOF	Employee
100024	Charlie	Bernard	Male	TOF	Employee
100025	Steven	Haladki	Male	TOF	Employee
100026	Robert	Lindsey	Male	TOF	Employee
100027	Calvin	McCullough	Male	TOF	Employee
100028	Hayden	Chase	Female	TOF	Employe
100029	Diane	Dixon	Female	TOF	Employee
100030	Zhang	Lee	Male	TOF	Employee

Table 7: Sample Employees

© 2015 Blind Squirrel Publishing, LLC, All Rights Reserved
www.dynamicsaxcompanions.com

Importing In Employees Using The Data Import Export Framework

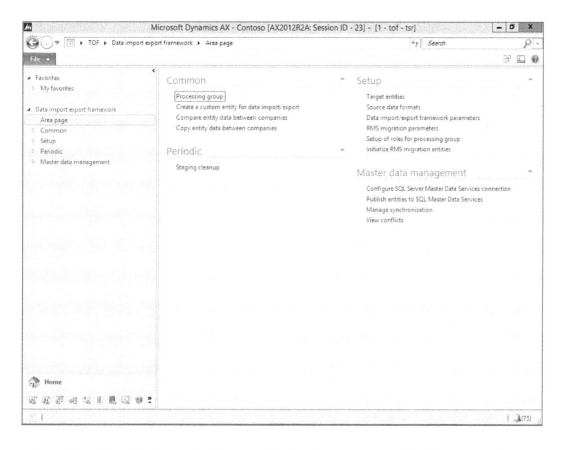

To do this, click on the **Processing Groups** within the **Common** group of the **Data Import Export Framework** area page.

© 2015 Blind Squirrel Publishing, LLC, All Rights Reserved
www.dynamicsaxcompanions.com

Importing In Employees Using The Data Import Export Framework

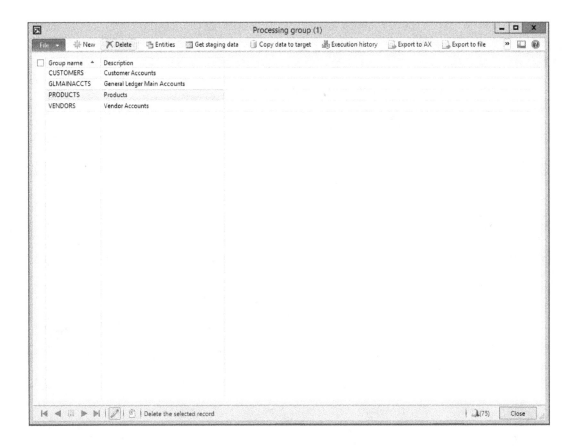

When the **Processing Group** list page is displayed, click on the **New** button in the menu bar to create a new record.

© 2015 Blind Squirrel Publishing, LLC, All Rights Reserved
www.dynamicsaxcompanions.com

Importing In Employees Using The Data Import Export Framework

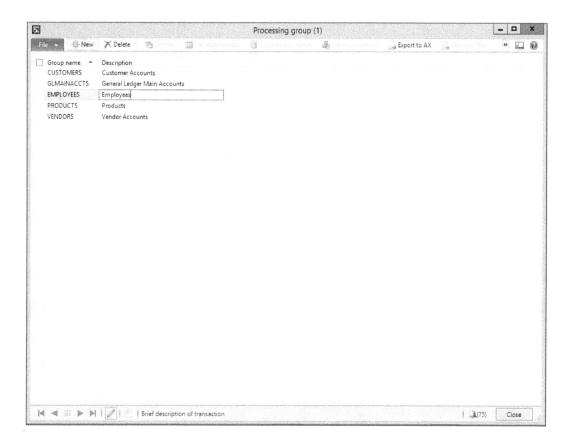

Then set the **Group Name** to **EMPLOYEES** and the **Description** to **Employees**.

© 2015 Blind Squirrel Publishing, LLC, All Rights Reserved
www.dynamicsaxcompanions.com

Importing In Employees Using The Data Import Export Framework

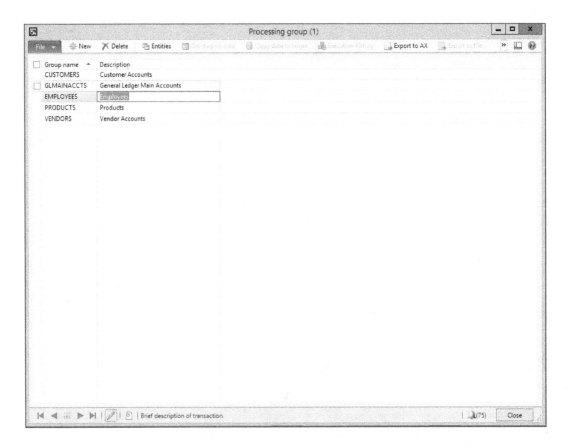

Save the record by pressing **CTRL+S** and that will enable you to click on the **Entities** button within the menu bar.

© 2015 Blind Squirrel Publishing, LLC, All Rights Reserved
www.dynamicsaxcompanions.com

Importing In Employees Using The Data Import Export Framework

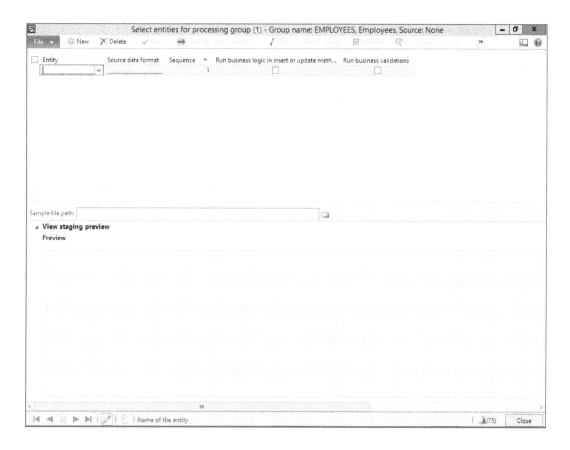

When the **Select Entities For Processing Groups** maintenance form is displayed, click on the **New** button in the menu bar to add a new **Entity** record.

© 2015 Blind Squirrel Publishing, LLC, All Rights Reserved
www.dynamicsaxcompanions.com

Importing In Employees Using The Data Import Export Framework

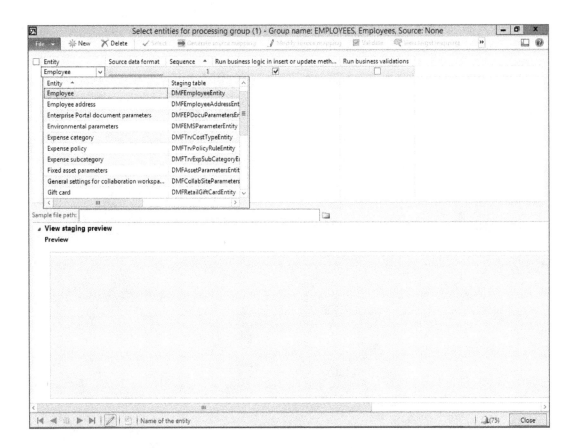

Click on the **Entity** dropdown list and select the **Employee** entity.

© 2015 Blind Squirrel Publishing, LLC, All Rights Reserved
www.dynamicsaxcompanions.com

Importing In Employees Using The Data Import Export Framework

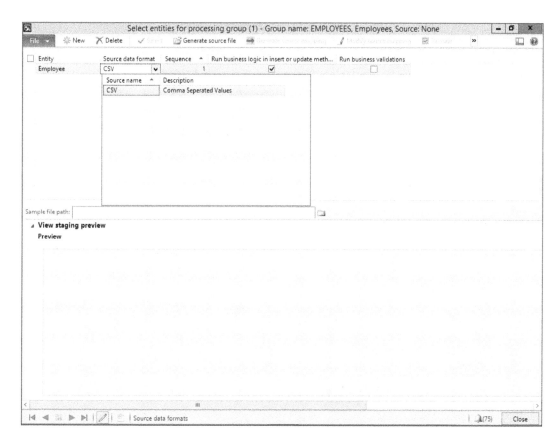

Then click on the **Source Data Format** dropdown list and select the **CSV** data format.

© 2015 Blind Squirrel Publishing, LLC, All Rights Reserved
www.dynamicsaxcompanions.com

Importing In Employees Using The Data Import Export Framework

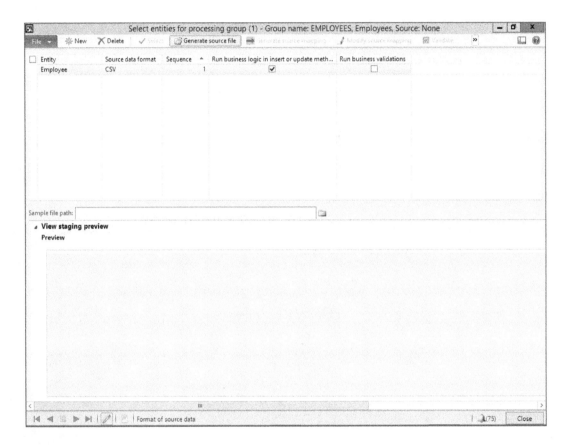

After you have done that, click on the **Generate Source File** button in the menui bar to start formatting the import file.

© 2015 Blind Squirrel Publishing, LLC, All Rights Reserved
www.dynamicsaxcompanions.com

Importing In Employees Using The Data Import Export Framework

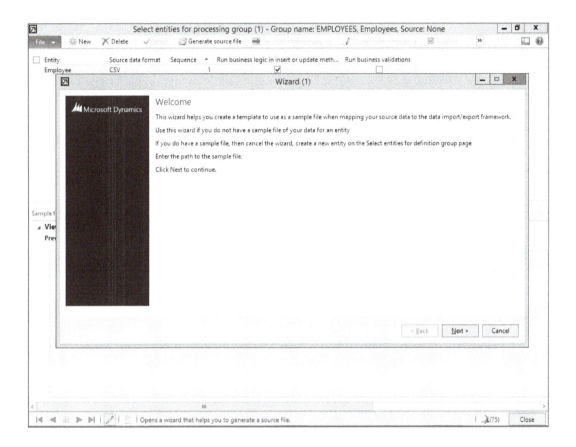

When the Import Wizard is displayed, click on the **Next** button to start the process.

© 2015 Blind Squirrel Publishing, LLC, All Rights Reserved
www.dynamicsaxcompanions.com

Importing In Employees Using The Data Import Export Framework

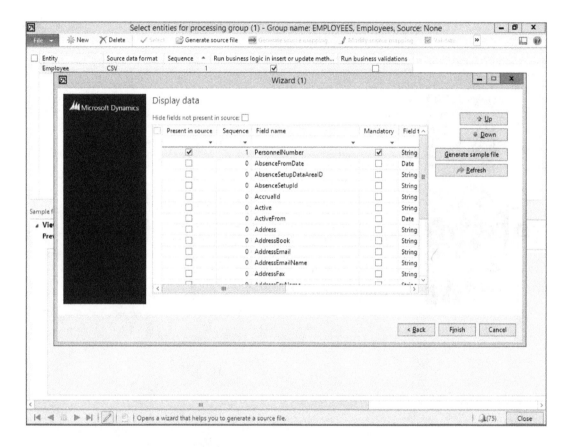

That will take you to the **Display Data** page where you will be able to see all of the fields that are available to be imported, and also the ones that have already been selected.

Note: If the search bar is not showing at the top of the form, then turn it on by pressing **CTRL+G**. This is going to make the following selections so much easier.

© 2015 Blind Squirrel Publishing, LLC, All Rights Reserved
www.dynamicsaxcompanions.com

Importing In Employees Using The Data Import Export Framework

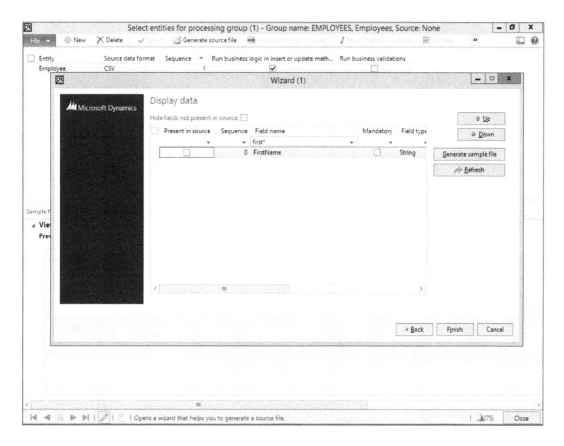

Type **first*** into the search field for the **Field Name**. This will filter out the records and you will see the **FirstName** field. Click on the **Present In Source** checkbox for the field.

© 2015 Blind Squirrel Publishing, LLC, All Rights Reserved
www.dynamicsaxcompanions.com

Importing In Employees Using The Data Import Export Framework

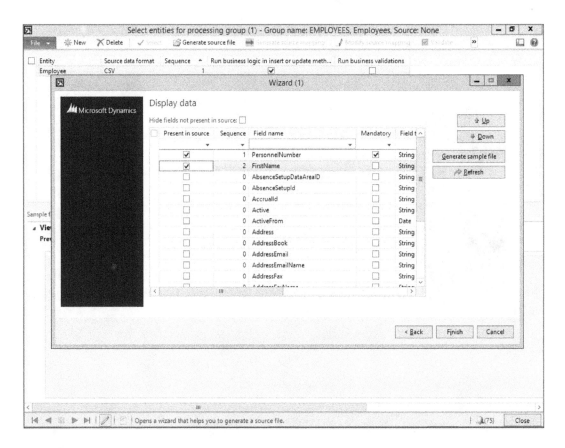

This will return you back to the field list and now you will have the **FirstName** field as an import field.

© 2015 Blind Squirrel Publishing, LLC, All Rights Reserved
www.dynamicsaxcompanions.com

Importing In Employees Using The Data Import Export Framework

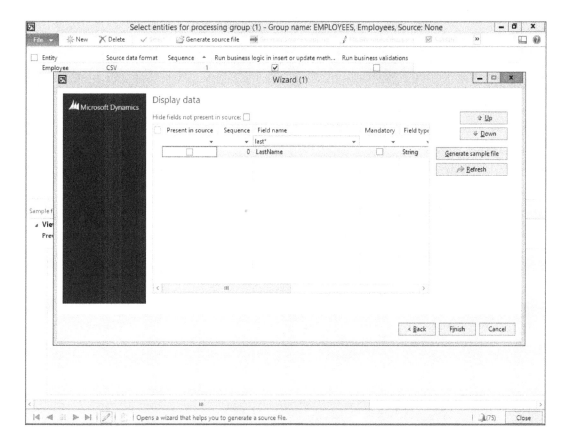

Next type **last*** into the search field for the **Field Name**. This will filter out the records and you will see the **LastName** field. Click on the **Present In Source** checkbox for the field.

© 2015 Blind Squirrel Publishing, LLC, All Rights Reserved
www.dynamicsaxcompanions.com

Importing In Employees Using The Data Import Export Framework

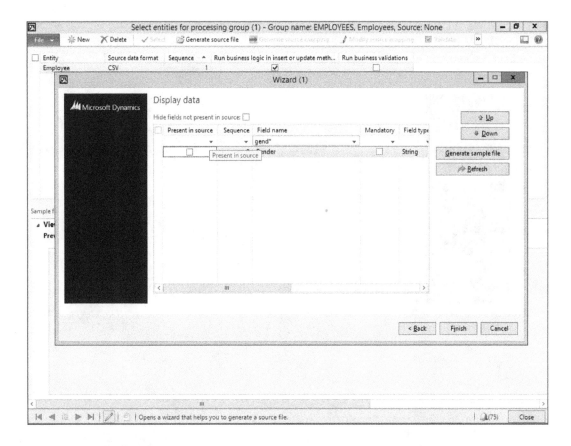

Now type **gender*** into the search field for the **Field Name**. This will filter out the records and you will see the **Gender** field. Click on the **Present In Source** checkbox for the field.

© 2015 Blind Squirrel Publishing, LLC, All Rights Reserved
www.dynamicsaxcompanions.com

Importing In Employees Using The Data Import Export Framework

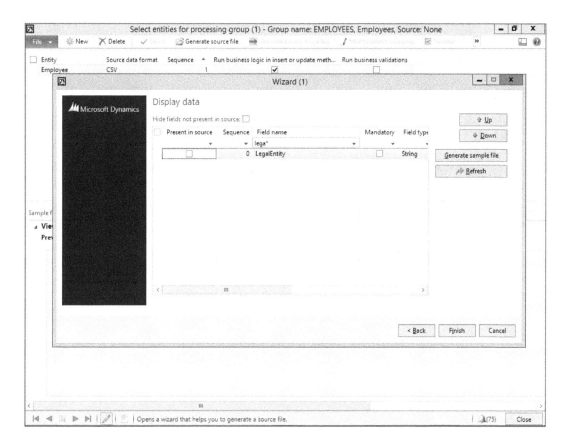

Next type **legal*** into the search field for the **Field Name**. This will filter out the records and you will see the **Legal Entity** field. Click on the **Present In Source** checkbox for the field.

© 2015 Blind Squirrel Publishing, LLC, All Rights Reserved
www.dynamicsaxcompanions.com

Importing In Employees Using The Data Import Export Framework

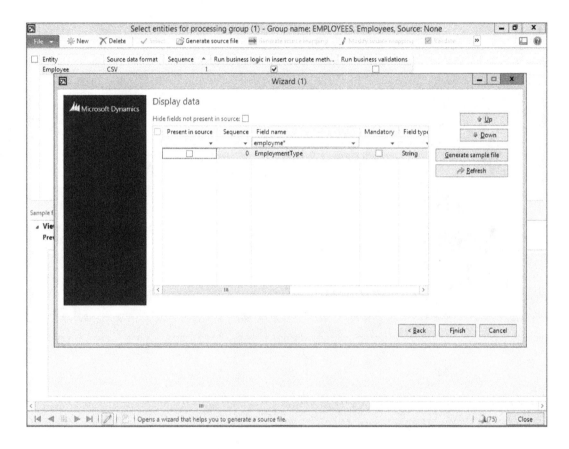

Finally type **Employme*** into the search field for the **Field Name**. This will filter out the records and you will see the **EmploymentType** field. Click on the **Present In Source** checkbox for the field.

© 2015 Blind Squirrel Publishing, LLC, All Rights Reserved
www.dynamicsaxcompanions.com

daxc

Importing In Employees Using The Data Import Export Framework

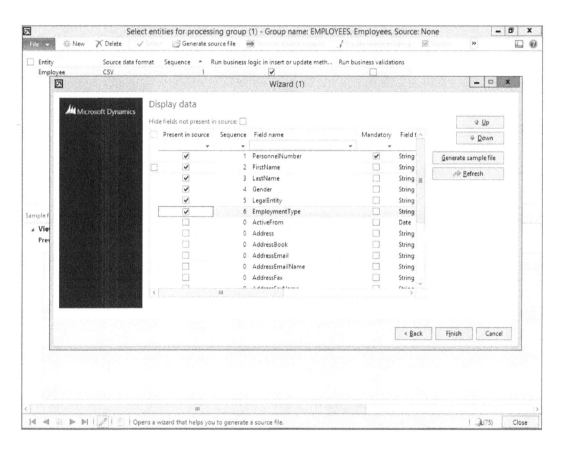

Now that you have all of the main fields that you need in the template, click on the **Generate Sample File** button

© 2015 Blind Squirrel Publishing, LLC, All Rights Reserved
www.dynamicsaxcompanions.com

Importing In Employees Using The Data Import Export Framework

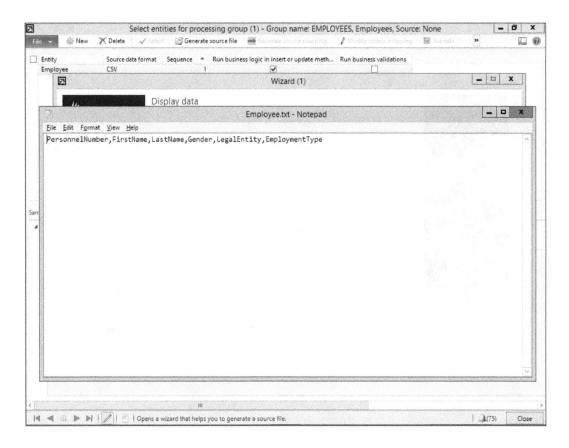

This will create your sample CSV file for the import. Just click on the **File** menu and select the **Save** option.

© 2015 Blind Squirrel Publishing, LLC, All Rights Reserved
www.dynamicsaxcompanions.com

Importing In Employees Using The Data Import Export Framework

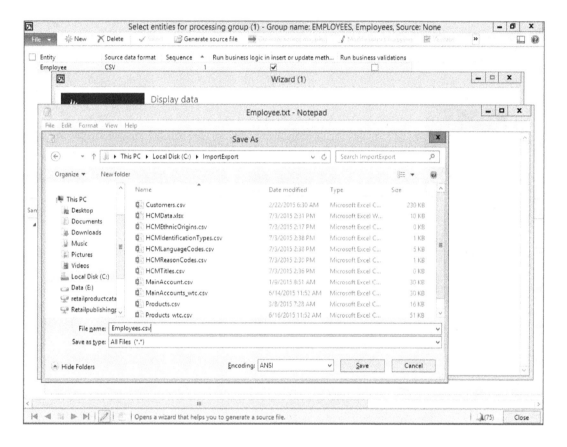

And when the **Save As** dialog box is displayed, navigate to the location where you are storing all of your import files, set the **Name** to **Employees.csv** and then click on the **Save** button.

© 2015 Blind Squirrel Publishing, LLC, All Rights Reserved
www.dynamicsaxcompanions.com

Importing In Employees Using The Data Import Export Framework

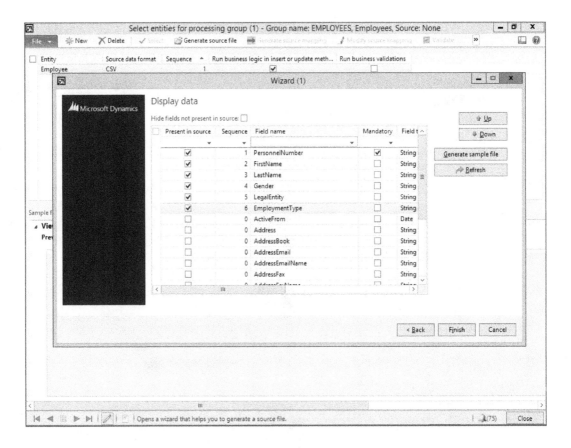

When you return back to the wizard, click on the **Finish** button to exit from the form.

© 2015 Blind Squirrel Publishing, LLC, All Rights Reserved
www.dynamicsaxcompanions.com

Importing In Employees Using The Data Import Export Framework

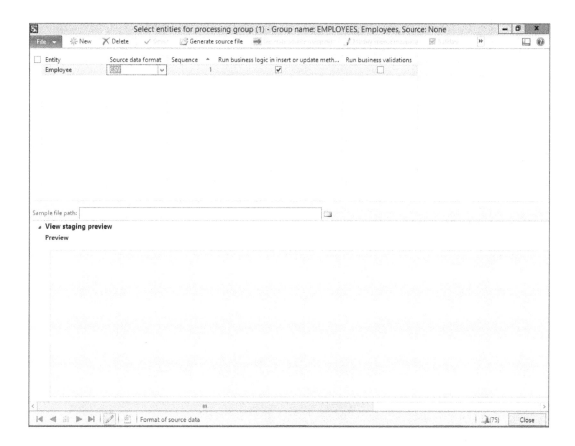

When you return back to the **Select Entities For Processing** form, click on the **Folder** icon to the right of the **Sample File Path** field.

Importing In Employees Using The Data Import Export Framework

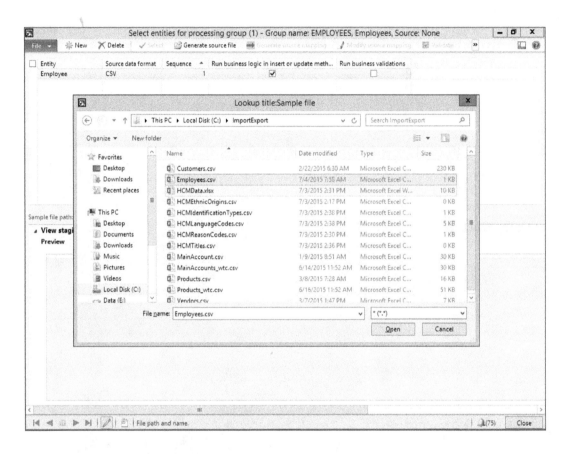

When the **Lookup Sample File** browser is displayed, navigate to the sample file that you just created and then click the **Open** button.

© 2015 Blind Squirrel Publishing, LLC, All Rights Reserved
www.dynamicsaxcompanions.com

Importing In Employees Using The Data Import Export Framework

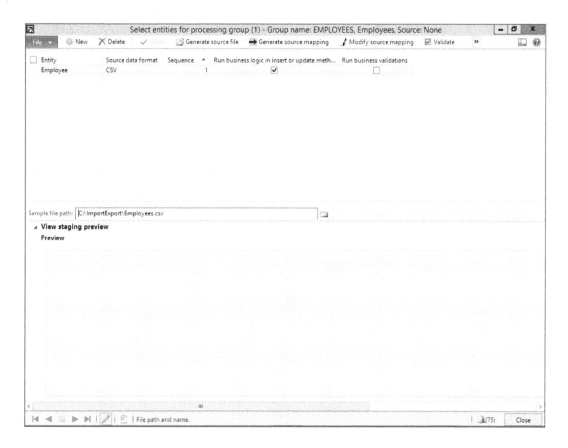

Now that you have linked the sample file to the mapping, click on the **Generate Source Mapping** button within the menu bar.

© 2015 Blind Squirrel Publishing, LLC, All Rights Reserved
www.dynamicsaxcompanions.com

Importing In Employees Using The Data Import Export Framework

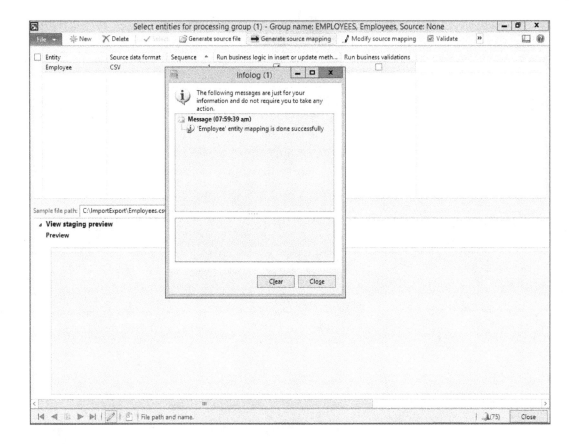

Next you should see an InfoLog that says that everything was correctly mapped and you can then click on the **Close** button to dismiss the form.

© 2015 Blind Squirrel Publishing, LLC, All Rights Reserved
www.dynamicsaxcompanions.com

Importing In Employees Using The Data Import Export Framework

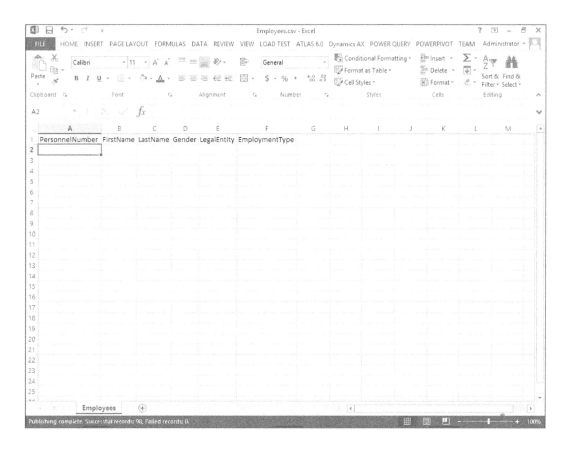

Now find the sample CSV file that you just created and open it up within Excel.

© 2015 Blind Squirrel Publishing, LLC, All Rights Reserved
www.dynamicsaxcompanions.com

Importing In Employees Using The Data Import Export Framework

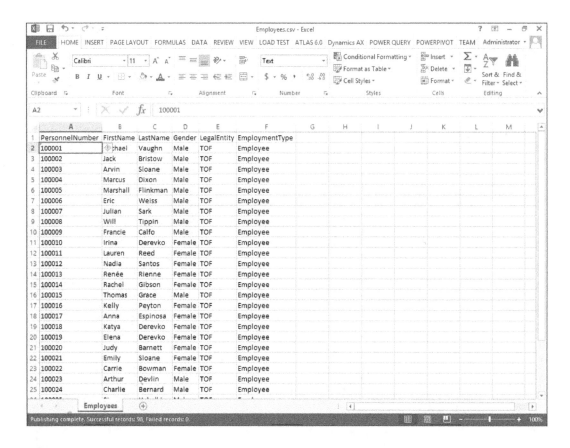

Now just paste in all of your employee information into the spreadsheet and save and close the file.

Note: If you are a covert spy operation, or if you just want to use the sample data that we created, then you can download it from the **Dynamics AX Companions** site. Here is the link to the resources page:

http://www.dynamicsaxcompanions.com/Bare-Bones-Configuration-Guides/Configuring-Human-Resources

© 2015 Blind Squirrel Publishing, LLC, All Rights Reserved
www.dynamicsaxcompanions.com

Importing In Employees Using The Data Import Export Framework

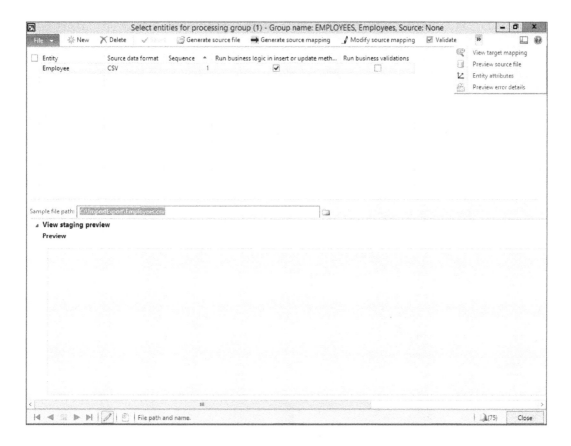

To make sure that everything looks good, click on the **Preview Source File** within the menu bar.

© 2015 Blind Squirrel Publishing, LLC, All Rights Reserved
www.dynamicsaxcompanions.com

Importing In Employees Using The Data Import Export Framework

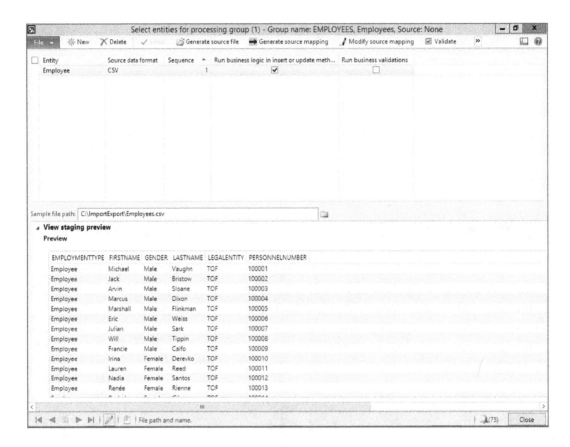

Within the **Preview** pane you should see all of your employees now show up.

Now click on the **Close** button to exit from the form.

© 2015 Blind Squirrel Publishing, LLC, All Rights Reserved
www.dynamicsaxcompanions.com

Importing In Employees Using The Data Import Export Framework

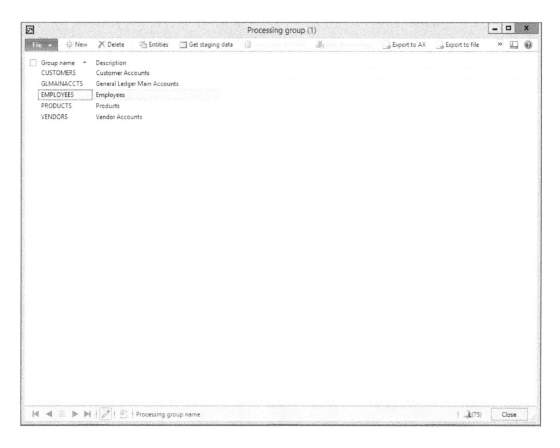

When you return to the **Processing Group** form, click on the **Get Staging Data** button in the menu bar.

© 2015 Blind Squirrel Publishing, LLC, All Rights Reserved
www.dynamicsaxcompanions.com

Importing In Employees Using The Data Import Export Framework

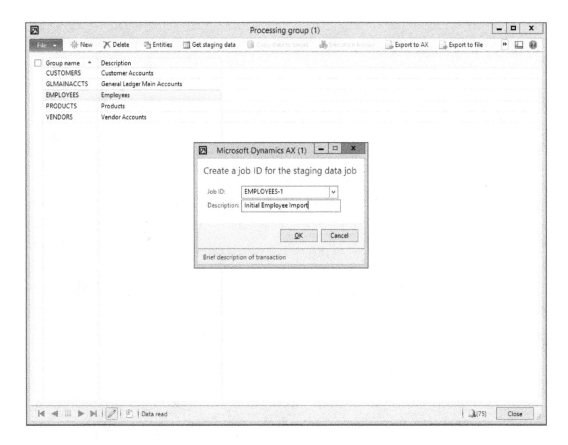

When the **Job Details** dialog box is displayed, enter in a better **Description** to describe the jobs function and then click on the **OK** button

© 2015 Blind Squirrel Publishing, LLC, All Rights Reserved
www.dynamicsaxcompanions.com

Importing In Employees Using The Data Import Export Framework

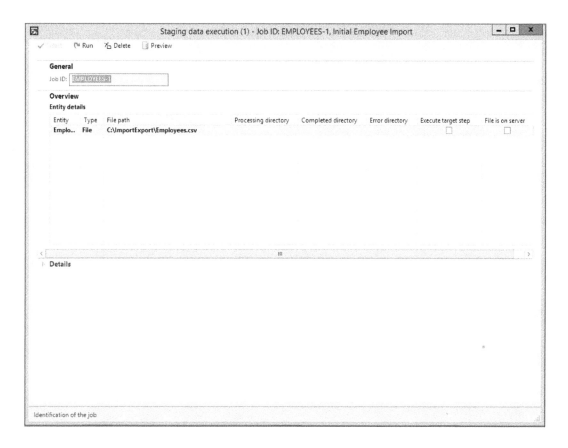

When the **Staging Data Execution** form is displayed, click on the **Preview** button to double check the data.

© 2015 Blind Squirrel Publishing, LLC, All Rights Reserved
www.dynamicsaxcompanions.com

Importing In Employees Using The Data Import Export Framework

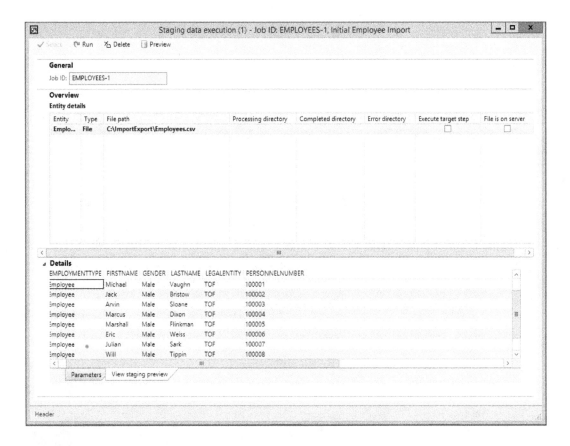

In the **Details** panel you should see the data again.

Note: This is a little bit more stringent a test than the first preview that we did, so it's a good idea to test it this way again.

© 2015 Blind Squirrel Publishing, LLC, All Rights Reserved
www.dynamicsaxcompanions.com

Importing In Employees Using The Data Import Export Framework

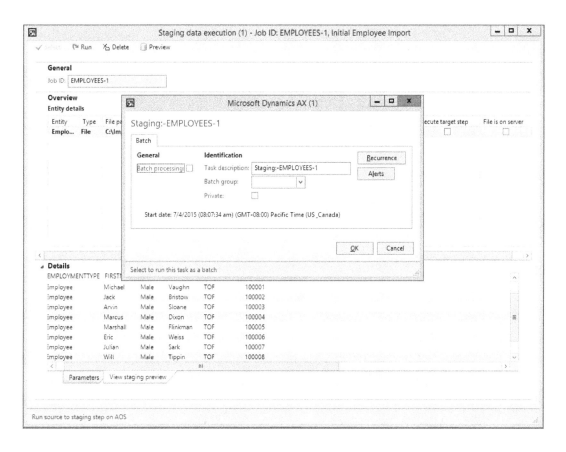

Now click on the **Run** button in the menu bar.

This will open up the **Processing** dialog box. All you need to do to kick off the process is to click on the **OK** button.

© 2015 Blind Squirrel Publishing, LLC, All Rights Reserved
www.dynamicsaxcompanions.com

Importing In Employees Using The Data Import Export Framework

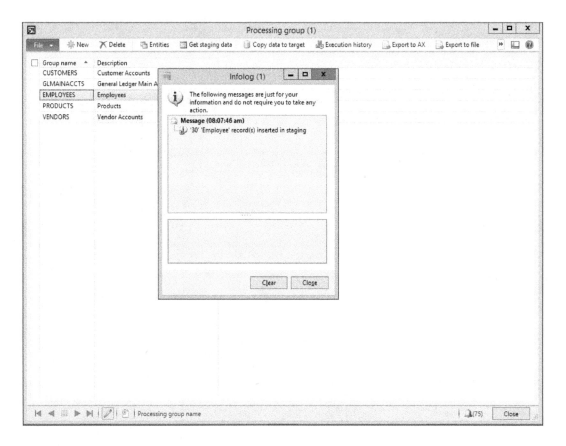

If everything goes well, then you will get a dialog box saying that the records were inserted into the **Staging** area and you can click on the **Close** button to exit from the form.

© 2015 Blind Squirrel Publishing, LLC, All Rights Reserved
www.dynamicsaxcompanions.com

Importing In Employees Using The Data Import Export Framework

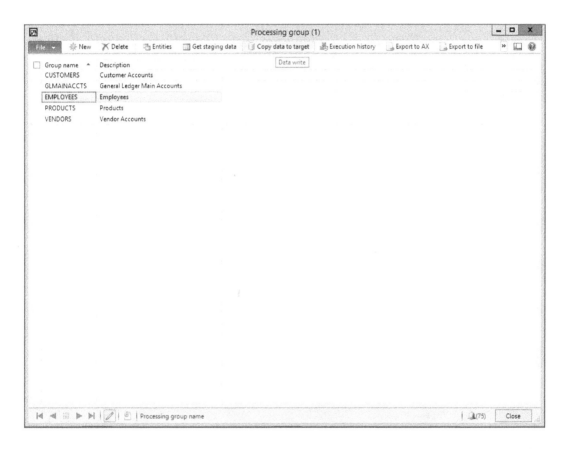

When you return back to the **Processing Group** form, click on the **Copy Data To Target** button in the menu bar.

© 2015 Blind Squirrel Publishing, LLC, All Rights Reserved
www.dynamicsaxcompanions.com

Importing In Employees Using The Data Import Export Framework

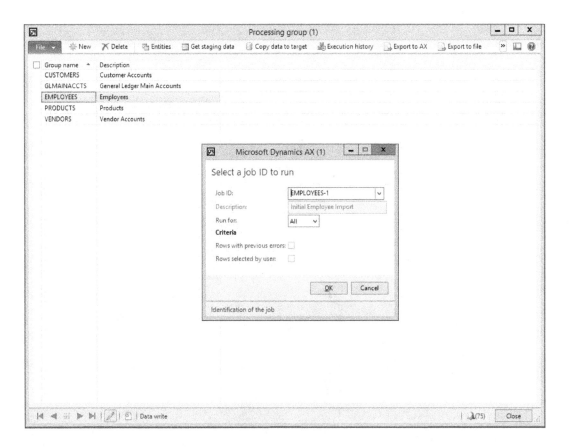

This will open up a dialog box where you can select the staging job that you just performed and then just click on the **OK** button.

© 2015 Blind Squirrel Publishing, LLC, All Rights Reserved
www.dynamicsaxcompanions.com

Importing In Employees Using The Data Import Export Framework

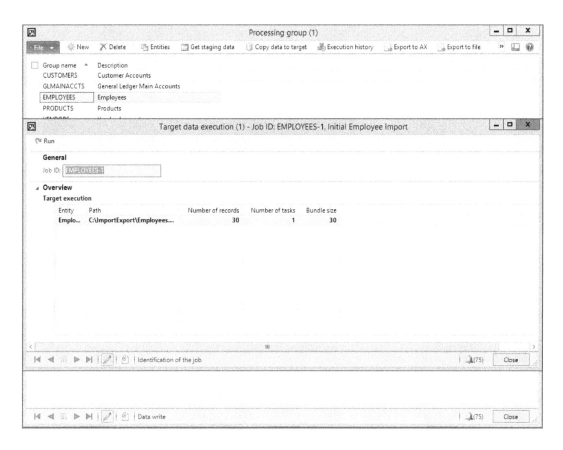

When the **Target Data Execution** dialog box is displayed, just click on the **Run** button in the menu bar.

© 2015 Blind Squirrel Publishing, LLC, All Rights Reserved
www.dynamicsaxcompanions.com

Importing In Employees Using The Data Import Export Framework

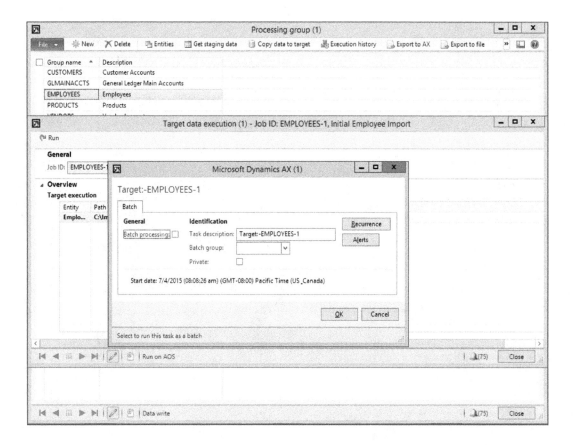

When the job details form is displayed, just click on the **OK** button.

© 2015 Blind Squirrel Publishing, LLC, All Rights Reserved
www.dynamicsaxcompanions.com

Importing In Employees Using The Data Import Export Framework

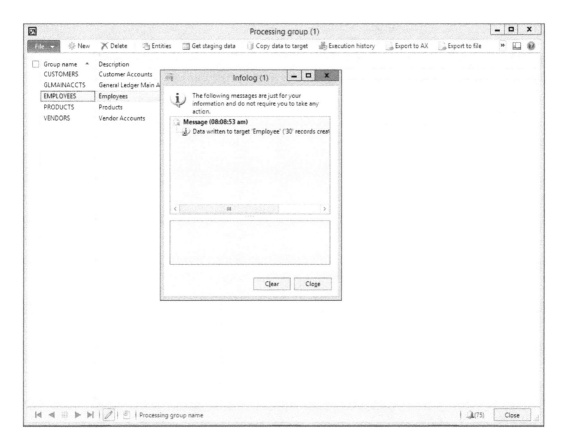

If all of your data is in the right place and valid then you should get a dialog box saying that the data has been loaded and you can click on the **Close** button to exit from the form.

© 2015 Blind Squirrel Publishing, LLC, All Rights Reserved
www.dynamicsaxcompanions.com

Importing In Employees Using The Data Import Export Framework

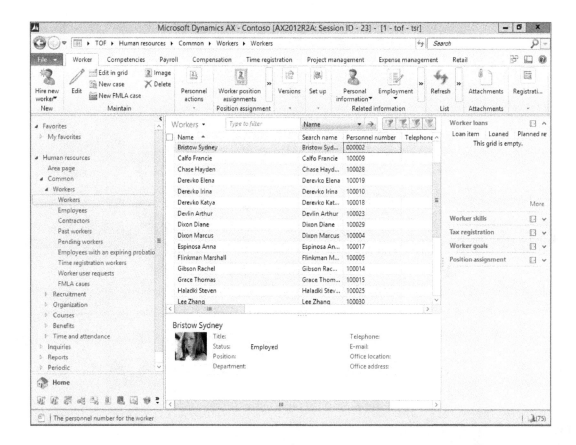

Now when you return back to the **Workers** form you will see that all of your other employees have been loaded into the system.

That is definitely easier than typing it in by hand.

© 2015 Blind Squirrel Publishing, LLC, All Rights Reserved
www.dynamicsaxcompanions.com

© 2015 Blind Squirrel Publishing, LLC, All Rights Reserved
www.dynamicsaxcompanions.com

Updating Worker Using Edit In Grid

After you have imported in your Workers into Dynamics AX, you may want to do a little polishing of the data and some small tweaks by hand. A great way to do this is to user the **Edit In Grid** feature which allows you to update the **Worker** details through a spreadsheet style grid rather than having to open up each individual **Worker** record.

© 2015 Blind Squirrel Publishing, LLC, All Rights Reserved
www.dynamicsaxcompanions.com

Updating Worker Using Edit In Grid

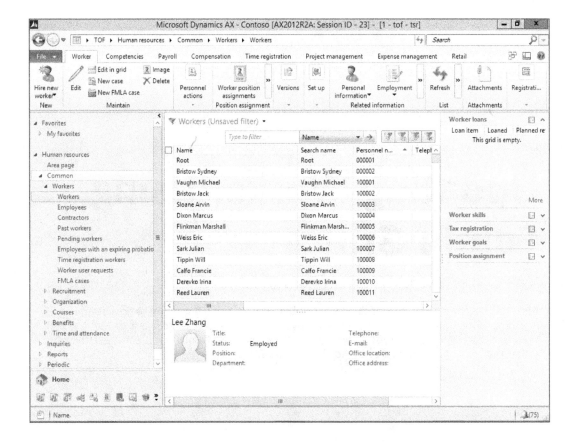

To do this, open up the **Workers** list page and click on the **Edit In Grid** button within the **Maintain** group of the **Worker** ribbon bar.

© 2015 Blind Squirrel Publishing, LLC, All Rights Reserved
www.dynamicsaxcompanions.com

Updating Worker Using Edit In Grid

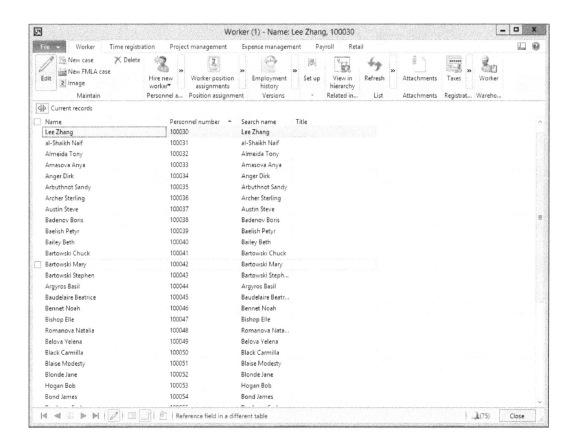

This will open up another worker view where you can just tab through the data and update it.

© 2015 Blind Squirrel Publishing, LLC, All Rights Reserved
www.dynamicsaxcompanions.com

Updating Worker Using Edit In Grid

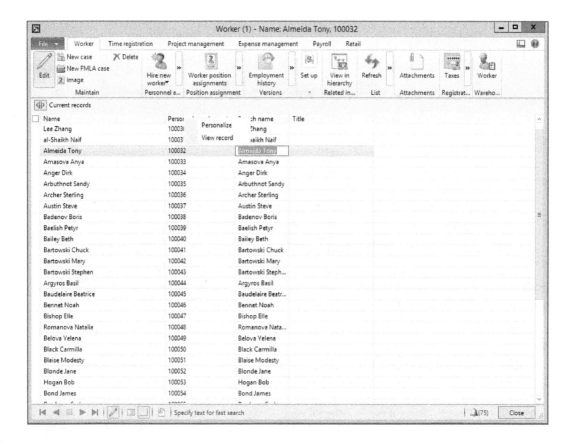

Before we start doing that though, let's add a few more fields to the grid to make this a little more useful as an updating tool. To do this, right-mouse-click on any of the fields in the grid and select the **Personalize** menu item from within the context menu.

© 2015 Blind Squirrel Publishing, LLC, All Rights Reserved
www.dynamicsaxcompanions.com

Updating Worker Using Edit In Grid

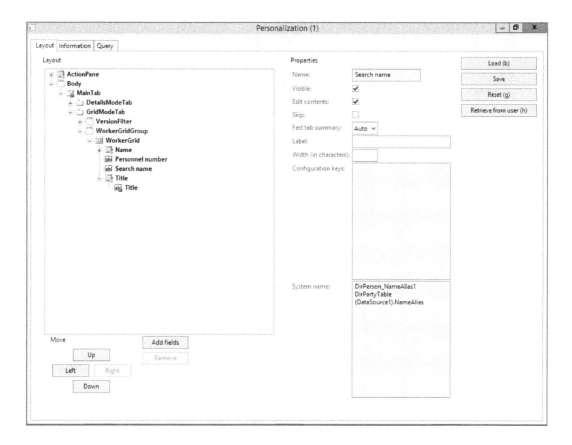

When the **Personalization** form is displayed, click on the **Add Fields** button below the **Layout** tree.

© 2015 Blind Squirrel Publishing, LLC, All Rights Reserved
www.dynamicsaxcompanions.com

Updating Worker Using Edit In Grid

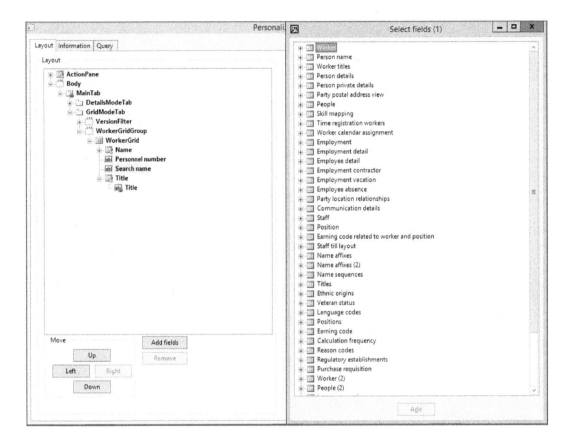

That will open up a list of all of the tables and fields that you can add to the form.

© 2015 Blind Squirrel Publishing, LLC, All Rights Reserved
www.dynamicsaxcompanions.com

Updating Worker Using Edit In Grid

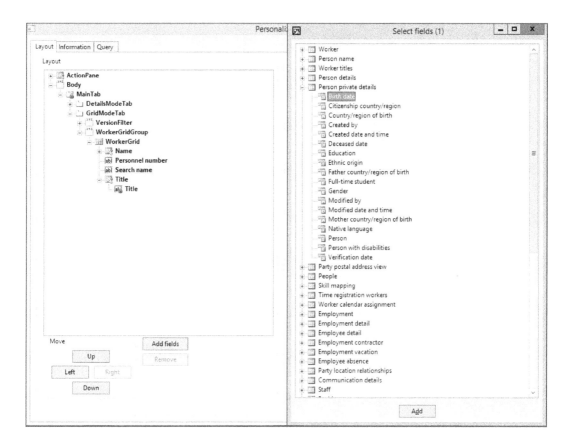

Expand the **Person Private Information** folder and you will be able to see all of the personal fields for the workers.

© 2015 Blind Squirrel Publishing, LLC, All Rights Reserved
www.dynamicsaxcompanions.com

Updating Worker Using Edit In Grid

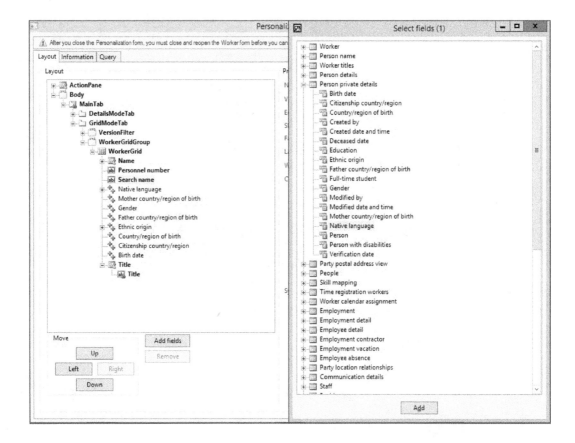

To add a field to the grid, just select it and then click the **Add** button. To start off, add the following fields:

Birth Date
Citizenship Country/Region
Country/Region of Birth
Father Country/Region of Birth
Mother Country/Region of Birth
Ethnic Origin
Gender
Native Language

© 2015 Blind Squirrel Publishing, LLC, All Rights Reserved
www.dynamicsaxcompanions.com

Updating Worker Using Edit In Grid

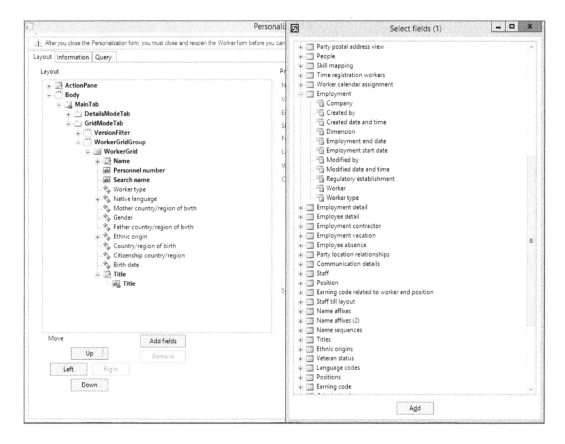

Then expand out the **Employment** field group and add the following field:

Worker Type

© 2015 Blind Squirrel Publishing, LLC, All Rights Reserved
www.dynamicsaxcompanions.com

Updating Worker Using Edit In Grid

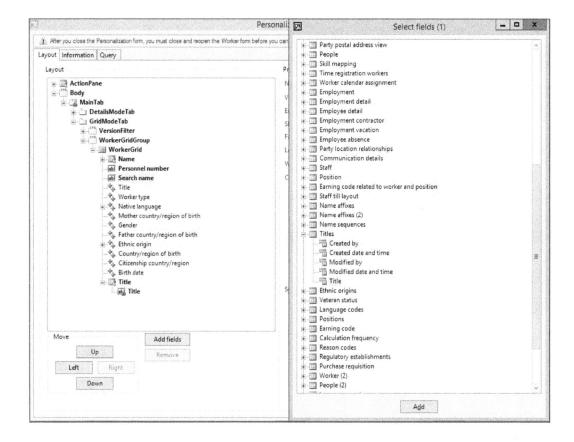

Finally expand out the **Title** field group and add the following field:

Title

When you are done just close the **Select Fields** form.

© 2015 Blind Squirrel Publishing, LLC, All Rights Reserved
www.dynamicsaxcompanions.com

Updating Worker Using Edit In Grid

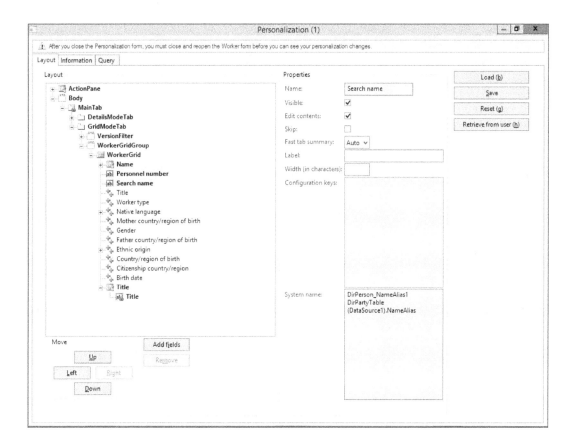

When you return back to the **Personalization** form you can just close out of the form.

© 2015 Blind Squirrel Publishing, LLC, All Rights Reserved
www.dynamicsaxcompanions.com

Updating Worker Using Edit In Grid

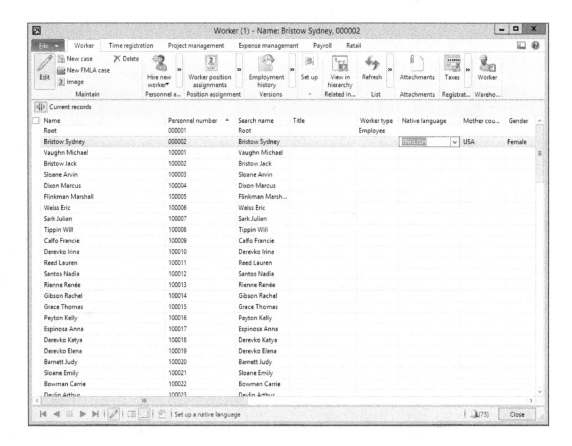

When you return to the **Edit In Grid** view you will notice that there are a lot more fields that you can update. Now you can just tab through the data and make your changes.

© 2015 Blind Squirrel Publishing, LLC, All Rights Reserved
www.dynamicsaxcompanions.com

Updating Worker Using Edit In Grid

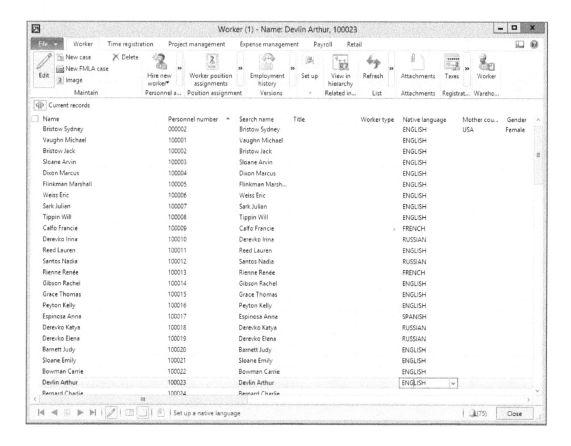

After you are done, just click on the **Close** button to exit out of the form.

© 2015 Blind Squirrel Publishing, LLC, All Rights Reserved
www.dynamicsaxcompanions.com

© 2015 Blind Squirrel Publishing, LLC, All Rights Reserved
www.dynamicsaxcompanions.com

CONFIGURING JOBS

Now that you have your employees configured, the next step is to model your organization by creating Jobs that you can assign to the workers.

© 2015 Blind Squirrel Publishing, LLC, All Rights Reserved
www.dynamicsaxcompanions.com

© 2015 Blind Squirrel Publishing, LLC, All Rights Reserved
www.dynamicsaxcompanions.com

Configuring Job Types

Before we start creating Jobs though we will want to start off by configuring a few codes, starting with **Job Types** which we will use to segregate jobs and also specify if they are exempt from Fair Labor Standards Act (FLSA) coverage.

Configuring Job Types

Job type	Description	Exempt status
AGENTS	Agents	Non-exempt
CLERICAL	Clerical	Non-exempt
DIRECTORS	Directors	Exempt
EXECUTIVES	Executives	Exempt
HOURLY	Hourly	Non-exempt
MANAGER	Managers	Exempt

© 2015 Blind Squirrel Publishing, LLC, All Rights Reserved
www.dynamicsaxcompanions.com

Configuring Job Types

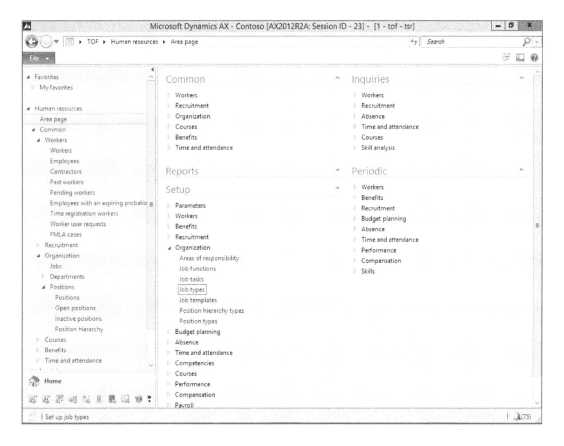

To do this, click on the **Job Types** menu item within the **Organization** folder of the **Setup** group within the **Human Resources** area.

© 2015 Blind Squirrel Publishing, LLC, All Rights Reserved
www.dynamicsaxcompanions.com

Configuring Job Types

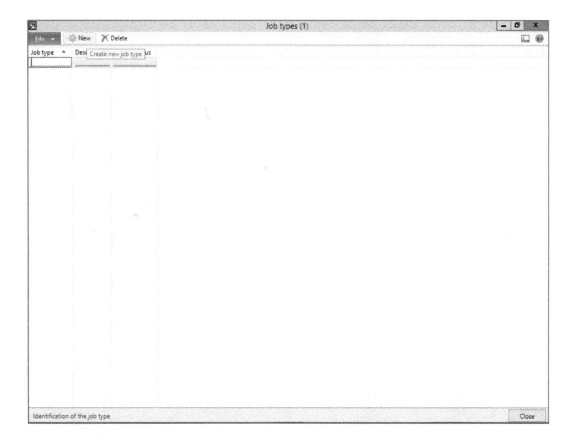

When the **Job Types** list page is displayed, click on the **New** button in the menu bar to create a new record.

© 2015 Blind Squirrel Publishing, LLC, All Rights Reserved
www.dynamicsaxcompanions.com

Configuring Job Types

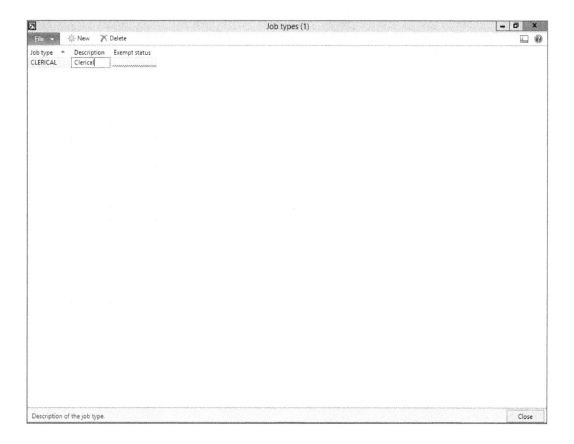

Set the **Job Type** code to **CLERICAL** and the **Description** to **Clerical**.

© 2015 Blind Squirrel Publishing, LLC, All Rights Reserved
www.dynamicsaxcompanions.com

Configuring Job Types

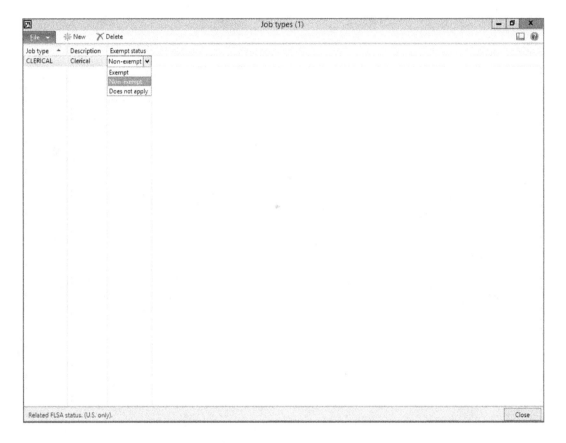

Then click on the **Exempt Status** dropdown list and select the **Non-Exempt** value to indicate that the position is non-exempt from the Fair Labor Standards Act (FLSA) coverage.

© 2015 Blind Squirrel Publishing, LLC, All Rights Reserved
www.dynamicsaxcompanions.com

Configuring Job Types

You can continue adding in all of the other **Job Types** by repeating the process.

When you are done, just click on the **Close** button to exit from the form

© 2015 Blind Squirrel Publishing, LLC, All Rights Reserved
www.dynamicsaxcompanions.com

© 2015 Blind Squirrel Publishing, LLC, All Rights Reserved
www.dynamicsaxcompanions.com

Configuring Job Functions

Next we will want to configure some **Job Functions** which you will then be able to use within your **Jobs** to help manage and track compensation levels.

Configuring Job Functions

Function	Description
0100	Officials and Manager
0200	Professionals
0300	Technicians
0400	Sales Workers
0500	Administrative Support Workers
0600	Craft Workers
0700	Operatives
0800	Laborers and Helpers
0900	Service Workers

Configuring Job Functions

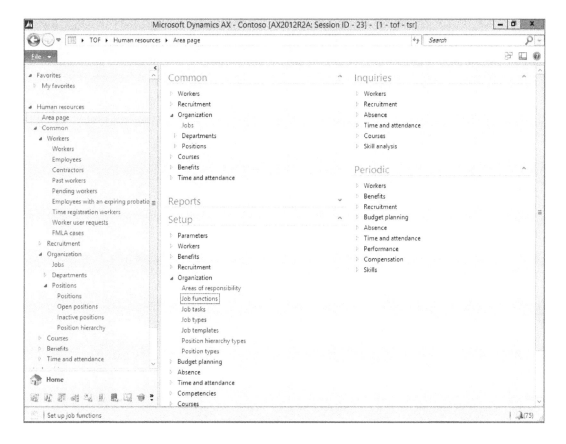

To do this click on the **Job Functions** menu item within the **Organization** folder of the **Setup** group within the **Human Resources** area page,

© 2015 Blind Squirrel Publishing, LLC, All Rights Reserved
www.dynamicsaxcompanions.com

Configuring Job Functions

When the **Job Functions** list page is displayed, click on the **New** button in the ribbon bar to create a new record.

© 2015 Blind Squirrel Publishing, LLC, All Rights Reserved
www.dynamicsaxcompanions.com

Configuring Job Functions

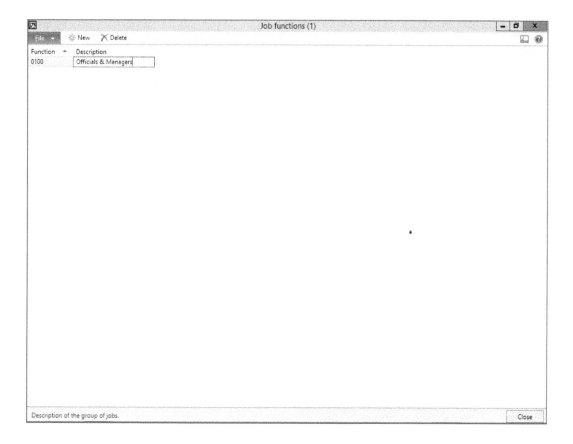

Then set the **Function** code to **0100** and the **Description** to **Officials & Managers**.

© 2015 Blind Squirrel Publishing, LLC, All Rights Reserved
www.dynamicsaxcompanions.com

Configuring Job Functions

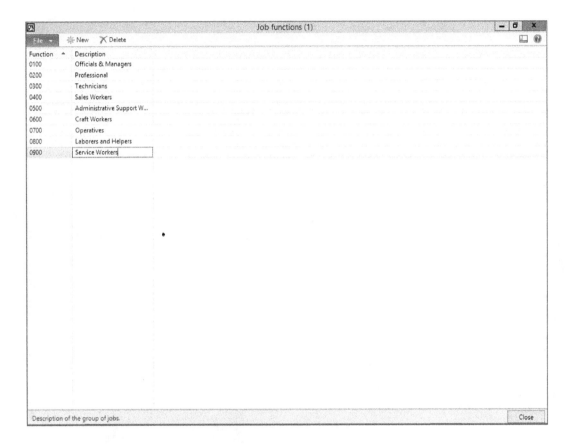

You can continue adding in all of the other **Job Functions** by repeating the process.

When you are done, just click on the **Close** button to exit from the form

© 2015 Blind Squirrel Publishing, LLC, All Rights Reserved
www.dynamicsaxcompanions.com

© 2015 Blind Squirrel Publishing, LLC, All Rights Reserved
www.dynamicsaxcompanions.com

© 2015 Blind Squirrel Publishing, LLC, All Rights Reserved
www.dynamicsaxcompanions.com

Configuring Job Tasks

Next we will want to configure our **Job Tasks** which we will assign to our **Jobs** to specify the tasks that are associated with the job.

© 2015 Blind Squirrel Publishing, LLC, All Rights Reserved
www.dynamicsaxcompanions.com

Configuring Job Tasks

Job task	Description
Accounting	Financials/Accounting
Compensation	Comp and benefits
Customer calls	Customer calls
Finance	Finance
Fixed Assets	Fixed Assets
Logistics	Manage Logistics
Manufacturing	Manufacturing
Project	Project management
Purchasing	Purchasing
Recruiting	Recruiting
Safety	Safety
Sales	Sales calls
Strategy	Strategy
Support	Customer support
Systems	Internal systems

© 2015 Blind Squirrel Publishing, LLC, All Rights Reserved
www.dynamicsaxcompanions.com

Configuring Job Tasks

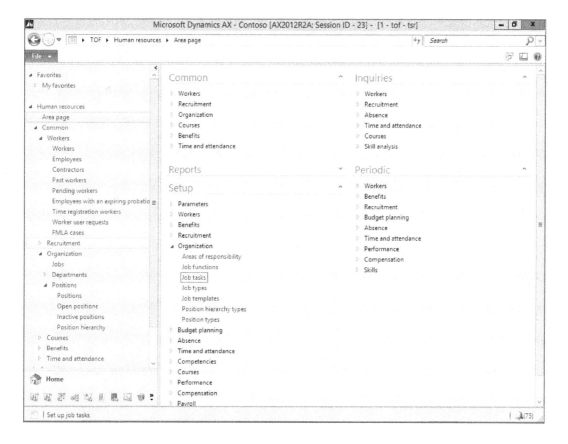

To do this, click on the **Job Tasks** menu item within the **Organization** folder of the **Setup** group of the **Human Resources** area.

© 2015 Blind Squirrel Publishing, LLC, All Rights Reserved
www.dynamicsaxcompanions.com

Configuring Job Tasks

When the **Job Tasks** form is displayed, click on the **New** button within the menu bar to create a new record.

© 2015 Blind Squirrel Publishing, LLC, All Rights Reserved
www.dynamicsaxcompanions.com

Configuring Job Tasks

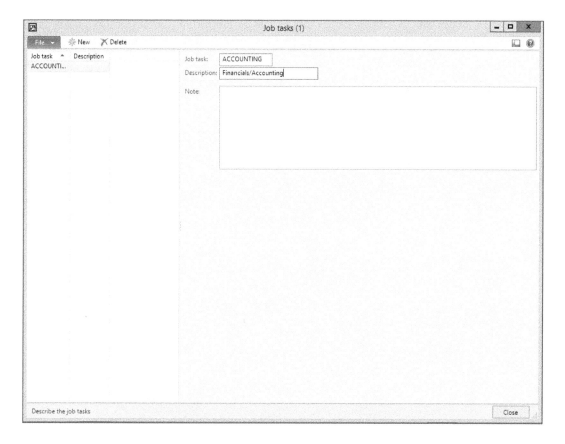

Now set the **Job Task** to **ACCOUNTING** and the **Description** to **Finance/Accounting.**

You can continue adding more **Job Tasks** by repeating the process and when you are done, just click on the **Close** button to exit from the form.

© 2015 Blind Squirrel Publishing, LLC, All Rights Reserved
www.dynamicsaxcompanions.com

© 2015 Blind Squirrel Publishing, LLC, All Rights Reserved
www.dynamicsaxcompanions.com

Importing Job Tasks Through Excel

To make the loading of the **Job Tasks** just a little bit easier, let's use Excel to import them in from a template file, and speed up the process a little.

© 2015 Blind Squirrel Publishing, LLC, All Rights Reserved
www.dynamicsaxcompanions.com

Importing Job Tasks Through Excel

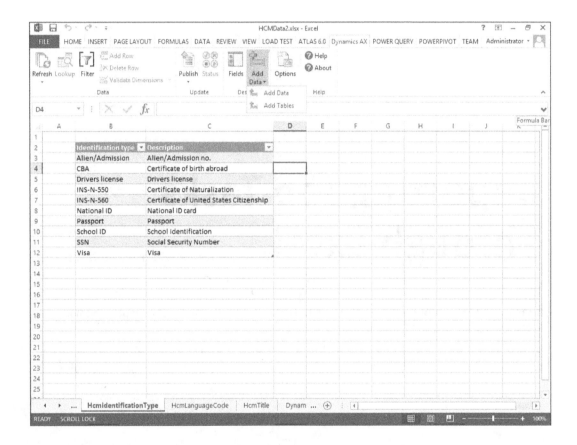

To do this, return to your Excel workbook that you used to import in the other codes and click on the **Add Data** button within the **Data** group of the **Dynamics AX** ribbon bar, and click on the **Add Tables** menu item again.

© 2015 Blind Squirrel Publishing, LLC, All Rights Reserved
www.dynamicsaxcompanions.com

Importing Job Tasks Through Excel

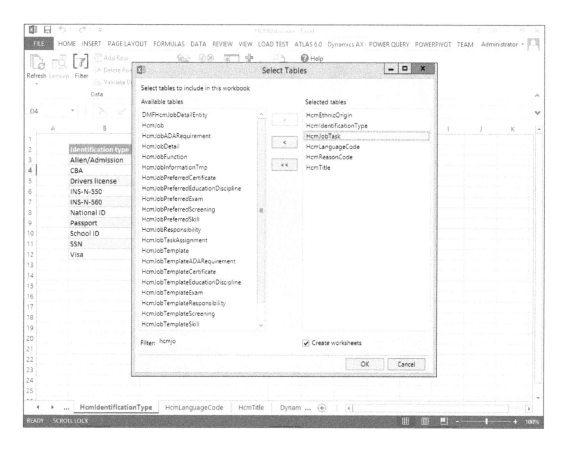

When the **Select Tables** dialog box is displayed, filter the table list down to the **HcmJobTask** table, click on the **>** button to add it to the **Selected Tables** group and then click on the **OK** button.

© 2015 Blind Squirrel Publishing, LLC, All Rights Reserved
www.dynamicsaxcompanions.com

Importing Job Tasks Through Excel

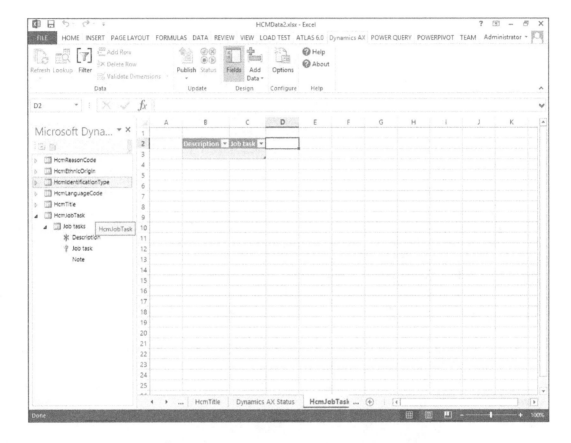

This will create a new worksheet for you linked to the **HcmJobTasks** table.

254

© 2015 Blind Squirrel Publishing, LLC, All Rights Reserved
www.dynamicsaxcompanions.com

Importing Job Tasks Through Excel

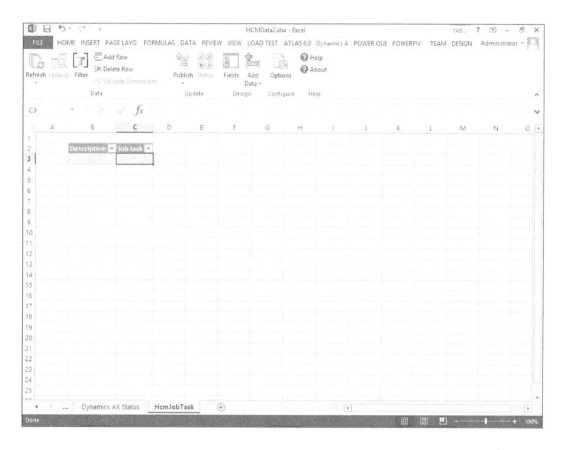

Now click on the **Fields** button within the **Updates** group of the **Dynamics AX** ribbon bar to exit from design mode into edit mode.

© 2015 Blind Squirrel Publishing, LLC, All Rights Reserved
www.dynamicsaxcompanions.com

Importing Job Tasks Through Excel

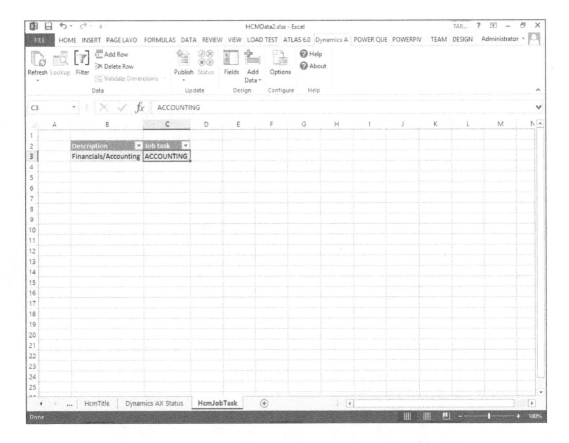

Then click on the **Refresh** button within the **Data** group of the **Dynamics AX** ribbon bar to refresh the data and you will be able to see the **Job Tasks** that you just added.

© 2015 Blind Squirrel Publishing, LLC, All Rights Reserved
www.dynamicsaxcompanions.com

Importing Job Tasks Through Excel

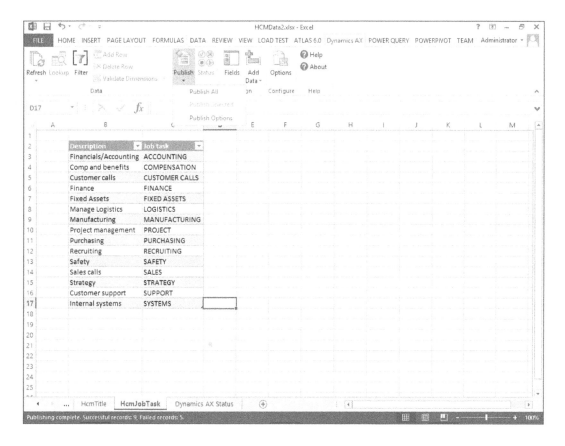

Now just paste in all of the **Job Tasks** that you want to import into Dynamics AX into the worksheet.

Then click on the **Publish** button within the **Update** group of the **Dynamics AX** ribbon bar and click on the **Publish All** menu item.

© 2015 Blind Squirrel Publishing, LLC, All Rights Reserved
www.dynamicsaxcompanions.com

Importing Job Tasks Through Excel

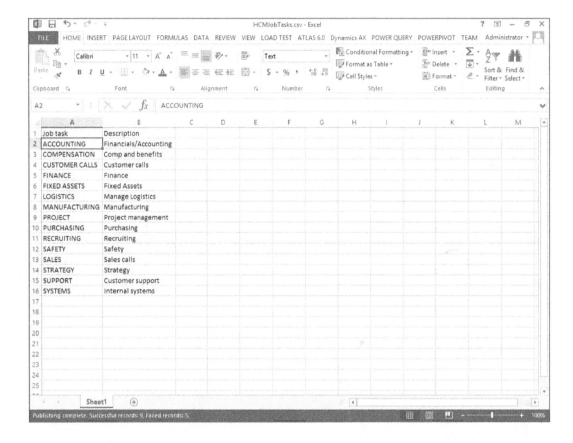

To save time, we have created a **CSV** file that contains all of the suggested **Job Tasks** that you might want to use and they are available for download from the **Dynamics AX Companions** site. Here is the link to the resources page:

http://www.dynamicsaxcompanions.com/Bare-Bones-Configuration-Guides/Configuring-Human-Resources

© 2015 Blind Squirrel Publishing, LLC, All Rights Reserved
www.dynamicsaxcompanions.com

Importing Job Tasks Through Excel

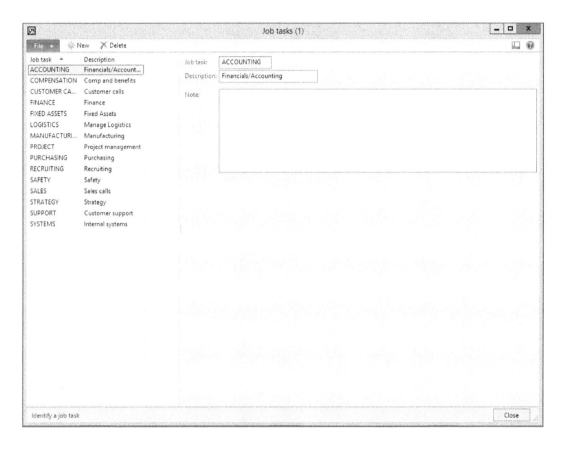

Now when you return back to your **Job Tasks** form you will notice that the **Job Tasks** are loaded for you

© 2015 Blind Squirrel Publishing, LLC, All Rights Reserved
www.dynamicsaxcompanions.com

© 2015 Blind Squirrel Publishing, LLC, All Rights Reserved
www.dynamicsaxcompanions.com

Configuring Jobs

Now that we have all of our codes configured we can start creating **Jobs** that we can assign our workers to.

© 2015 Blind Squirrel Publishing, LLC, All Rights Reserved
www.dynamicsaxcompanions.com

Configuring Jobs

HcmJobTask_JobTaskId	JobId	RatingLevelId	Description	HcmTitle_TitleId	HcmJobType_JobTypeId
ACCOUNTING	Account Manager	B1	Account Manager	Account Manager	MANAGERS
ACCOUNTING	Accountant	B1	Accountant	Accountant	CLERICAL
ACCOUNTING	Accounting Manager	B1	Accounting Manager	Accounting Manager	MANAGERS
ACCOUNTING	Allocation Specialist	B1	Allocation Specialist	Allocation Specialist	CLERICAL
ACCOUNTING	AP Coordinator	B1	AP Coordinator	Accounts Payable Coordinator	HOURLY
ACCOUNTING	Application Developer	B1	Business Application Developer	Business Application Developer	HOURLY
ACCOUNTING	AR Administrator	B1	Accounts Receivable Administrator	AR Administrator	MANAGERS
ACCOUNTING	AR Coordinator	B1	AR Coordinator	Accounts Receivable Coordn.	CLERICAL
ACCOUNTING	Attorney	B1	Attorney	Attorney	DIRECTORS
ACCOUNTING	Budget Manager	B1	Budget Manager	Budget Manager	MANAGERS
ACCOUNTING	Business Manager	B1	Business Manager	Business Manager	MANAGERS
ACCOUNTING	Business System Dev	B1	Business System Developer	Business System Developer	MANAGERS
ACCOUNTING	Catalog Manager	B1	Catalog Manager	Catalog Manager	MANAGERS
ACCOUNTING	Category Manager	B1	Category Manager	Category Manager	MANAGERS
ACCOUNTING	CFO	B1	Chief Financial Officer	Chief Financial Officer	EXECUTIVES

© 2015 Blind Squirrel Publishing, LLC, All Rights Reserved
www.dynamicsaxcompanions.com

Configuring Jobs

HcmJobTask_JobTaskId	JobId	RatingLevelId	Description	HcmTitle_TitleId	HcmJobType_JobTypeId
ACCOUNTING	Client Services Mgr	B1	Manager of Client Services	Manager of Client Services	HOURLY
ACCOUNTING	Comp & Ben Specialist	B1	Compensation & Benefits Specialist	Compensation & Benefits Cons.	MANAGERS
ACCOUNTING	Consultant	B1	Consultant	Consultant	HOURLY
ACCOUNTING	Contract consultant	B1	Contract consultant	Consultant	HOURLY
ACCOUNTING	Controller	B1	Controller	Controller	EXECUTIVES
ACCOUNTING	Credit & Collections Mgr	B1	Credit and Collections Manager	Credit and Collections Manager	MANAGERS
ACCOUNTING	Customer Service Mgr	B1	Customer Service Manager	Customer Service Manager	MANAGERS
ACCOUNTING	Customer Service Rep	B1	Customer Service Representative	Customer Service Rep	HOURLY
ACCOUNTING	Dedicated Sales Rep	B1	Dedicated Sales Representative	Dedicated Sales Representative	HOURLY
ACCOUNTING	Design & Construct Mgr	B1	Design & Construction Manager	Design & Construction Manager	MANAGERS
ACCOUNTING	Dispatcher	B1	Dispatcher	Dispatcher	HOURLY
ACCOUNTING	E-Commerce Manager	B1	E-Commerce Manager	E-Commerce Manager	MANAGERS
ACCOUNTING	Finance Manager	B1	Manager of Finance	Manager of Finance	MANAGERS
ACCOUNTING	Fleet Manager	B1	Fleet Manager	Fleet Manager	MANAGERS
ACCOUNTING	HR Assistant	B1	HR Assistant	HR Assistant	CLERICAL
ACCOUNTING	HR Director	B1	Human Resource Director	Director of Human Resources	EXECUTIVES

© 2015 Blind Squirrel Publishing, LLC, All Rights Reserved
www.dynamicsaxcompanions.com

Configuring Jobs

HcmJobTask_JobTaskId	JobId	RatingLevelId	Description	HcmTitle_TitleId	HcmJobType_JobTypeId
ACCOUNTING	HR Generalist	B1	HR Generalist	HR Generalist	HOURLY
ACCOUNTING	Human Resources Manager	B1	Manager of Human Resources	Manager of Human Resources	MANAGERS
ACCOUNTING	In-house Developer	B1	In-house Developer	In-house Developer	HOURLY
ACCOUNTING	Invent & Allocate Mgr	B1	Inventory & Allocation Manager	Inventory & Allocation Manager	MANAGERS
ACCOUNTING	IT Engineer	B1	IT Engineer	IT Engineer	HOURLY
ACCOUNTING	IT Manager	B1	IT Manager	IT Manager	MANAGERS
ACCOUNTING	Lean Officer	B1	Lean Officer	Lean Officer	DIRECTORS
ACCOUNTING	Lease Administrator	B1	Lease Administrator	Lease Administrator	HOURLY
ACCOUNTING	Loss Prevention Manager	B1	Loss Prevention Manager	Loss Prevention Manager	MANAGERS
ACCOUNTING	Machine Operator	B1	Machine Operator	Machine Operator	HOURLY
ACCOUNTING	Manager of Legal	B1	Manager of Legal	Manager of Legal	MANAGERS
ACCOUNTING	Managing Partner	B1	Managing Partner	Managing Partner	
ACCOUNTING	Marketing Assistant	B1	Marketing Assistant	Marketing Assistant	
ACCOUNTING	Marketing Director	B1	Director of Marketing	Director of Marketing	DIRECTORS
ACCOUNTING	Marketing Executive	B1	Marketing Executive	Marketing Executive	EXECUTIVES
ACCOUNTING	Marketing Manager	B1	Marketing Manager	Marketing Manager	MANAGERS
ACCOUNTING	Marketing Staff	B1	Marketing Staff	Marketing Staff	HOURLY
ACCOUNTING	Materials Manager	B1	Materials Manager	Materials Manager	HOURLY

© 2015 Blind Squirrel Publishing, LLC, All Rights Reserved
www.dynamicsaxcompanions.com

Configuring Jobs

HcmJobTask_JobTaskId	JobId	RatingLevelId	Description	HcmTitle_TitleId	HcmJobType_JobTypeId
ACCOUNTING	Merchandising Director	B1	Merchandising Director	Merchandising Director	DIRECTORS
ACCOUNTING	Mgr of Category Mgrs	B1	Mgr of Category Mgrs	Mgr of Category Mgrs	DIRECTORS
ACCOUNTING	Operations Manager	B1	Operations Manager	Operations Manager	MANAGERS
ACCOUNTING	Order Processor	B1	Order Processor	Order Processor	HOURLY
ACCOUNTING	Outbound Technician	B1	Outbound Technician	Outbound Technician	HOURLY
ACCOUNTING	Payroll Administrator	B1	Payroll Administrator	Payroll Administrator	
ACCOUNTING	Picker	B1	Picker	Picker	HOURLY
ACCOUNTING	Practice Manager	B1	Practice Manager	Practice Manager	MANAGERS
ACCOUNTING	President	B1	President	President	EXECUTIVES
ACCOUNTING	Principal Consultant	B1	Principal Consultant	Principal Consultant	MANAGERS
ACCOUNTING	Process Engineer	B1	Process Engineer	Process Engineer	MANAGERS
ACCOUNTING	Procurement Specialist	B1	Procurement Specialist	Procurement Specialist	HOURLY
ACCOUNTING	Product Designer	B1	Product Designer	Product Designer	
ACCOUNTING	Production Manager	B1	Production Manager	Production Manager	MANAGERS
ACCOUNTING	Production Planner	B1	Production Planner	Production Planner	MANAGERS
ACCOUNTING	Project Division Mgr	B1	Project Division Mgr	Project Division Mgr	DIRECTORS
ACCOUNTING	Project Manager	B1	Project Manager	Project Manager	MANAGERS
ACCOUNTING	Project Team Member	B1	Project Team Member	Project Team Member	HOURLY

© 2015 Blind Squirrel Publishing, LLC, All Rights Reserved
www.dynamicsaxcompanions.com

Configuring Jobs

HcmJobTask_JobTaskId	JobId	RatingLevelId	Description	HcmTitle_TitleId	HcmJobType_JobTypeId
ACCOUNTING	Purchasing Agent	B1	Purchasing Agent	Purchasing Agent	HOURLY
ACCOUNTING	Purchasing Manager	B1	Purchasing Manager	Purchasing Manager	MANAGERS
ACCOUNTING	Quality Controller	B1	Quality Controller	Quality Controller	HOURLY
ACCOUNTING	Receptionist	B1	Receptionist	Receptionist	HOURLY
ACCOUNTING	Recruiting Specialist	B1	Recruiting and Staffing Consultant	Recruiting&Staffing Consulant	
ACCOUNTING	Regional Manager	B1	Regional Manager	Regional Manager	MANAGERS
ACCOUNTING	Resource Manager	B1	Resource Manager	Resource Manager	HOURLY
ACCOUNTING	Retail Director	B1	Retail Director	Retail Director	MANAGERS
ACCOUNTING	Sales & Marketing Mng	B1	Manager of Sales and Marketing	Manager of Sales & Marketing	MANAGERS
ACCOUNTING	Sales Associate	B1	Sales Associate	Sales Associate	HOURLY
ACCOUNTING	Sales Assotiate - Russia	B1	Sales Assotiate - Russia	Sales Assotiate - Russia	HOURLY
ACCOUNTING	Sales Manager	B1	Sales Manager	Sales Manager	MANAGERS
ACCOUNTING	Senior Consultant	B1	Senior Consultant	Senior Consultant	HOURLY
ACCOUNTING	Shipping & Receiving	B1	Shipping & Receiving Staff	Shipping & Receiving Staff	HOURLY
ACCOUNTING	Shop Supervisor	B1	Shop Supervisor	Shop Supervisor	MANAGERS
ACCOUNTING	Store Cashier	B1	Store Cashier	Store Cashier	EXECUTIVES
ACCOUNTING	Store Designer	B1	Store Designer	Store Designer	HOURLY
ACCOUNTING	Store Manager	B1	Store Manager	Store Manager	MANAGERS
ACCOUNTING	Store Manager - Russia	B1	Store Manager - Russia	Store Manager - Russia	MANAGERS
ACCOUNTING	Store Merchandiser	B1	Store Merchandiser	Store Merchandiser	HOURLY

© 2015 Blind Squirrel Publishing, LLC, All Rights Reserved
www.dynamicsaxcompanions.com

Configuring Jobs

HcmJobTask_JobTaskId	JobId	RatingLevelId	Description	HcmTitle_TitleId	HcmJobType_JobTypeId
ACCOUNTING	Systems Consultant	B1	Systems Consultant	Systems Consultant	HOURLY
ACCOUNTING	Training & Dev Consult	B1	Training & Development Consultant	Training & Development Cons.	
ACCOUNTING	Transport Coordinator	B1	Transport Coordinator	Transport Coordinator	HOURLY
ACCOUNTING	Treasurer	B1	Treasurer	Treasurer	MANAGERS
ACCOUNTING	Value Stream Manager	B1	Value Stream Manager	Value Stream Manager	MANAGERS
ACCOUNTING	VP of Fin & Admin	B1	Vice President of Finance and Administration	VP of Finance & Administration	EXECUTIVES
ACCOUNTING	VP of Human Resources	B1	Vice President of Human Resources	VP of Human Resources	EXECUTIVES
ACCOUNTING	VP of Operations	B1	Vice President of Operations	VP of Operations	EXECUTIVES
ACCOUNTING	Warehouse Manager	B1	Warehouse Manager	Warehouse Manager	MANAGERS
ACCOUNTING	Warehouse Worker	B1	Warehouse Worker	Warehouse Worker	HOURLY
ACCOUNTING	Waterspider	B1	Waterspider	Waterspider	HOURLY

© 2015 Blind Squirrel Publishing, LLC, All Rights Reserved
www.dynamicsaxcompanions.com

Configuring Jobs

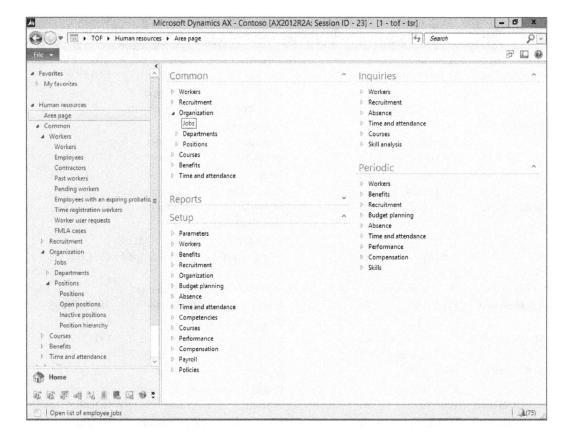

To do this, click on the **Jobs** menu item within the **Organization** folder of the **Common** group within the **Human Resources** area page.

© 2015 Blind Squirrel Publishing, LLC, All Rights Reserved
www.dynamicsaxcompanions.com

Configuring Jobs

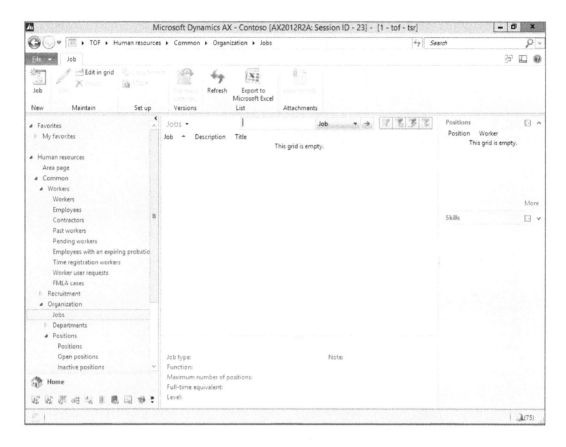

When the **Jobs** list page is displayed, just click on the **Job** button within the **New** group of the **Job** ribbon bar.

© 2015 Blind Squirrel Publishing, LLC, All Rights Reserved
www.dynamicsaxcompanions.com

Configuring Jobs

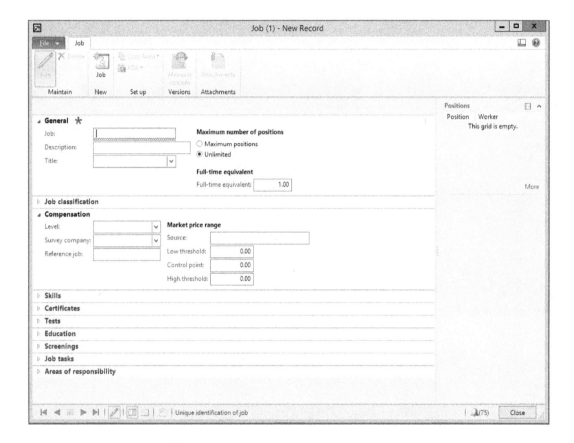

This will open up the **Job Details** form.

© 2015 Blind Squirrel Publishing, LLC, All Rights Reserved
www.dynamicsaxcompanions.com

Configuring Jobs

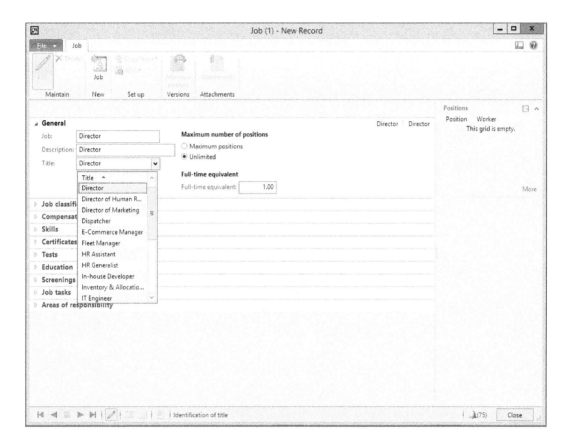

Set the **Job** code to **Director** and the **Description** to **Director**.

Then click on the **Title** dropdown list and select the **Director** title for the job.

© 2015 Blind Squirrel Publishing, LLC, All Rights Reserved
www.dynamicsaxcompanions.com

Configuring Jobs

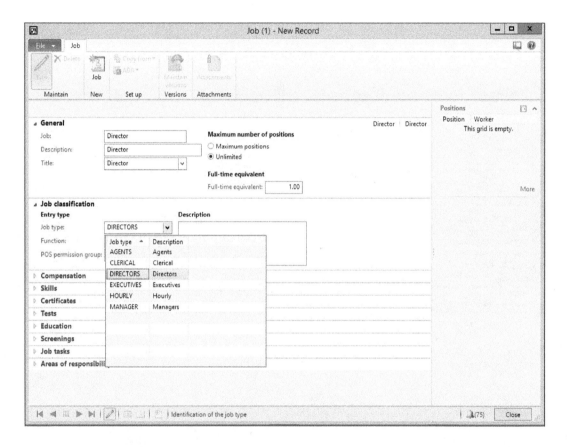

Now expand out the **Job Classification** fast tab, and click on the **Job Type** dropdown list and select the **DIRECTORS** job type.

© 2015 Blind Squirrel Publishing, LLC, All Rights Reserved
www.dynamicsaxcompanions.com

Configuring Jobs

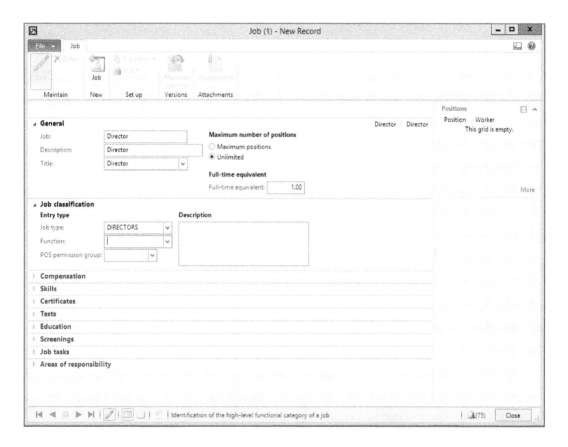

You can keep on tweaking the job if you want and then when you are done, click on the **Close** button to exit from the form.

© 2015 Blind Squirrel Publishing, LLC, All Rights Reserved
www.dynamicsaxcompanions.com

© 2015 Blind Squirrel Publishing, LLC, All Rights Reserved
www.dynamicsaxcompanions.com

Importing Jobs Using The Data Import Export Framework

If you have a handful of **Jobs** then adding them by hand is not a big deal, but if you have a lot of **Jobs** that you want to load into Dynamics AX, then you will probably want to use the Data Import Export Framework within Dynamics AX to load the data in from a spreadsheet.

© 2015 Blind Squirrel Publishing, LLC, All Rights Reserved
www.dynamicsaxcompanions.com

Importing Jobs Using The Data Import Export Framework

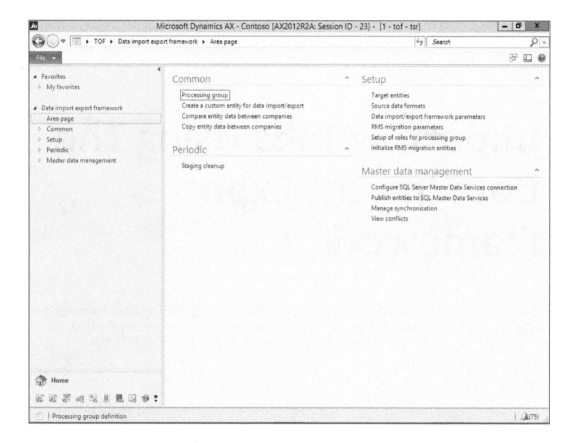

To do this, click on the **Processing Group** menu item within the **Common** group of the **Data Import Export Framework** area page.

© 2015 Blind Squirrel Publishing, LLC, All Rights Reserved
www.dynamicsaxcompanions.com

Importing Jobs Using The Data Import Export Framework

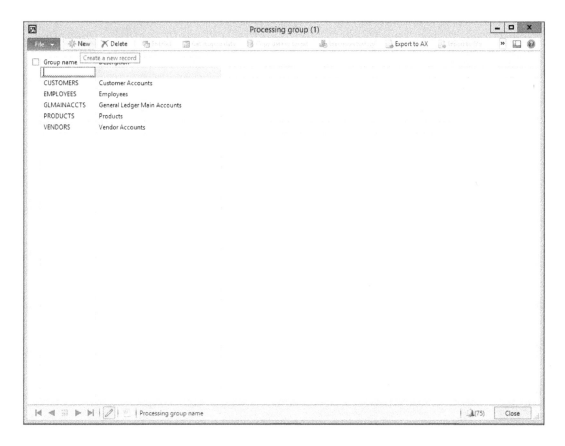

When the **Processing Group** list form is displayed, click on the **New** button in the menu bar to create a new record.

© 2015 Blind Squirrel Publishing, LLC, All Rights Reserved
www.dynamicsaxcompanions.com

Importing Jobs Using The Data Import Export Framework

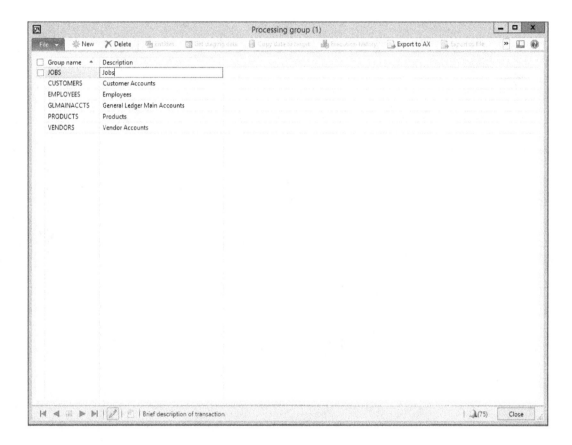

Then set the **Group Name** to **JOBS** and the **Description** to **Jobs**.

© 2015 Blind Squirrel Publishing, LLC, All Rights Reserved
www.dynamicsaxcompanions.com

Importing Jobs Using The Data Import Export Framework

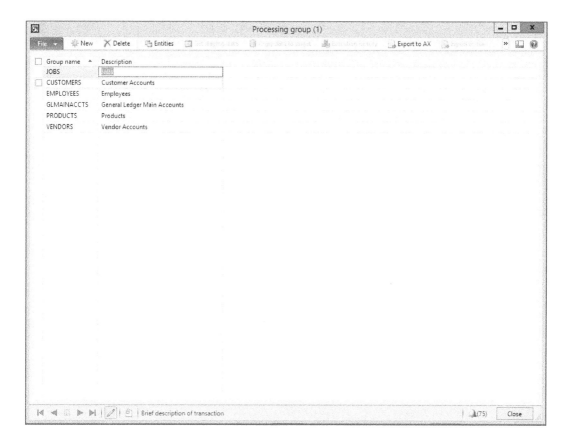

Save the record by pressing **CTRL+S** and that will enable you to click on the **Entities** button in the menu bar.

© 2015 Blind Squirrel Publishing, LLC, All Rights Reserved
www.dynamicsaxcompanions.com

Importing Jobs Using The Data Import Export Framework

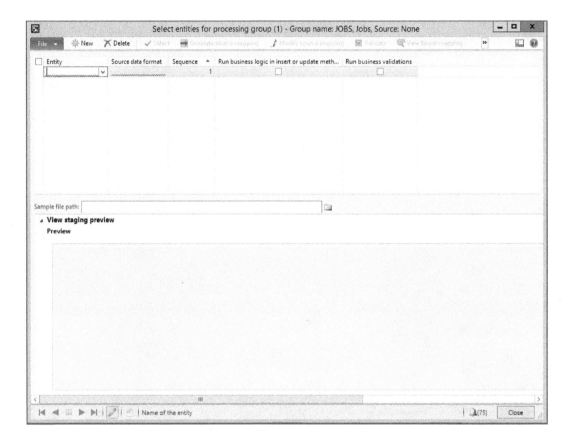

When the **Select Entities for Processing Group** maintenance form is displayed click on the **New** button in the menu bar to create a new record.

© 2015 Blind Squirrel Publishing, LLC, All Rights Reserved
www.dynamicsaxcompanions.com

Importing Jobs Using The Data Import Export Framework

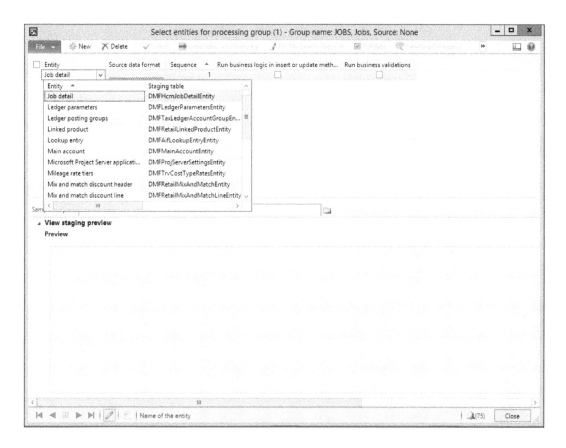

Then click on the **Entity** dropdown list and select the **Job Detail** entity.

© 2015 Blind Squirrel Publishing, LLC, All Rights Reserved
www.dynamicsaxcompanions.com

Importing Jobs Using The Data Import Export Framework

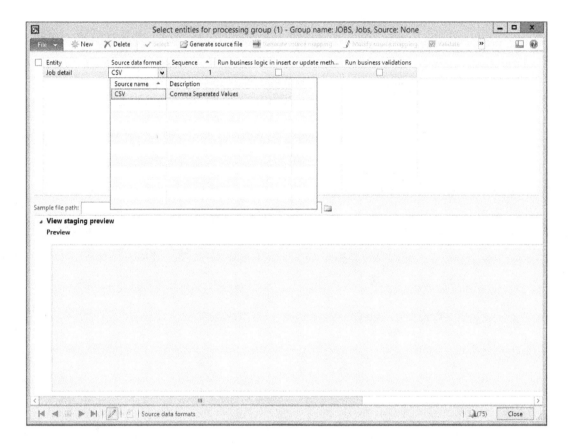

Then click on the **Source Data Format** dropdown list and select the **CSV** data format.

© 2015 Blind Squirrel Publishing, LLC, All Rights Reserved
www.dynamicsaxcompanions.com

Importing Jobs Using The Data Import Export Framework

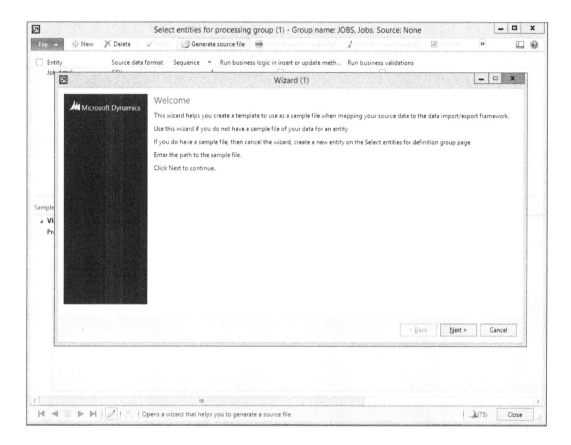

Now click on the **Generate Source File** button in the menu bar.

When the setup wizard is displayed, just click on the **Next** button to skip through the welcome page.

© 2015 Blind Squirrel Publishing, LLC, All Rights Reserved
www.dynamicsaxcompanions.com

Importing Jobs Using The Data Import Export Framework

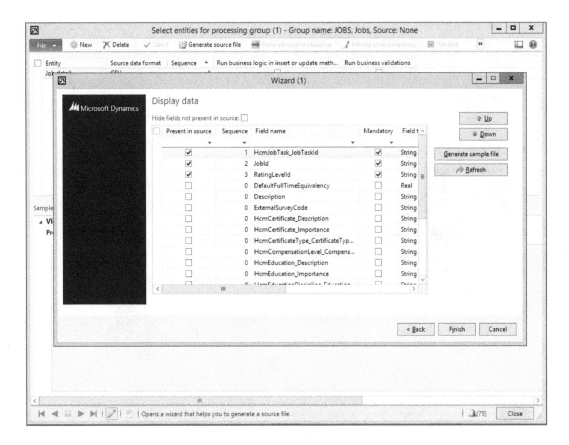

That will take you to the **Display Data** page where you will be able to see all of the fields that are available to be imported, and also the ones that have already been selected.

© 2015 Blind Squirrel Publishing, LLC, All Rights Reserved
www.dynamicsaxcompanions.com

Importing Jobs Using The Data Import Export Framework

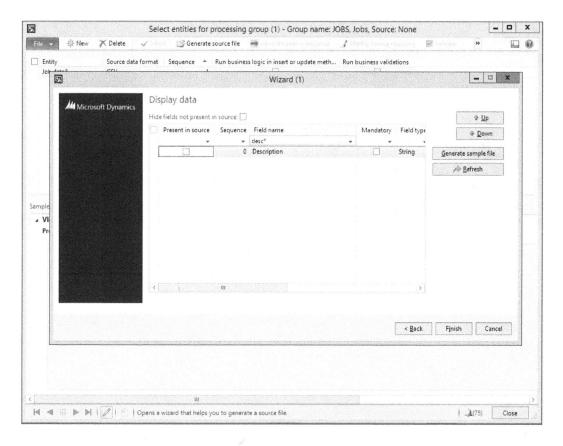

Type **desc*** into the search field for the **Field Name**. This will filter out the records and you will see the **Description** field. Click on the **Present In Source** checkbox for the field.

© 2015 Blind Squirrel Publishing, LLC, All Rights Reserved
www.dynamicsaxcompanions.com

Importing Jobs Using The Data Import Export Framework

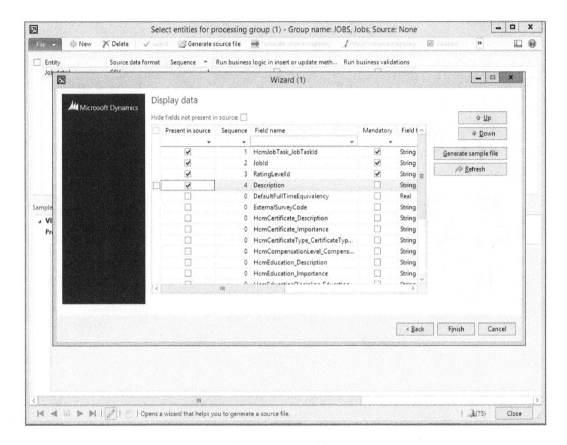

This will return you back to the field list and now you will have the **Description** field as an import field.

© 2015 Blind Squirrel Publishing, LLC, All Rights Reserved
www.dynamicsaxcompanions.com

Importing Jobs Using The Data Import Export Framework

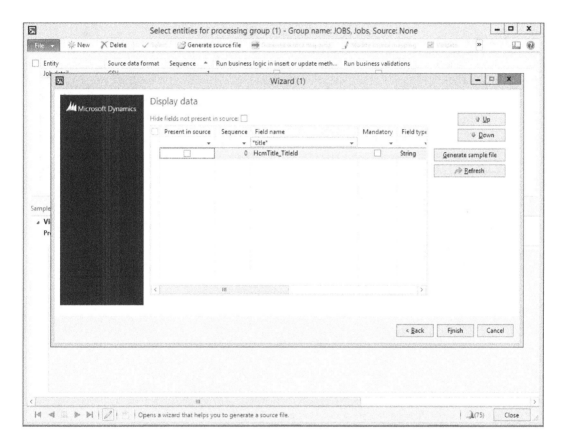

Now type ***title*** into the search field for the **Field Name**. This will filter out the records and you will see the **HCMTitle_TitleId** field. Click on the **Present In Source** checkbox for the field.

© 2015 Blind Squirrel Publishing, LLC, All Rights Reserved
www.dynamicsaxcompanions.com

Importing Jobs Using The Data Import Export Framework

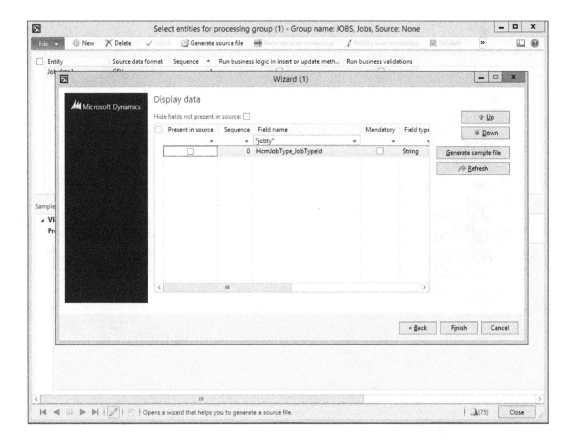

Now type ***jobtype*** into the search field for the **Field Name**. This will filter out the records and you will see the **HCMJobType_JobTypeId** field. Click on the **Present In Source** checkbox for the field.

© 2015 Blind Squirrel Publishing, LLC, All Rights Reserved
www.dynamicsaxcompanions.com

Importing Jobs Using The Data Import Export Framework

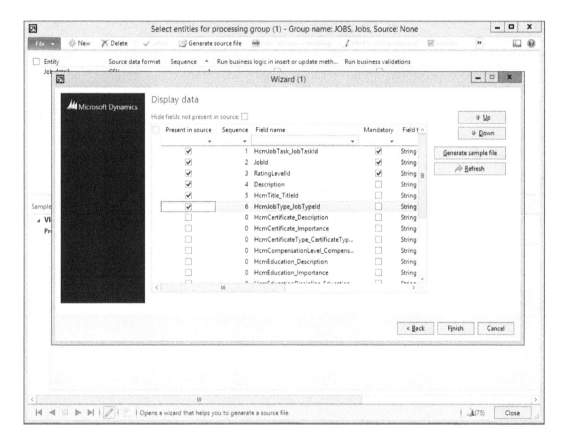

Now that you have all of the main fields that you need in the template, click on the **Generate Sample File** button

© 2015 Blind Squirrel Publishing, LLC, All Rights Reserved
www.dynamicsaxcompanions.com

Importing Jobs Using The Data Import Export Framework

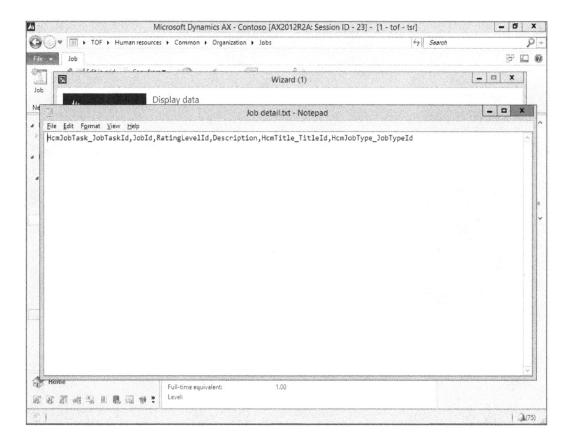

This will create your sample CSV file for the import. Just click on the **File** menu and select the **Save** option.

© 2015 Blind Squirrel Publishing, LLC, All Rights Reserved
www.dynamicsaxcompanions.com

Importing Jobs Using The Data Import Export Framework

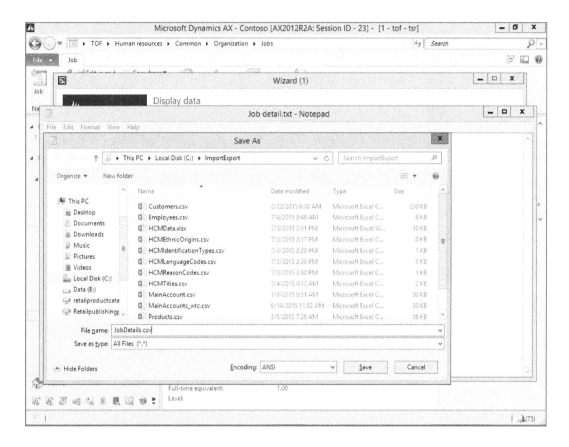

And when the **Save As** dialog box is displayed, navigate to the location where you are storing all of your import files, set the **Name** to **JobDetails.csv** and then click on the **Save** button.

© 2015 Blind Squirrel Publishing, LLC, All Rights Reserved
www.dynamicsaxcompanions.com

Importing Jobs Using The Data Import Export Framework

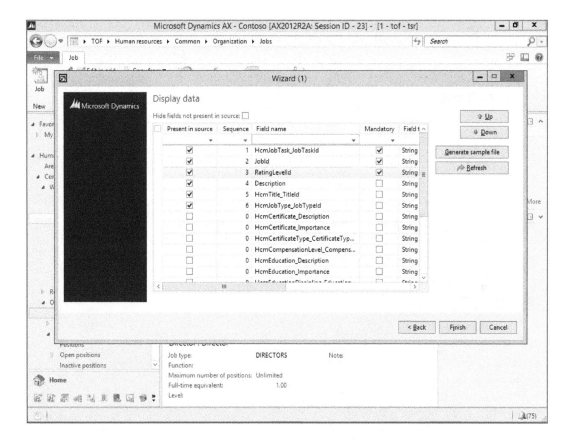

When you return back to the wizard, click on the **Finish** button to exit from the form.

© 2015 Blind Squirrel Publishing, LLC, All Rights Reserved
www.dynamicsaxcompanions.com

Importing Jobs Using The Data Import Export Framework

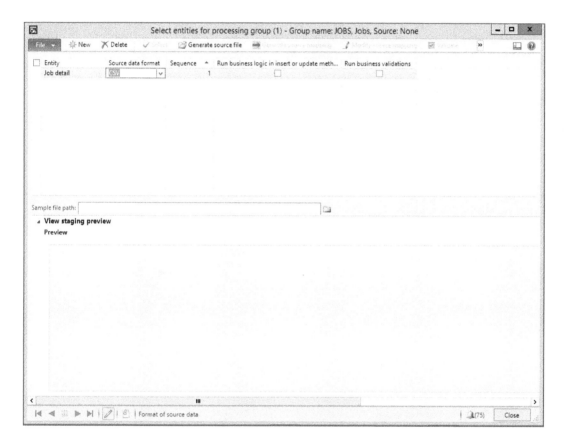

When you return back to the **Select Entities For Processing** form, click on the **Folder** icon to the right of the **Sample File Path** field.

© 2015 Blind Squirrel Publishing, LLC, All Rights Reserved
www.dynamicsaxcompanions.com

Importing Jobs Using The Data Import Export Framework

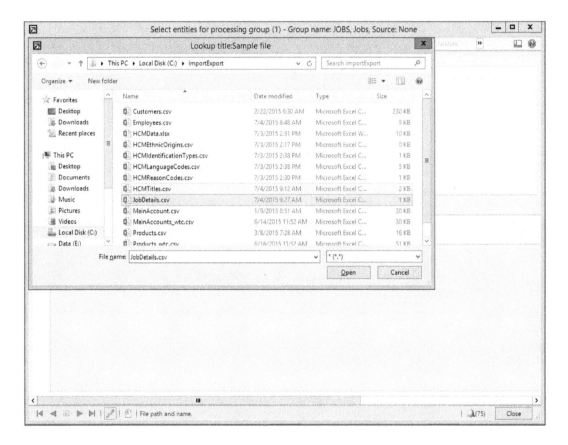

When the **Lookup Sample File** browser is displayed, navigate to the sample file that you just created and then click the **Open** button.

© 2015 Blind Squirrel Publishing, LLC, All Rights Reserved
www.dynamicsaxcompanions.com

Importing Jobs Using The Data Import Export Framework

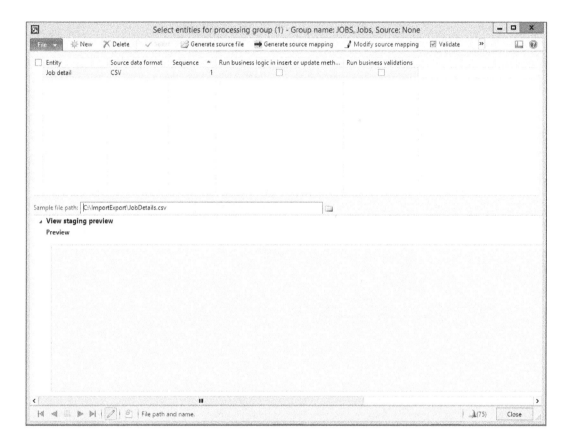

Now that you have linked the sample file to the mapping, click on the **Generate Source Mapping** button within the menu bar.

© 2015 Blind Squirrel Publishing, LLC, All Rights Reserved
www.dynamicsaxcompanions.com

Importing Jobs Using The Data Import Export Framework

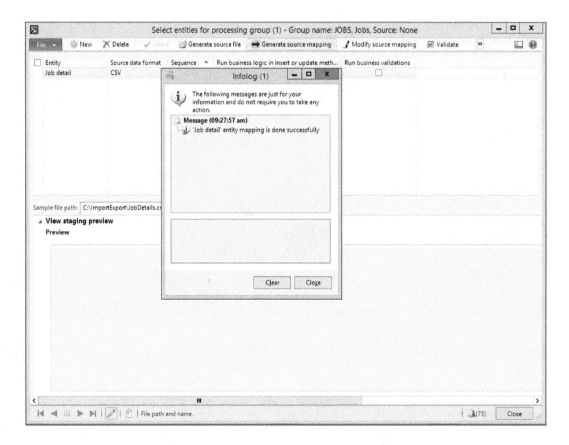

Next you should see an InfoLog that says that everything was correctly mapped and you can then click on the **Close** button to dismiss the form.

© 2015 Blind Squirrel Publishing, LLC, All Rights Reserved
www.dynamicsaxcompanions.com

Importing Jobs Using The Data Import Export Framework

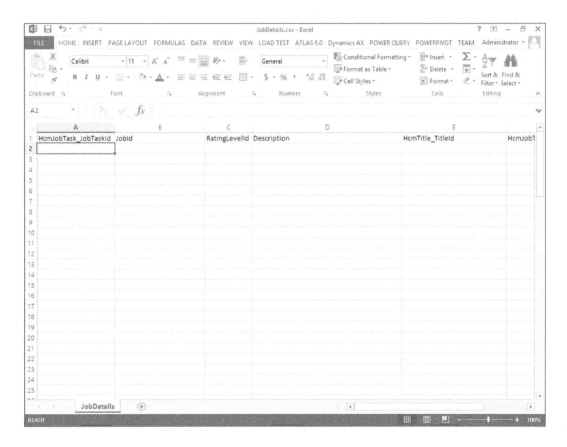

Now find the sample CSV file that you just created and open it up within Excel.

© 2015 Blind Squirrel Publishing, LLC, All Rights Reserved
www.dynamicsaxcompanions.com

Importing Jobs Using The Data Import Export Framework

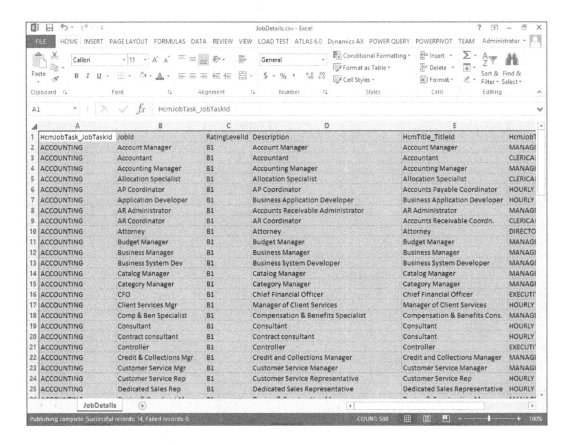

Now just paste in all of your **Job Details** into the spreadsheet and save and close the file.

Note: If you want to use the sample data that we created, then you can download it from the **Dynamics AX Companions** site. Here is the link to the resources page:

http://www.dynamicsaxcompanions.com/Bare-Bones-Configuration-Guides/Configuring-Human-Resources

© 2015 Blind Squirrel Publishing, LLC, All Rights Reserved
www.dynamicsaxcompanions.com

Importing Jobs Using The Data Import Export Framework

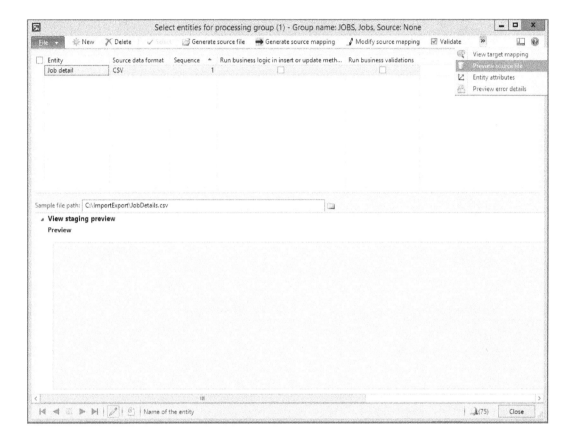

To make sure that everything looks good, click on the **Preview Source File** within the menu bar.

© 2015 Blind Squirrel Publishing, LLC, All Rights Reserved
www.dynamicsaxcompanions.com

Importing Jobs Using The Data Import Export Framework

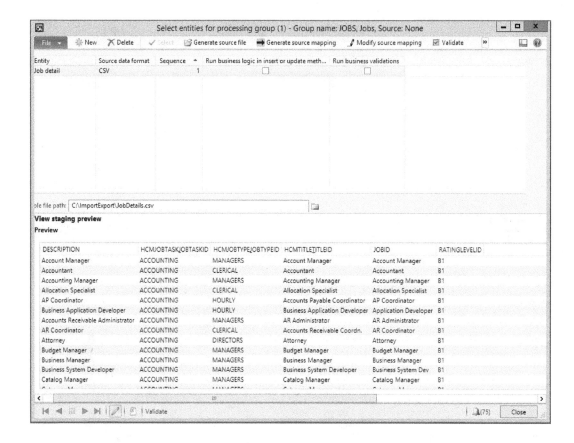

Within the **Preview** pane you should see all of your job details now show up.

Now click on the **Close** button to exit from the form.

© 2015 Blind Squirrel Publishing, LLC, All Rights Reserved
www.dynamicsaxcompanions.com

Importing Jobs Using The Data Import Export Framework

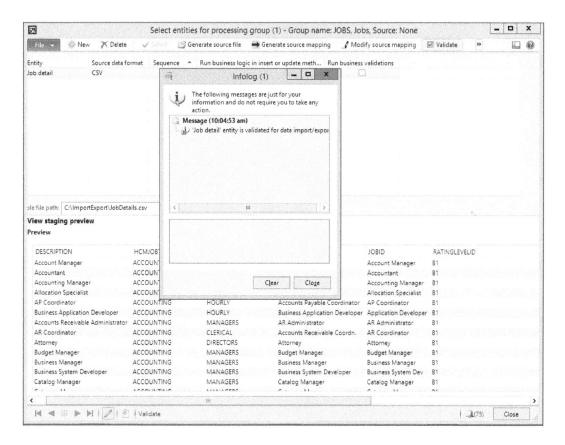

If you want to double check the data then you can click on the **Validate** button in the menu bar, and if the data is all looking good then you will get an InfoLog telling you that it all looks good.

© 2015 Blind Squirrel Publishing, LLC, All Rights Reserved
www.dynamicsaxcompanions.com

Importing Jobs Using The Data Import Export Framework

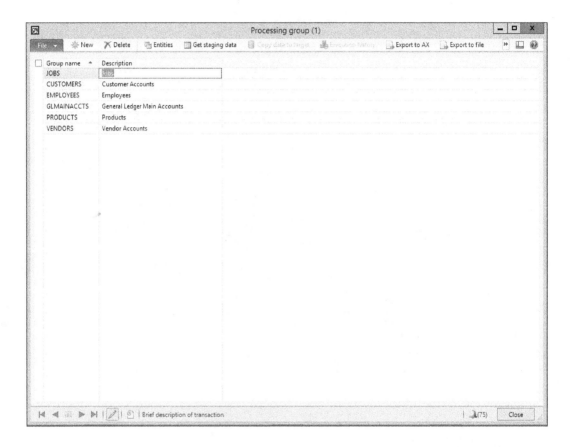

When you return to the **Processing Group** form, click on the **Get Staging Data** button in the menu bar.

© 2015 Blind Squirrel Publishing, LLC, All Rights Reserved
www.dynamicsaxcompanions.com

Importing Jobs Using The Data Import Export Framework

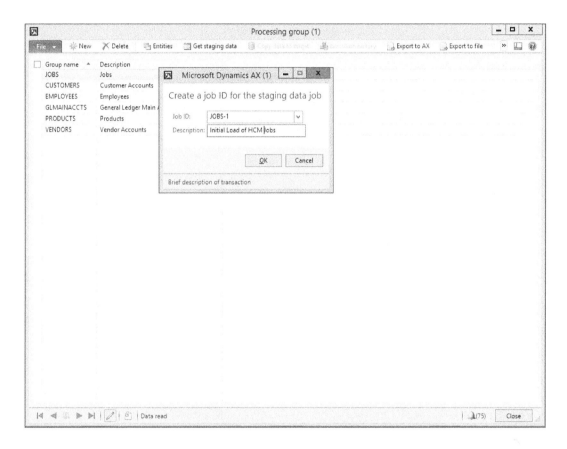

When the **Job Details** dialog box is displayed, enter in a better **Description** to describe the jobs function and then click on the **OK** button

© 2015 Blind Squirrel Publishing, LLC, All Rights Reserved
www.dynamicsaxcompanions.com

Importing Jobs Using The Data Import Export Framework

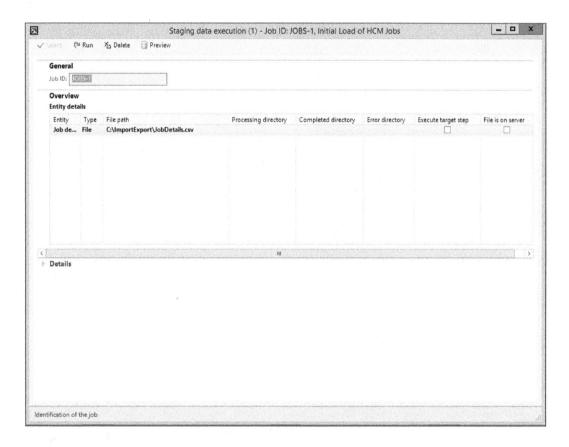

When the **Staging Data Execution** form is displayed, click on the **Preview** button to double check the data.

© 2015 Blind Squirrel Publishing, LLC, All Rights Reserved
www.dynamicsaxcompanions.com

Importing Jobs Using The Data Import Export Framework

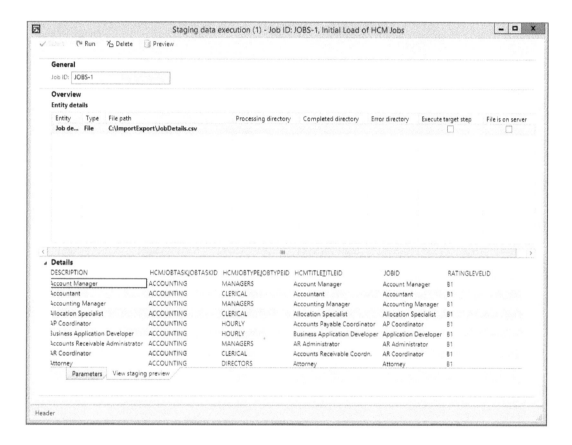

In the **Details** panel you should see the data again.

Note: This is a little bit more stringent a test than the first preview that we did, so it's a good idea to test it this way again.

© 2015 Blind Squirrel Publishing, LLC, All Rights Reserved
www.dynamicsaxcompanions.com

Importing Jobs Using The Data Import Export Framework

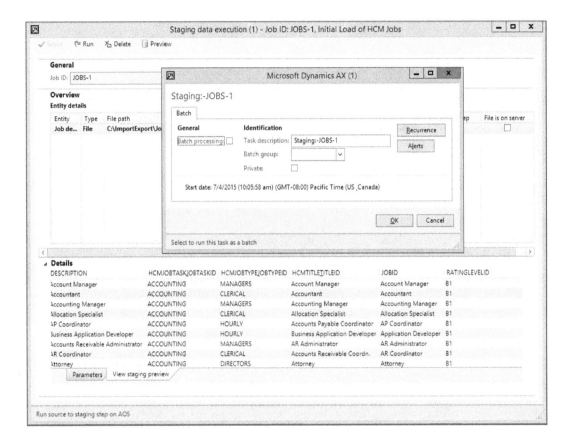

Now click on the **Run** button in the menu bar.

This will open up the **Processing** dialog box. All you need to do to kick off the process is to click on the **OK** button.

© 2015 Blind Squirrel Publishing, LLC, All Rights Reserved
www.dynamicsaxcompanions.com

Importing Jobs Using The Data Import Export Framework

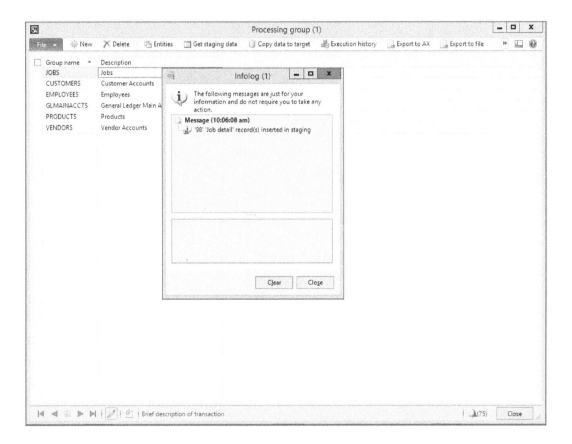

If everything goes well, then you will get a dialog box saying that the records were inserted into the **Staging** area and you can click on the **Close** button to exit from the form.

© 2015 Blind Squirrel Publishing, LLC, All Rights Reserved
www.dynamicsaxcompanions.com

Importing Jobs Using The Data Import Export Framework

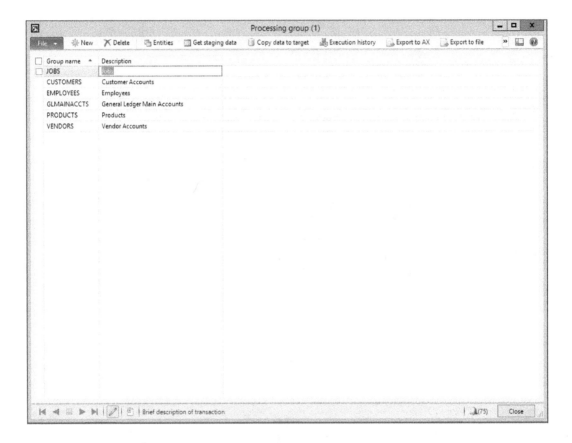

When you return back to the **Processing Group** form, click on the **Copy Data To Target** button in the menu bar.

© 2015 Blind Squirrel Publishing, LLC, All Rights Reserved
www.dynamicsaxcompanions.com

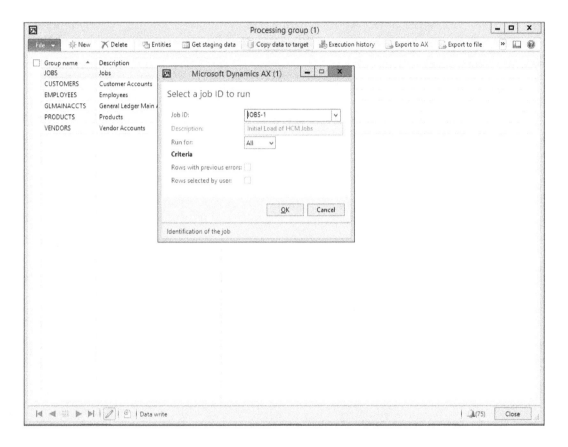

This will open up a dialog box where you can select the staging job that you just performed and then just click on the **OK** button.

© 2015 Blind Squirrel Publishing, LLC, All Rights Reserved
www.dynamicsaxcompanions.com

Importing Jobs Using The Data Import Export Framework

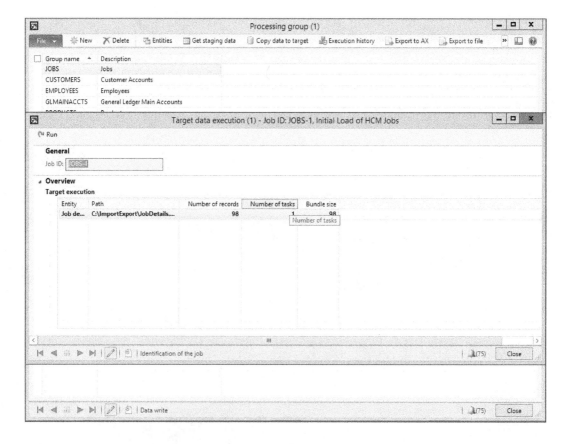

When the **Target Data Execution** dialog box is displayed, just click on the **Run** button in the menu bar.

© 2015 Blind Squirrel Publishing, LLC, All Rights Reserved
www.dynamicsaxcompanions.com

Importing Jobs Using The Data Import Export Framework

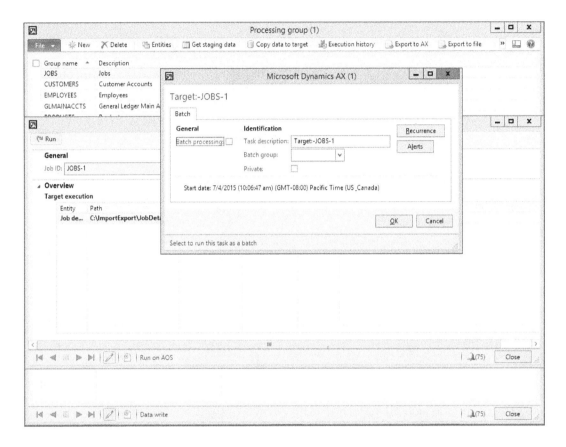

When the job details form is displayed, just click on the **OK** button.

© 2015 Blind Squirrel Publishing, LLC, All Rights Reserved
www.dynamicsaxcompanions.com

Importing Jobs Using The Data Import Export Framework

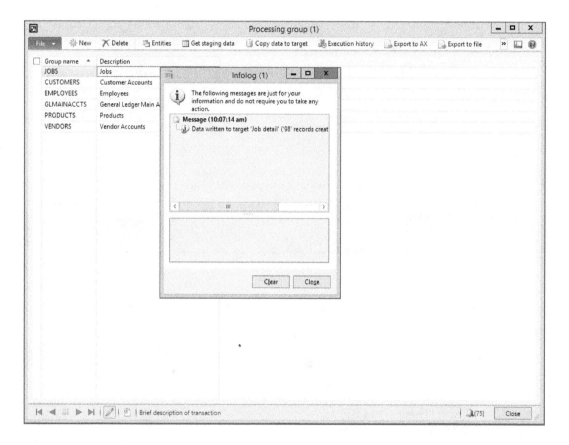

If all of your data is in the right place and valid then you should get a dialog box saying that the data has been loaded and you can click on the **Close** button to exit from the form.

© 2015 Blind Squirrel Publishing, LLC, All Rights Reserved
www.dynamicsaxcompanions.com

Importing Jobs Using The Data Import Export Framework

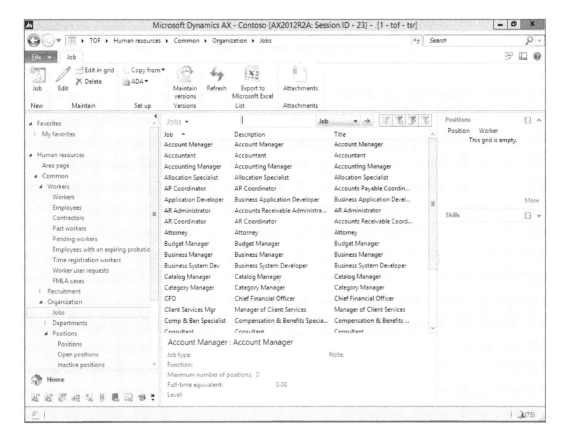

Now if you return back to the **Jobs** list page you will notice that there are a lot more jobs that you can assign your workers to.

© 2015 Blind Squirrel Publishing, LLC, All Rights Reserved
www.dynamicsaxcompanions.com

Importing Jobs Using The Data Import Export Framework

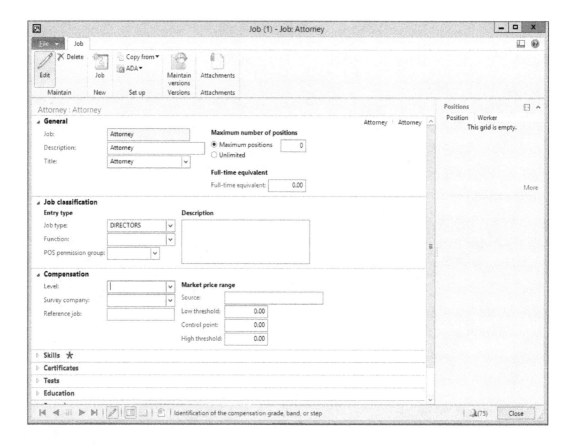

And if you open up the **Job Details** then you will also see that the key information has been populated for you.

That was a lot easier than doing it by hand.

© 2015 Blind Squirrel Publishing, LLC, All Rights Reserved
www.dynamicsaxcompanions.com

© 2015 Blind Squirrel Publishing, LLC, All Rights Reserved
www.dynamicsaxcompanions.com

© 2015 Blind Squirrel Publishing, LLC, All Rights Reserved
www.dynamicsaxcompanions.com

CONFIGURING POSITIONS AND POSITION HIERARCHIES

Now that we have created our jobs we can start creating the **Positions** and also the **Position Hierarchies** that will allow us to create reporting structures within the organization.

© 2015 Blind Squirrel Publishing, LLC, All Rights Reserved
www.dynamicsaxcompanions.com

© 2015 Blind Squirrel Publishing, LLC, All Rights Reserved
www.dynamicsaxcompanions.com

Creating Position Types

Before we create our **Positions** though there is a little bit of setup that we need to perform. The first place that we will start is to set up a couple of **Position Types** that we will use to identify Full-time and Part-time positions.

Creating Position Types

Position type	Description of the position type	Classification of the position type
Full-time	Full-time employee	Full-time
Part-time	Part-time employee	Part-time

© 2015 Blind Squirrel Publishing, LLC, All Rights Reserved
www.dynamicsaxcompanions.com

Creating Position Types

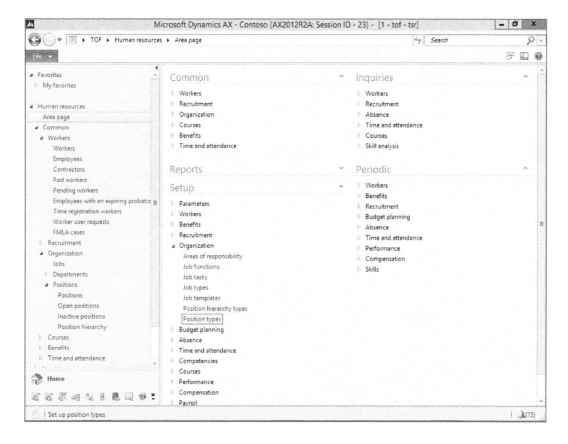

To do this, click on the **Position Types** menu item within the **Organization** folder of the **Setup** group within the **Human Resources** area page.

© 2015 Blind Squirrel Publishing, LLC, All Rights Reserved
www.dynamicsaxcompanions.com

Creating Position Types

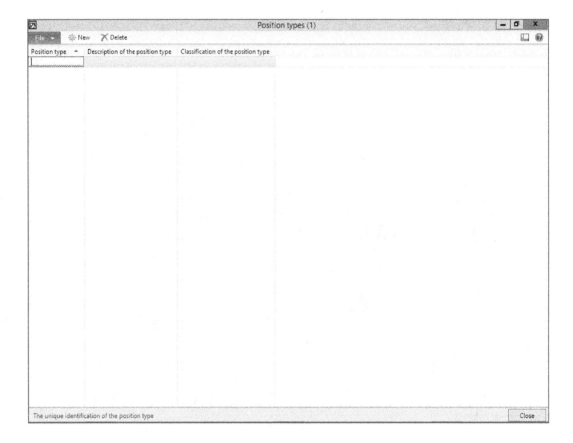

When the **Position Types** maintenance form is displayed, click on the **New** button to create a new record.

© 2015 Blind Squirrel Publishing, LLC, All Rights Reserved
www.dynamicsaxcompanions.com

Creating Position Types

Then set the **Position Type** code to **Full-time** and the **Description** to **Full-time Employee**.

© 2015 Blind Squirrel Publishing, LLC, All Rights Reserved
www.dynamicsaxcompanions.com

Creating Position Types

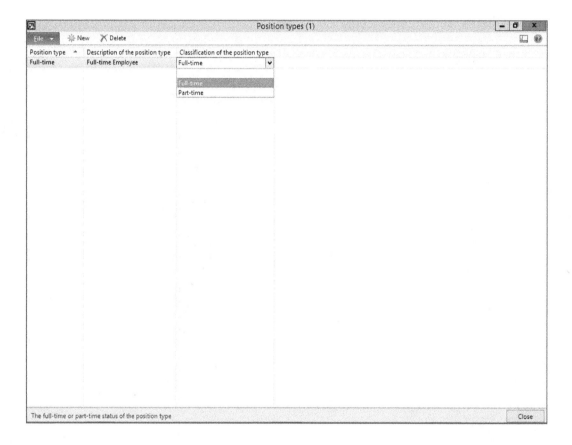

Then click on the **Classification of the Position Type** dropdown list and select the **Full-time**

© 2015 Blind Squirrel Publishing, LLC, All Rights Reserved
www.dynamicsaxcompanions.com

Creating Position Types

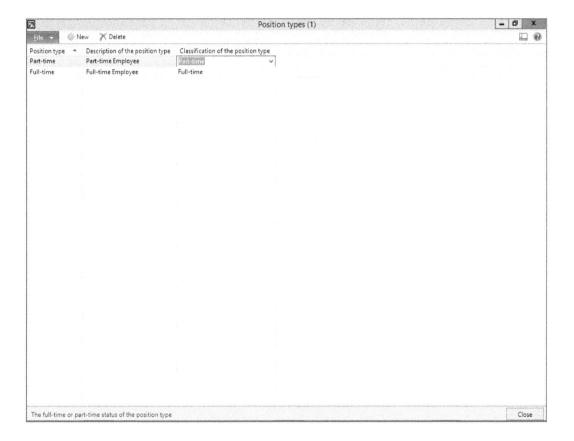

Click on the **New** button in the menu bar to create another new record, set the **Position Type** to **Part-time**, the **Description** to **Part-time Employee** and the **Classification of the Position Type** to **Part-time.**

After you have done that, click on the **Close** button to exit from the form.

© 2015 Blind Squirrel Publishing, LLC, All Rights Reserved
www.dynamicsaxcompanions.com

© 2015 Blind Squirrel Publishing, LLC, All Rights Reserved
www.dynamicsaxcompanions.com

Configuring Position Hierarchy Types

Next we will want to create a **Position Hierarchy Type** that we will be able to use to create alternative reporting structures.

© 2015 Blind Squirrel Publishing, LLC, All Rights Reserved
www.dynamicsaxcompanions.com

Configuring Position Hierarchy Types

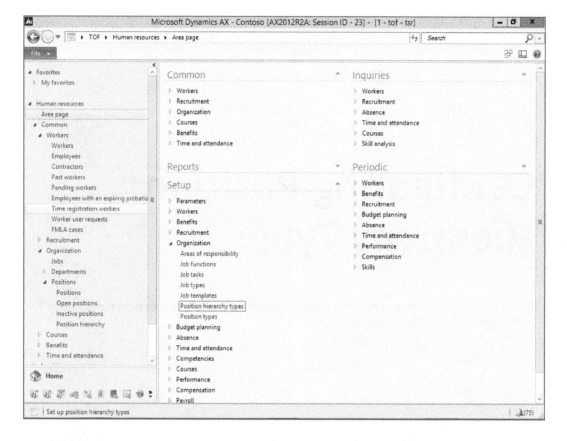

To do this, click on the **Position Hierarchy Types** menu item within the **Organization** folder of the **Setup** group within the **Human Resources** area page.

© 2015 Blind Squirrel Publishing, LLC, All Rights Reserved
www.dynamicsaxcompanions.com

Configuring Position Hierarchy Types

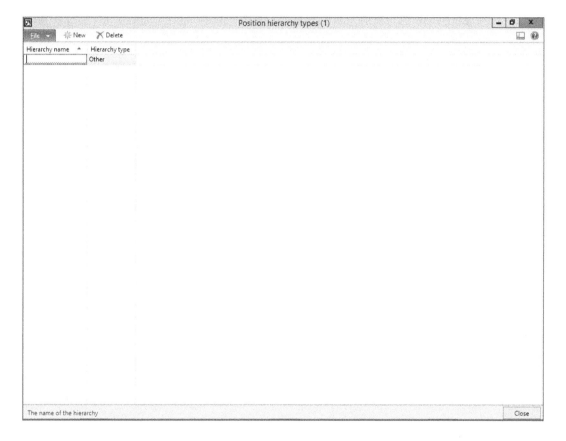

When the **Position Hierarchy Types** list page is displayed, click on the **New** button to create a new record.

© 2015 Blind Squirrel Publishing, LLC, All Rights Reserved
www.dynamicsaxcompanions.com

Configuring Position Hierarchy Types

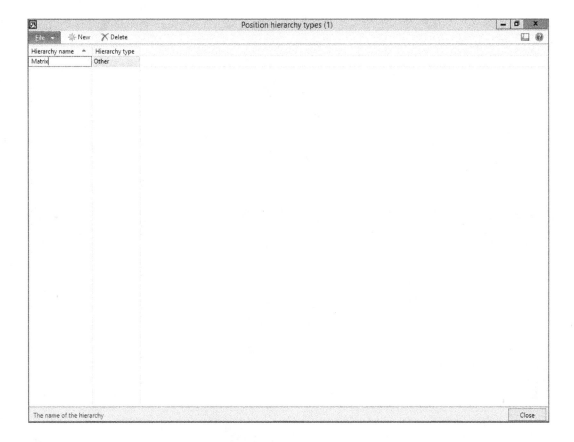

Then set the **Hierarchy Name** to **Matrix**.

© 2015 Blind Squirrel Publishing, LLC, All Rights Reserved
www.dynamicsaxcompanions.com

Configuring Position Hierarchy Types

Click on the **New** button in the menu bar again to create another record and then set the **Hierarchy Name** to **Project.**

When you have done that, click on the **Close** button to exit from the form.

© 2015 Blind Squirrel Publishing, LLC, All Rights Reserved
www.dynamicsaxcompanions.com

© 2015 Blind Squirrel Publishing, LLC, All Rights Reserved
www.dynamicsaxcompanions.com

Creating Positions

Now we can start creating our **Positions** that we will then be able to assign jobs to and then place our workers into.

© 2015 Blind Squirrel Publishing, LLC, All Rights Reserved
www.dynamicsaxcompanions.com

Creating Positions

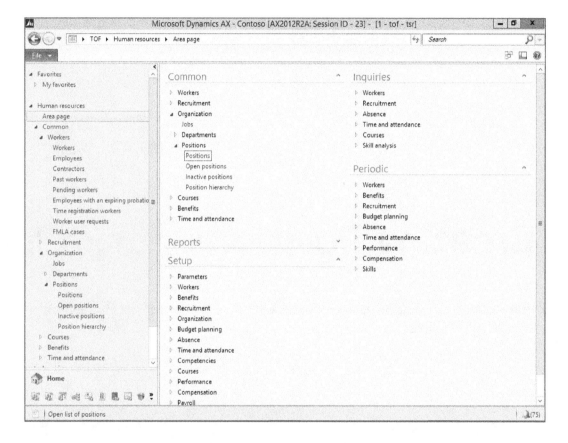

To do this, click on the **Positions** menu item within the **Positions** sub-folder of the **Organization** folder within the **Common** group of the **Human Resources** area page.

© 2015 Blind Squirrel Publishing, LLC, All Rights Reserved
www.dynamicsaxcompanions.com

Creating Positions

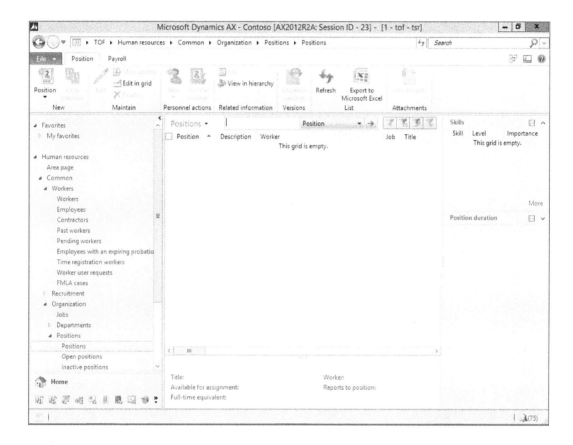

When the **Positions** list page is displayed, click on the **Position** button within the **New** group of the **Position** ribbon bar to create a new record.

Creating Positions

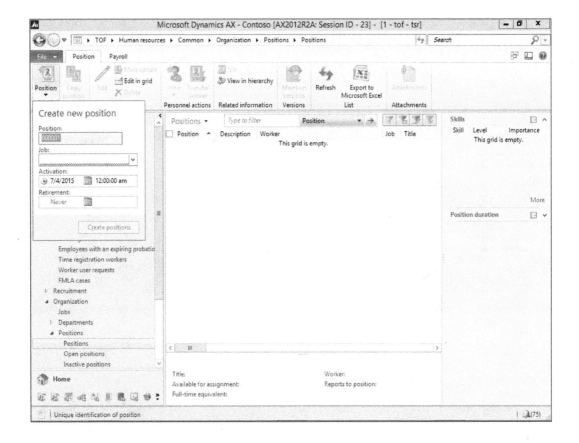

This will open up the **Create New Position** quick entry form.

© 2015 Blind Squirrel Publishing, LLC, All Rights Reserved
www.dynamicsaxcompanions.com

Creating Positions

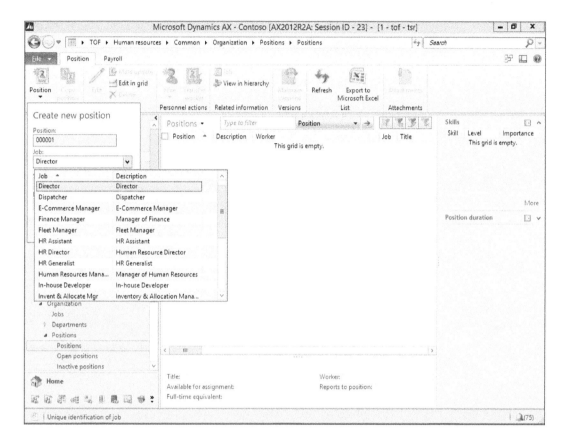

Click on the **Job** dropdown list and select the **Job** of **Director** from the list of available jobs.

© 2015 Blind Squirrel Publishing, LLC, All Rights Reserved
www.dynamicsaxcompanions.com

Creating Positions

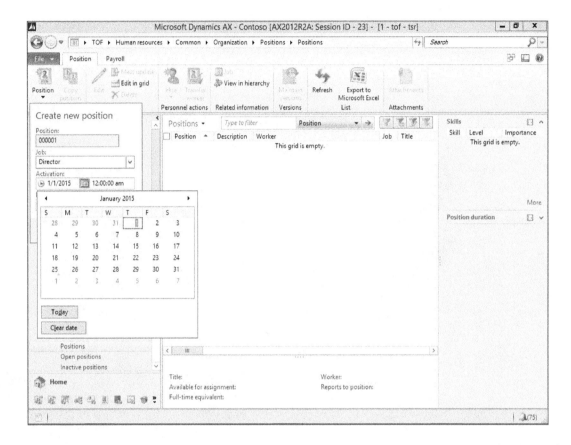

Then click on the **Activation** date picker and select the date that you want to make the **Position** active.

© 2015 Blind Squirrel Publishing, LLC, All Rights Reserved
www.dynamicsaxcompanions.com

Creating Positions

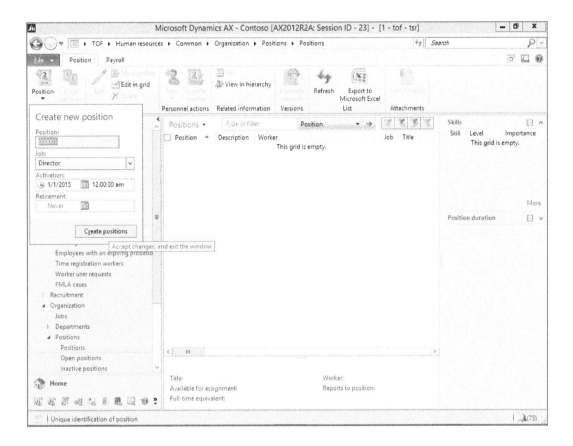

Then click on the **Create Position** button to create the **Position** record.

© 2015 Blind Squirrel Publishing, LLC, All Rights Reserved
www.dynamicsaxcompanions.com

Creating Positions

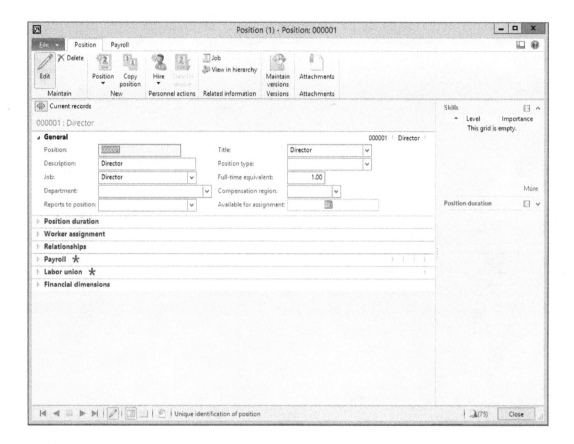

This will open up the **Position Details** form with a lot more information for you to maintain against the **Position**.

© 2015 Blind Squirrel Publishing, LLC, All Rights Reserved
www.dynamicsaxcompanions.com

Creating Positions

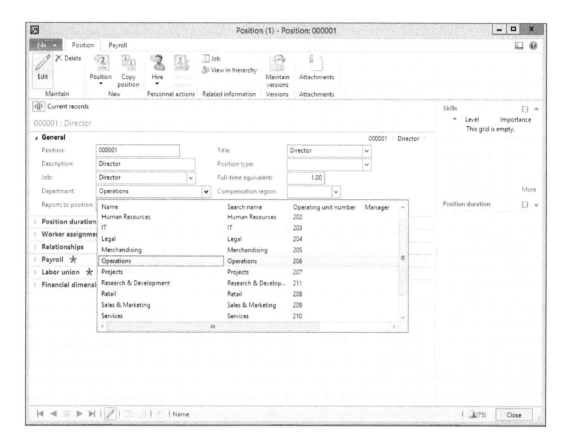

You can click on the **Department** field dropdown list and assign the **Position** to the **Operations** department.

© 2015 Blind Squirrel Publishing, LLC, All Rights Reserved
www.dynamicsaxcompanions.com

Creating Positions

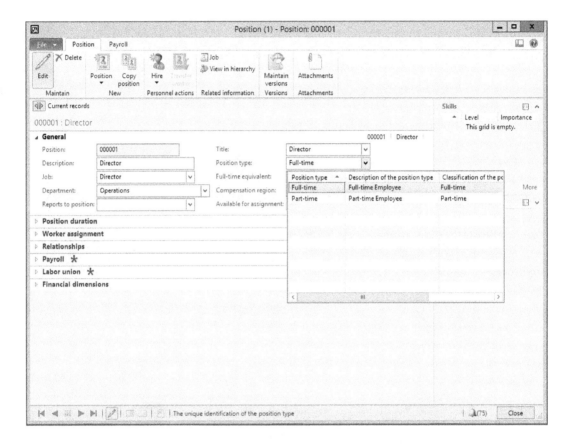

Also, if you click on the **Position Type** dropdown list you can select the **Full-time** option that you just created earlier.

© 2015 Blind Squirrel Publishing, LLC, All Rights Reserved
www.dynamicsaxcompanions.com

Creating Positions

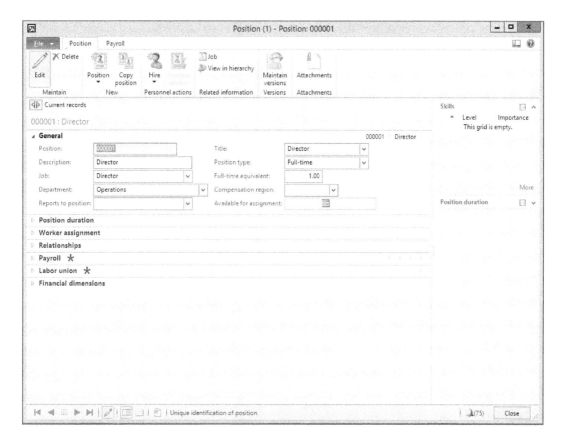

Once you have done this, click on the **View In Hierarchy** button within the **Related Information** group of the **Position** ribbon bar.

© 2015 Blind Squirrel Publishing, LLC, All Rights Reserved
www.dynamicsaxcompanions.com

Creating Positions

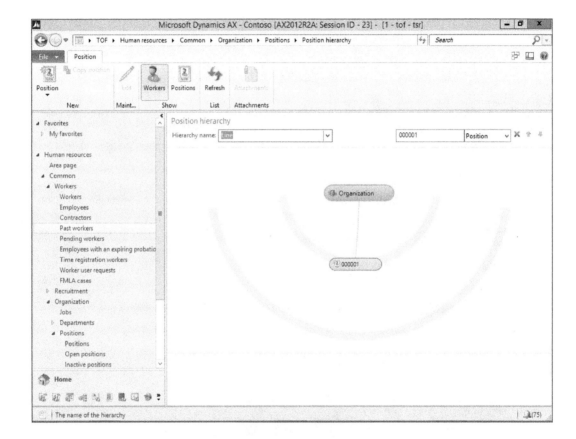

That will show you your **Organization Hierarchy** graphically.

I think we need to add more positions for sure.

© 2015 Blind Squirrel Publishing, LLC, All Rights Reserved
www.dynamicsaxcompanions.com

© 2015 Blind Squirrel Publishing, LLC, All Rights Reserved
www.dynamicsaxcompanions.com

© 2015 Blind Squirrel Publishing, LLC, All Rights Reserved
www.dynamicsaxcompanions.com

Importing Positions Using The Data Import Export Framework

If you have all of your **Positions** and **Position Reporting Structures** filed away as a spreadsheet then rather than building all of the positions by hand, you can take advantage of the **Data Import Export Framework** and import the **Positions** into Dynamics AX through a template.

© 2015 Blind Squirrel Publishing, LLC, All Rights Reserved
www.dynamicsaxcompanions.com

Importing Positions Using The Data Import Export Framework

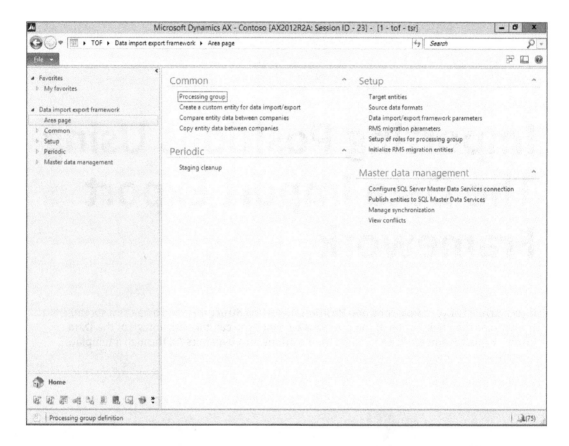

To do this, click on the **Processing Group** menu item within the **Common** group of the **Data Import Export Framework** area page.

© 2015 Blind Squirrel Publishing, LLC, All Rights Reserved
www.dynamicsaxcompanions.com

Importing Positions Using The Data Import Export Framework

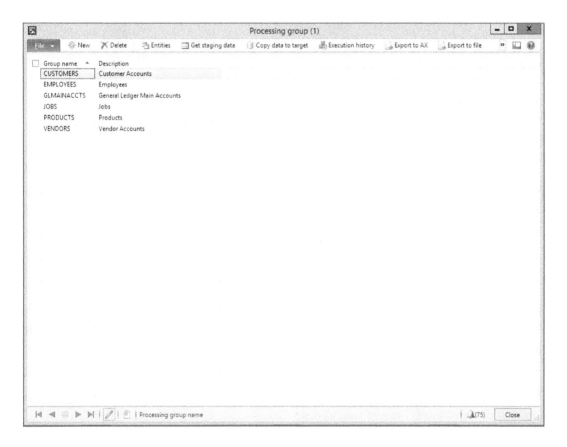

When the **Processing Group** list page is displayed, click on the **New** button in the menu bar to create a new roecord.

© 2015 Blind Squirrel Publishing, LLC, All Rights Reserved
www.dynamicsaxcompanions.com

Importing Positions Using The Data Import Export Framework

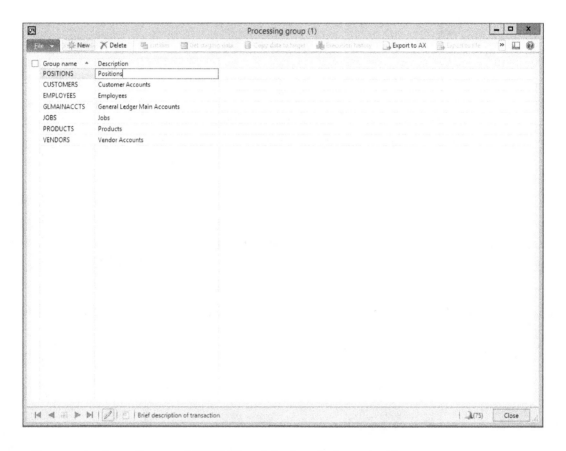

Then set the **Group Name** to **POSITIONS** and the **Description** to **Positions**.

© 2015 Blind Squirrel Publishing, LLC, All Rights Reserved
www.dynamicsaxcompanions.com

Importing Positions Using The Data Import Export Framework

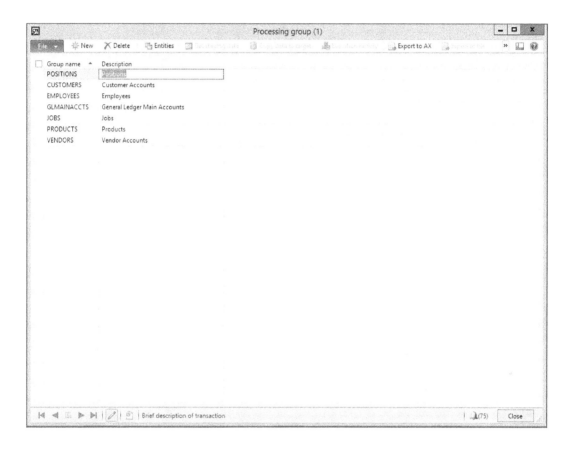

Save the record by pressing **CTRL+S** and that will enable you to click on the **Entities** button in the menu bar.

© 2015 Blind Squirrel Publishing, LLC, All Rights Reserved
www.dynamicsaxcompanions.com

Importing Positions Using The Data Import Export Framework

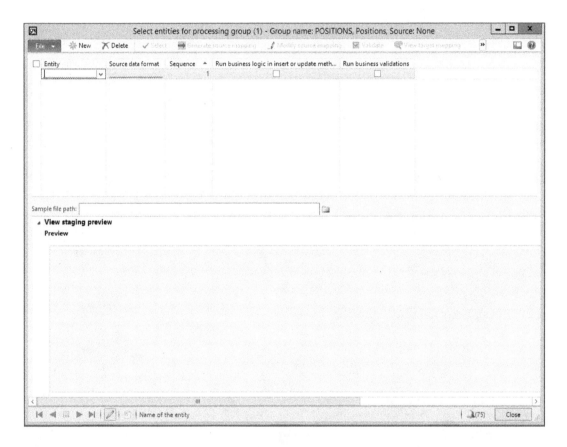

When the **Select Entities for Processing Group** maintenance form is displayed click on the **New** button in the menu bar to create a new record.

© 2015 Blind Squirrel Publishing, LLC, All Rights Reserved
www.dynamicsaxcompanions.com

Importing Positions Using The Data Import Export Framework

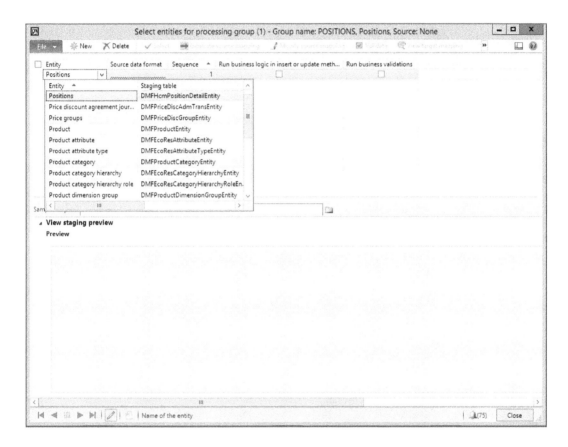

Then click on the **Entity** dropdown list and select the **Positions** entity.

© 2015 Blind Squirrel Publishing, LLC, All Rights Reserved
www.dynamicsaxcompanions.com

Importing Positions Using The Data Import Export Framework

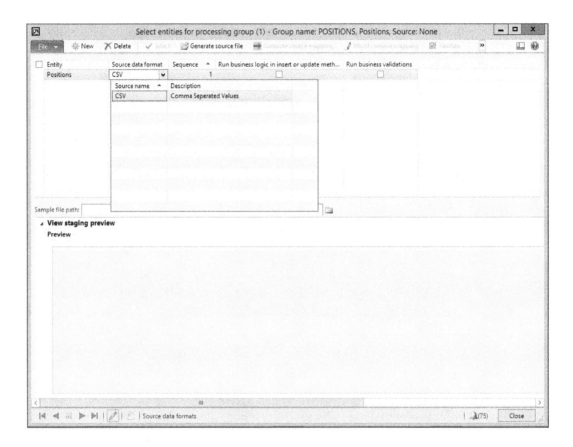

Then click on the **Source Data Format** dropdown list and select the **CSV** data format.

© 2015 Blind Squirrel Publishing, LLC, All Rights Reserved
www.dynamicsaxcompanions.com

Importing Positions Using The Data Import Export Framework

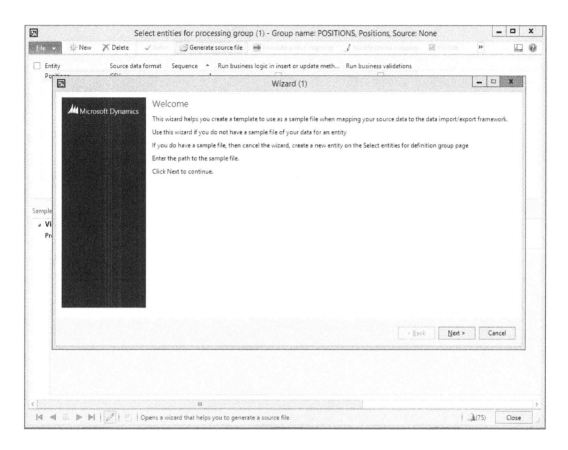

Now click on the **Generate Source File** button in the menu bar.

When the setup wizard is displayed, just click on the **Next** button to skip through the welcome page.

© 2015 Blind Squirrel Publishing, LLC, All Rights Reserved
www.dynamicsaxcompanions.com

Importing Positions Using The Data Import Export Framework

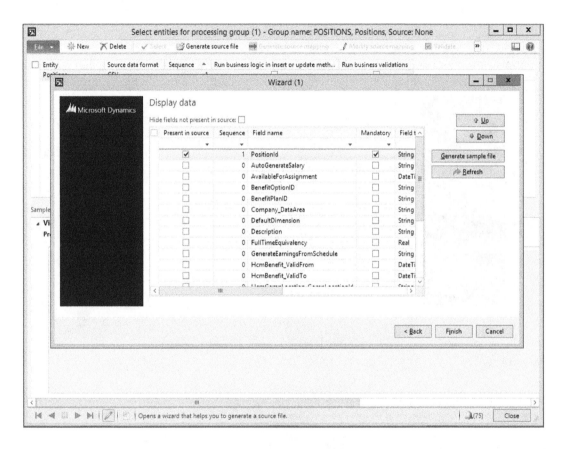

That will take you to the **Display Data** page where you will be able to see all of the fields that are available to be imported, and also the ones that have already been selected.

© 2015 Blind Squirrel Publishing, LLC, All Rights Reserved
www.dynamicsaxcompanions.com

Importing Positions Using The Data Import Export Framework

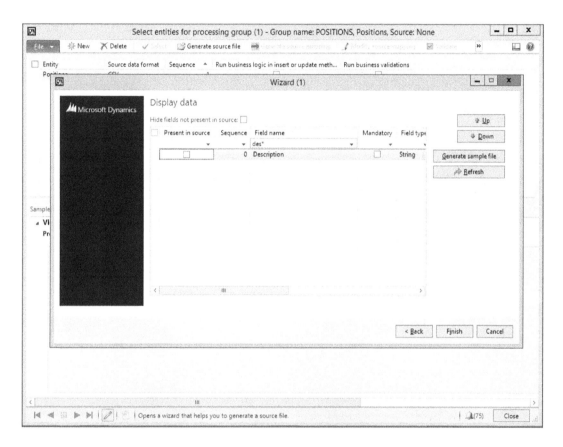

Type **desc*** into the search field for the **Field Name**. This will filter out the records and you will see the **Description** field. Click on the **Present In Source** checkbox for the field.

© 2015 Blind Squirrel Publishing, LLC, All Rights Reserved
www.dynamicsaxcompanions.com

Importing Positions Using The Data Import Export Framework

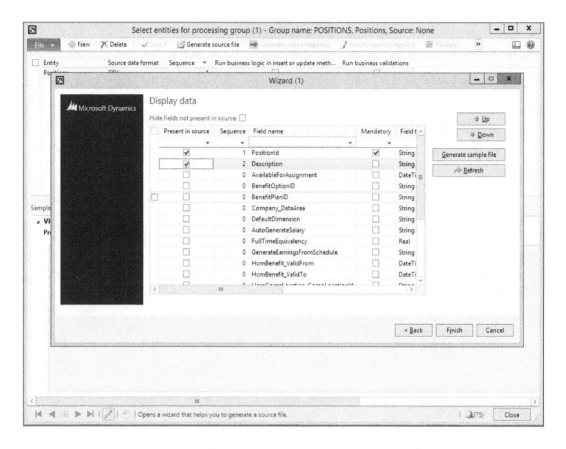

This will return you back to the field list and now you will have the **Description** field as an import field.

© 2015 Blind Squirrel Publishing, LLC, All Rights Reserved
www.dynamicsaxcompanions.com

Importing Positions Using The Data Import Export Framework

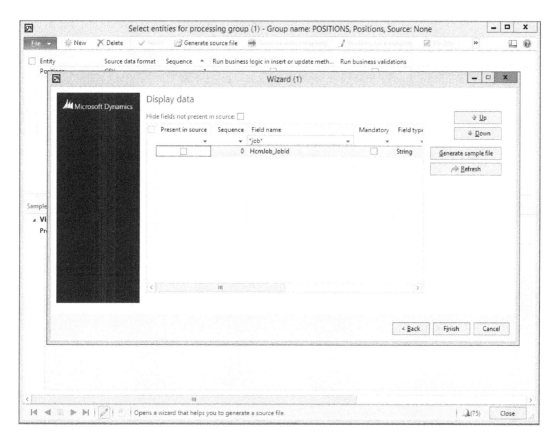

Now type ***job*** into the search field for the **Field Name**. This will filter out the records and you will see the **HCMJob_JobId** field. Click on the **Present In Source** checkbox for the field.

© 2015 Blind Squirrel Publishing, LLC, All Rights Reserved
www.dynamicsaxcompanions.com

Importing Positions Using The Data Import Export Framework

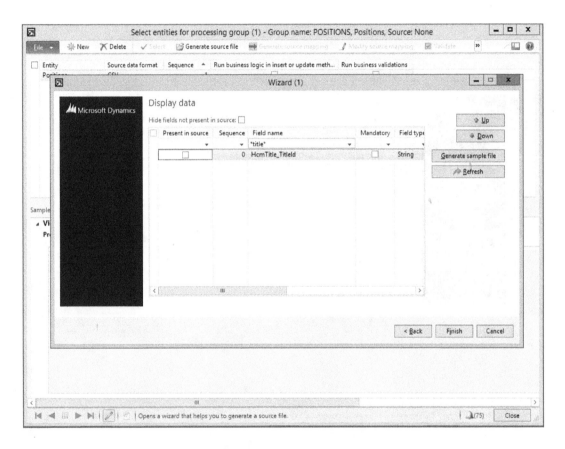

Now type ***title*** into the search field for the **Field Name**. This will filter out the records and you will see the **HCMTitle_TitleId** field. Click on the **Present In Source** checkbox for the field.

© 2015 Blind Squirrel Publishing, LLC, All Rights Reserved
www.dynamicsaxcompanions.com

Importing Positions Using The Data Import Export Framework

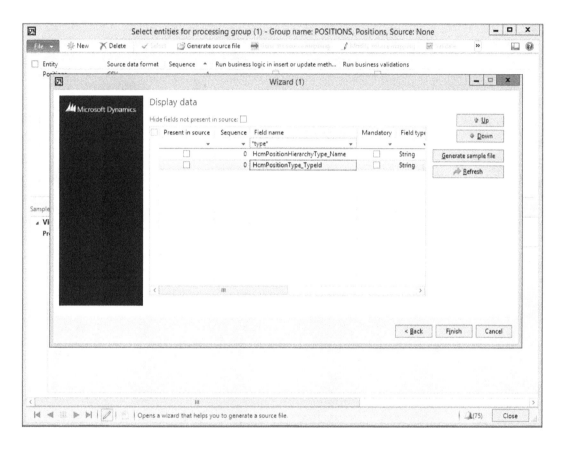

Now type ***type*** into the search field for the **Field Name**. This will filter out the records and you will see the **HCMPositionType_TypeId** field. Click on the **Present In Source** checkbox for the field.

© 2015 Blind Squirrel Publishing, LLC, All Rights Reserved
www.dynamicsaxcompanions.com

Importing Positions Using The Data Import Export Framework

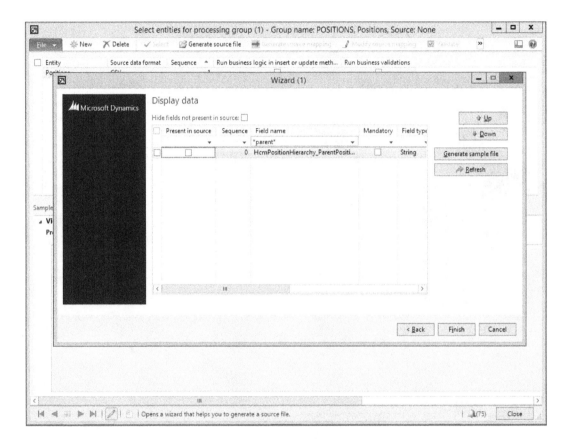

Now type ***parent*** into the search field for the **Field Name**. This will filter out the records and you will see the **HCMPositionHierarchy_ParentPositionId** field. Click on the **Present In Source** checkbox for the field.

Importing Positions Using The Data Import Export Framework

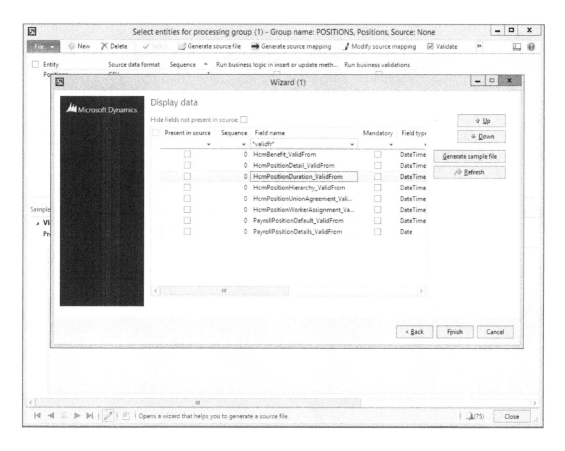

Now type ***validfr*** into the search field for the **Field Name**. This will filter out the records and you will see the **HCMPositionDuration_ValidFrom** field. Click on the **Present In Source** checkbox for the field.

© 2015 Blind Squirrel Publishing, LLC, All Rights Reserved
www.dynamicsaxcompanions.com

Importing Positions Using The Data Import Export Framework

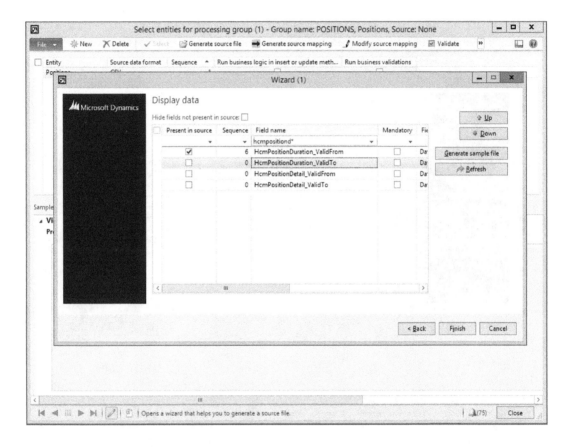

Now type ***hcmpositiond*** into the search field for the **Field Name**. This will filter out the records and you will see the **HCMPositionDuration_ValidTo** field. Click on the **Present In Source** checkbox for the field.

© 2015 Blind Squirrel Publishing, LLC, All Rights Reserved
www.dynamicsaxcompanions.com

Importing Positions Using The Data Import Export Framework

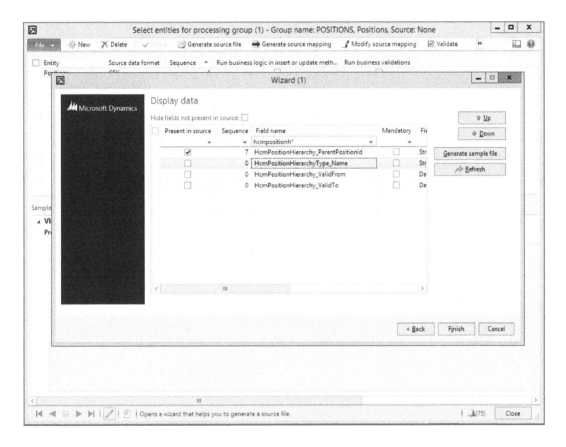

Now type **hcmpositionh*** into the search field for the **Field Name**. This will filter out the records and you will see the **HCMPositionHierarchyType_Name** field. Click on the **Present In Source** checkbox for the field.

© 2015 Blind Squirrel Publishing, LLC, All Rights Reserved
www.dynamicsaxcompanions.com

Importing Positions Using The Data Import Export Framework

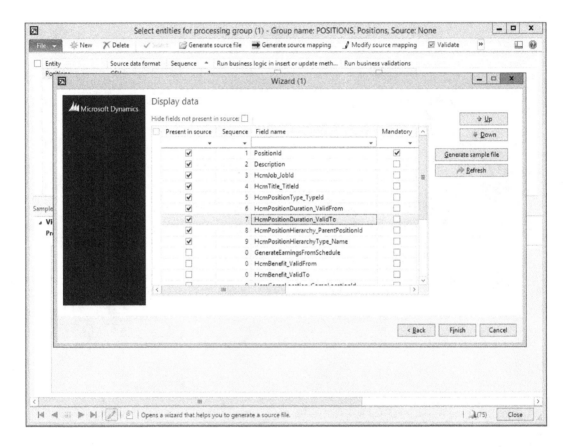

Now that you have all of the main fields that you need in the template, click on the **Generate Sample File** button

© 2015 Blind Squirrel Publishing, LLC, All Rights Reserved
www.dynamicsaxcompanions.com

Importing Positions Using The Data Import Export Framework

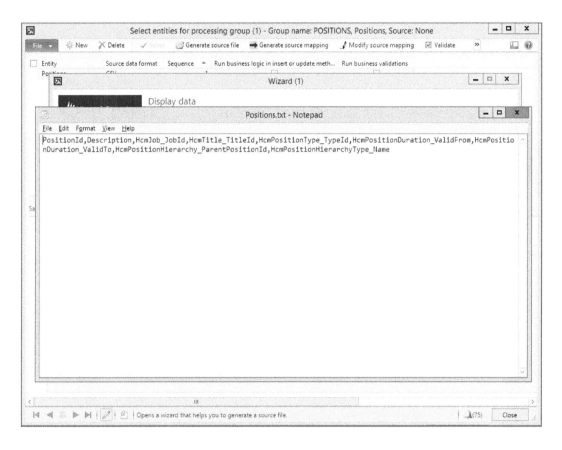

This will create your sample CSV file for the import. Just click on the **File** menu and select the **Save** option.

© 2015 Blind Squirrel Publishing, LLC, All Rights Reserved
www.dynamicsaxcompanions.com

Importing Positions Using The Data Import Export Framework

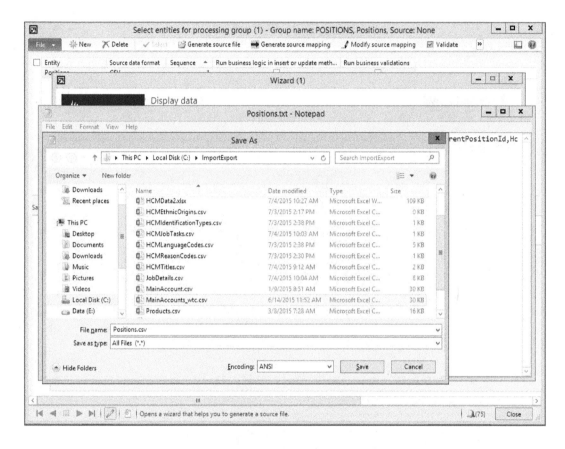

And when the **Save As** dialog box is displayed, navigate to the location where you are storing all of your import files, set the **Name** to **Positions.csv** and then click on the **Save** button.

© 2015 Blind Squirrel Publishing, LLC, All Rights Reserved
www.dynamicsaxcompanions.com

Importing Positions Using The Data Import Export Framework

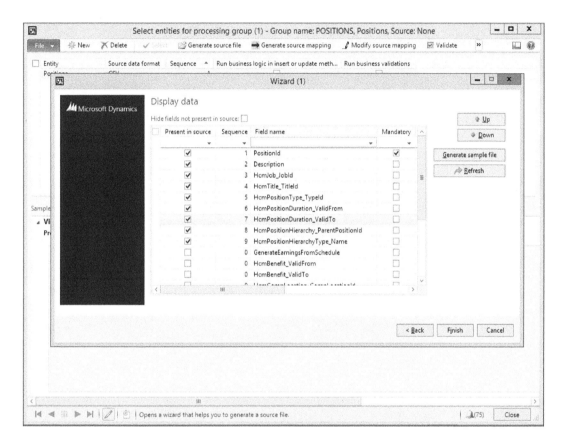

When you return back to the wizard, click on the **Finish** button to exit from the form.

© 2015 Blind Squirrel Publishing, LLC, All Rights Reserved
www.dynamicsaxcompanions.com

Importing Positions Using The Data Import Export Framework

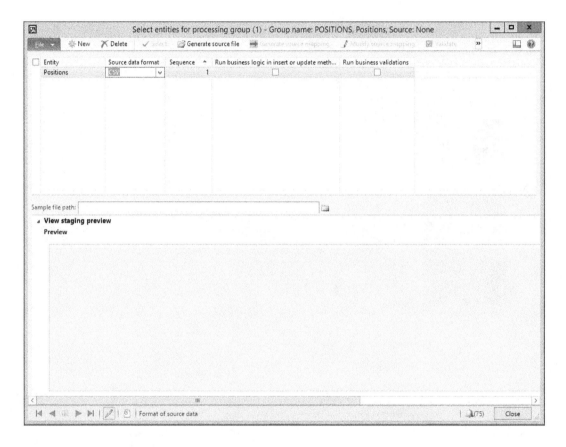

When you return back to the **Select Entities For Processing** form, click on the **Folder** icon to the right of the **Sample File Path** field.

© 2015 Blind Squirrel Publishing, LLC, All Rights Reserved
www.dynamicsaxcompanions.com

Importing Positions Using The Data Import Export Framework

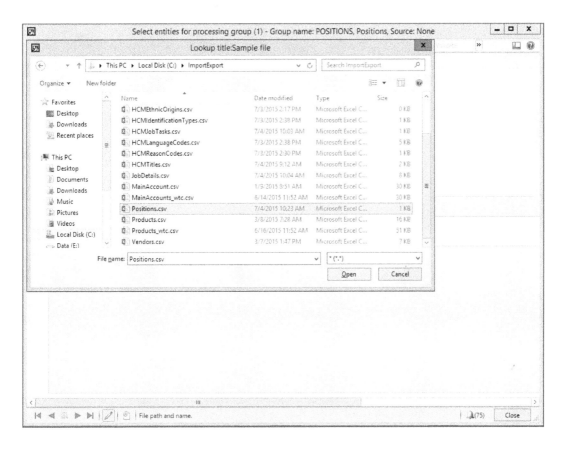

When the **Lookup Sample File** browser is displayed, navigate to the sample file that you just created and then click the **Open** button.

© 2015 Blind Squirrel Publishing, LLC, All Rights Reserved
www.dynamicsaxcompanions.com

Importing Positions Using The Data Import Export Framework

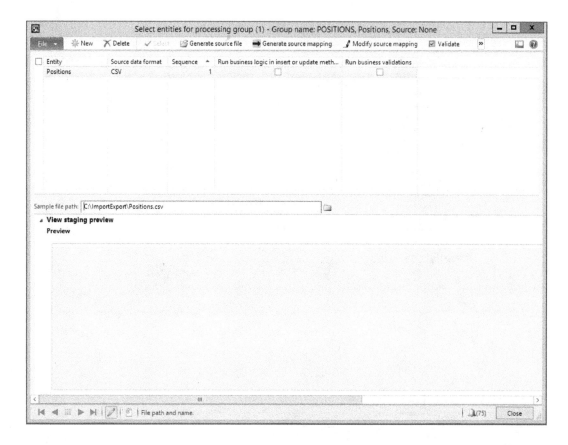

Now that you have linked the sample file to the mapping, click on the **Generate Source Mapping** button within the menu bar.

© 2015 Blind Squirrel Publishing, LLC, All Rights Reserved
www.dynamicsaxcompanions.com

Importing Positions Using The Data Import Export Framework

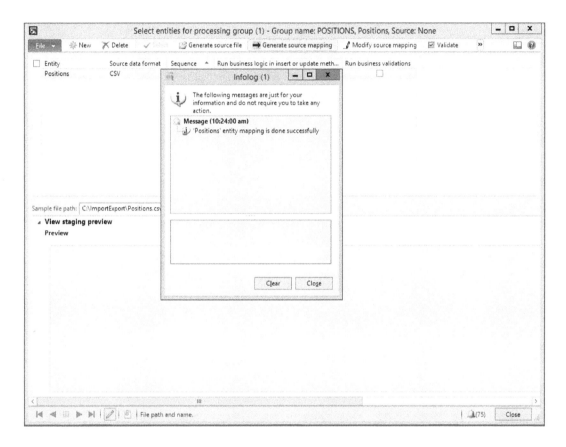

Next you should see an InfoLog that says that everything was correctly mapped and you can then click on the **Close** button to dismiss the form.

© 2015 Blind Squirrel Publishing, LLC, All Rights Reserved
www.dynamicsaxcompanions.com

Importing Positions Using The Data Import Export Framework

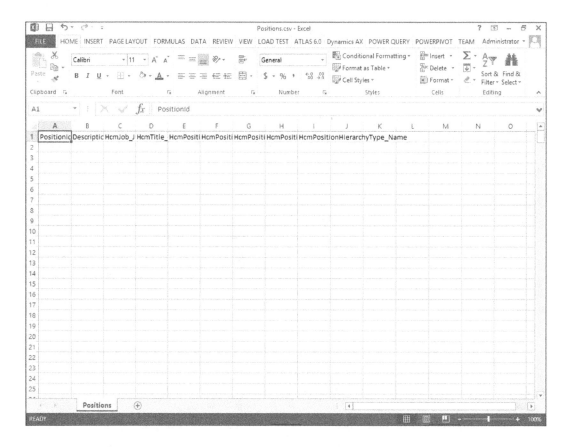

Now find the sample CSV file that you just created and open it up within Excel.

© 2015 Blind Squirrel Publishing, LLC, All Rights Reserved
www.dynamicsaxcompanions.com

Importing Positions Using The Data Import Export Framework

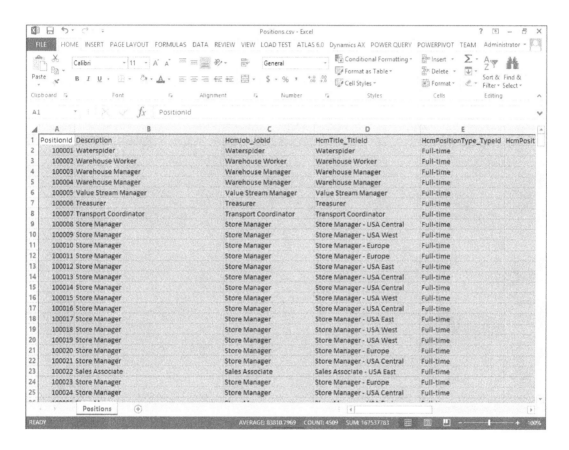

Now just paste in all of your **Job Details** into the spreadsheet and save and close the file.

Note: If you want to use the sample data that we created, then you can download it from the **Dynamics AX Companions** site. Here is the link to the resources page:

http://www.dynamicsaxcompanions.com/Bare-Bones-Configuration-Guides/Configuring-Human-Resources

© 2015 Blind Squirrel Publishing, LLC, All Rights Reserved
www.dynamicsaxcompanions.com

Importing Positions Using The Data Import Export Framework

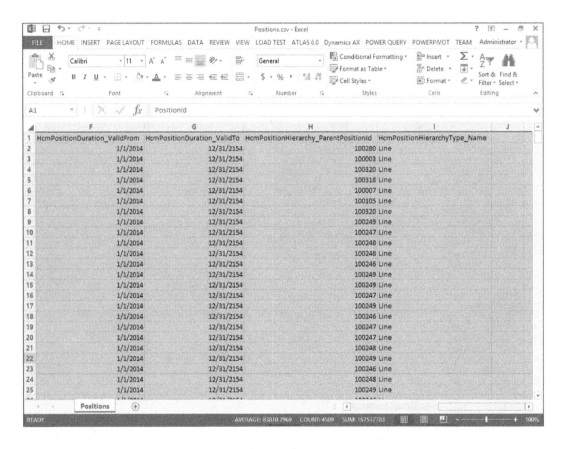

This template has a few more columns than the others so you may want to scroll over and make sure that all of the fields are populated including the **Parent Position** column.

© 2015 Blind Squirrel Publishing, LLC, All Rights Reserved
www.dynamicsaxcompanions.com

Importing Positions Using The Data Import Export Framework

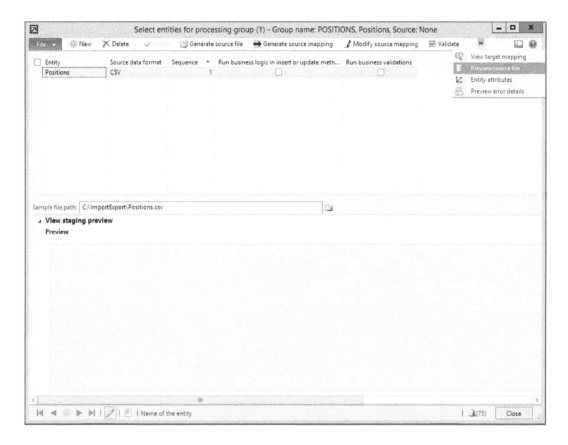

To make sure that everything looks good, click on the **Preview Source File** within the menu bar.

© 2015 Blind Squirrel Publishing, LLC, All Rights Reserved
www.dynamicsaxcompanions.com

Importing Positions Using The Data Import Export Framework

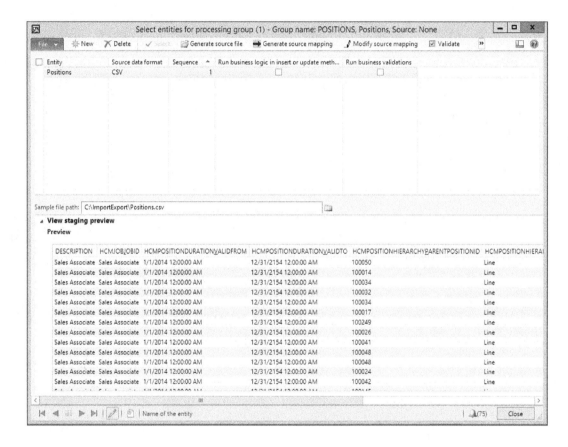

Within the **Preview** pane you should see all of your **Positions** now show up.

Now click on the **Close** button to exit from the form.

© 2015 Blind Squirrel Publishing, LLC, All Rights Reserved
www.dynamicsaxcompanions.com

Importing Positions Using The Data Import Export Framework

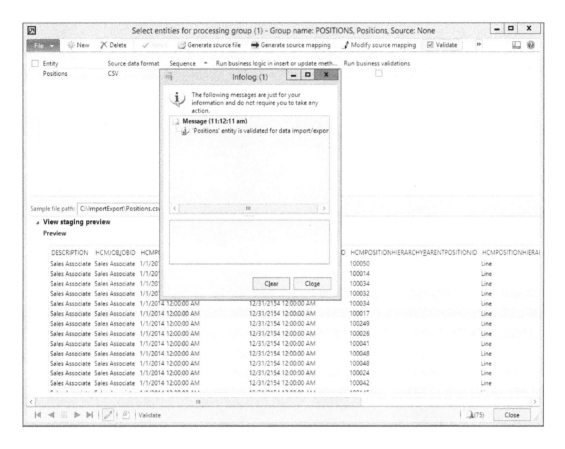

If you want to double check the data then you can click on the **Validate** button in the menu bar, and if the data is all looking good then you will get an InfoLog telling you that it all looks good.

© 2015 Blind Squirrel Publishing, LLC, All Rights Reserved
www.dynamicsaxcompanions.com

Importing Positions Using The Data Import Export Framework

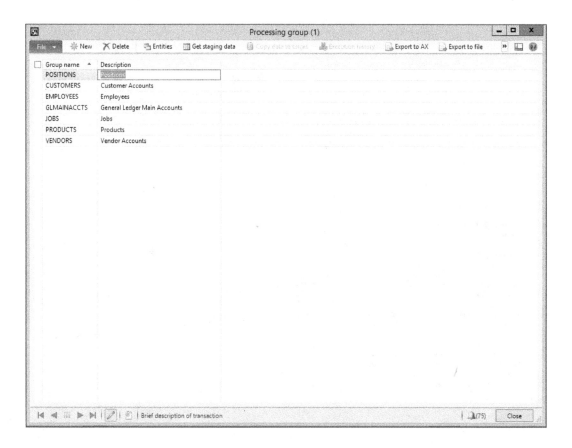

When you return to the **Processing Group** form, click on the **Get Staging Data** button in the menu bar.

© 2015 Blind Squirrel Publishing, LLC, All Rights Reserved
www.dynamicsaxcompanions.com

Importing Positions Using The Data Import Export Framework

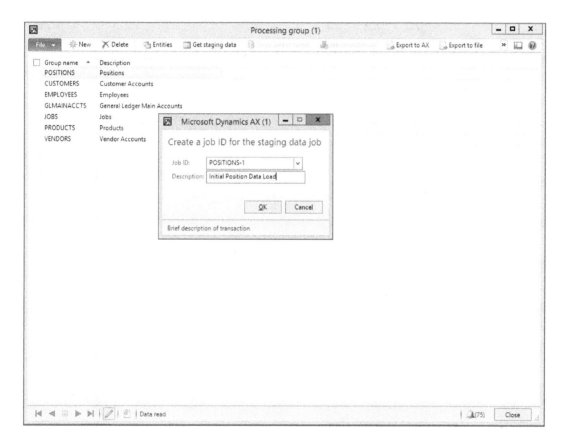

When the **Job Details** dialog box is displayed, enter in a better **Description** to describe the jobs function and then click on the **OK** button

© 2015 Blind Squirrel Publishing, LLC, All Rights Reserved
www.dynamicsaxcompanions.com

Importing Positions Using The Data Import Export Framework

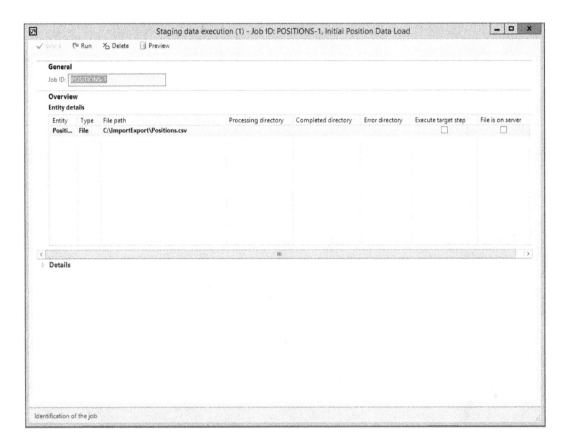

When the **Staging Data Execution** form is displayed, click on the **Preview** button to double check the data.

© 2015 Blind Squirrel Publishing, LLC, All Rights Reserved
www.dynamicsaxcompanions.com

Importing Positions Using The Data Import Export Framework

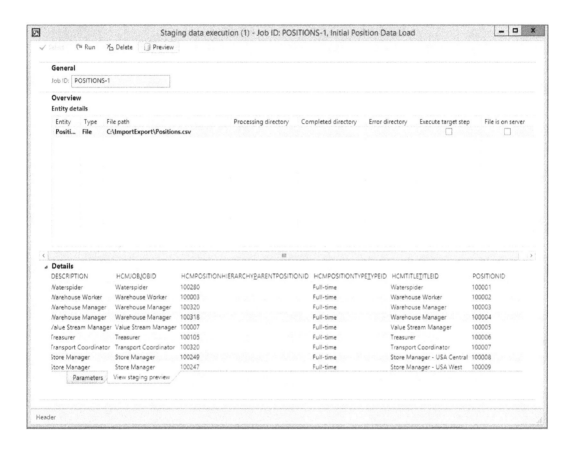

In the **Details** panel you should see the data again.

Note: This is a little bit more stringent a test than the first preview that we did, so it's a good idea to test it this way again.

© 2015 Blind Squirrel Publishing, LLC, All Rights Reserved
www.dynamicsaxcompanions.com

Importing Positions Using The Data Import Export Framework

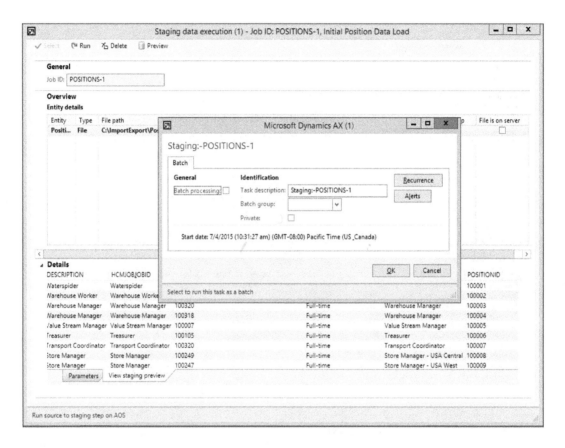

Now click on the **Run** button in the menu bar.

This will open up the **Processing** dialog box. All you need to do to kick off the process is to click on the **OK** button.

© 2015 Blind Squirrel Publishing, LLC, All Rights Reserved
www.dynamicsaxcompanions.com

Importing Positions Using The Data Import Export Framework

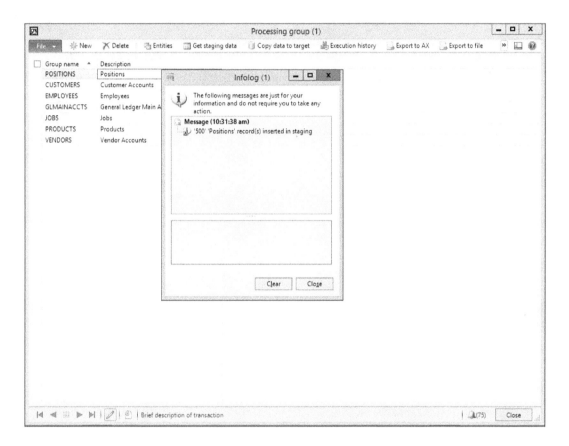

If everything goes well, then you will get a dialog box saying that the records were inserted into the **Staging** area and you can click on the **Close** button to exit from the form.

© 2015 Blind Squirrel Publishing, LLC, All Rights Reserved
www.dynamicsaxcompanions.com

Importing Positions Using The Data Import Export Framework

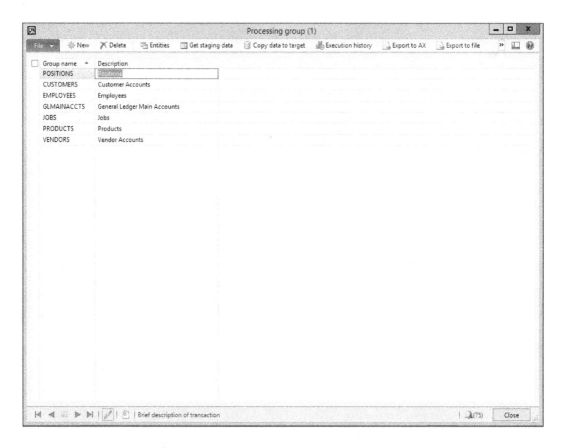

When you return back to the **Processing Group** form, click on the **Copy Data To Target** button in the menu bar.

Importing Positions Using The Data Import Export Framework

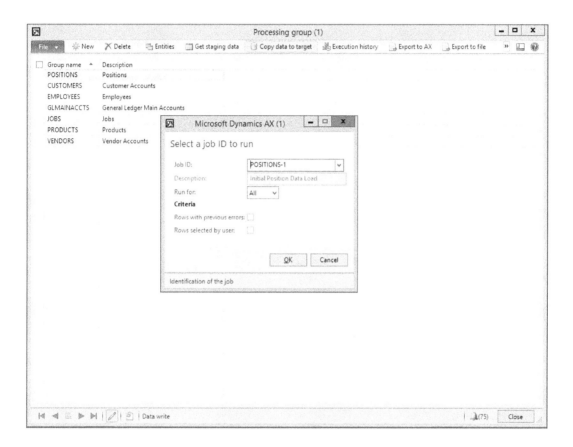

This will open up a dialog box where you can select the staging job that you just performed and then just click on the **OK** button.

© 2015 Blind Squirrel Publishing, LLC, All Rights Reserved
www.dynamicsaxcompanions.com

Importing Positions Using The Data Import Export Framework

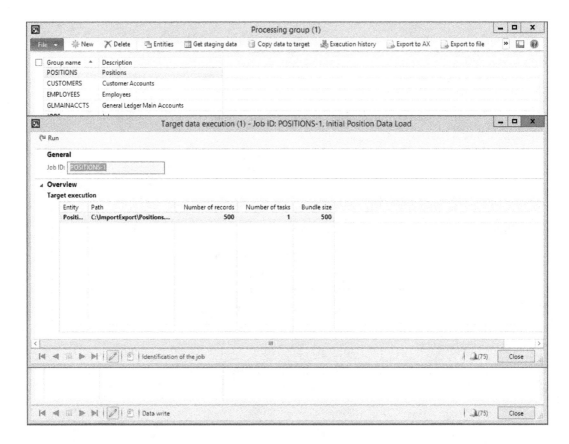

When the **Target Data Execution** dialog box is displayed, just click on the **Run** button in the menu bar.

© 2015 Blind Squirrel Publishing, LLC, All Rights Reserved
www.dynamicsaxcompanions.com

Importing Positions Using The Data Import Export Framework

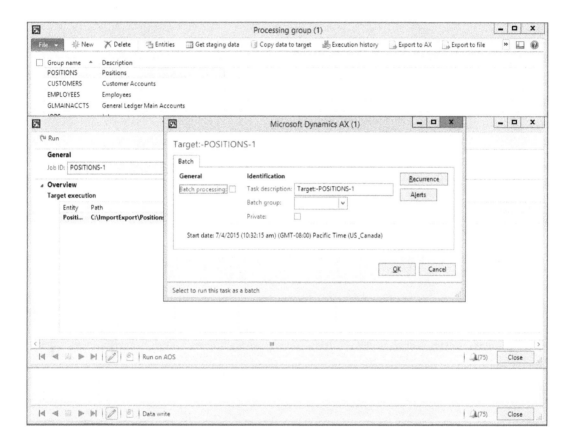

When the job details form is displayed, just click on the **OK** button.

© 2015 Blind Squirrel Publishing, LLC, All Rights Reserved
www.dynamicsaxcompanions.com

Importing Positions Using The Data Import Export Framework

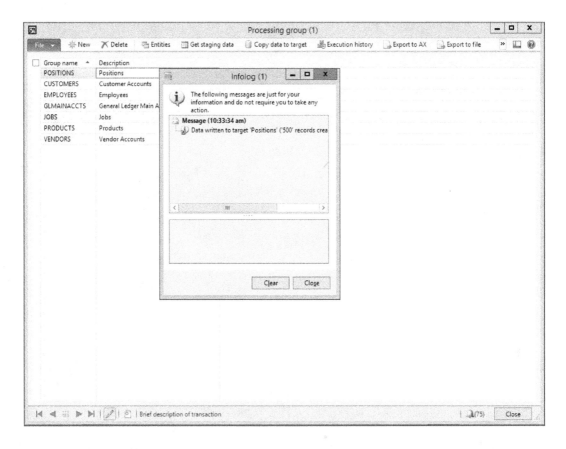

If all of your data is in the right place and valid then you should get a dialog box saying that the data has been loaded and you can click on the **Close** button to exit from the form.

Importing Positions Using The Data Import Export Framework

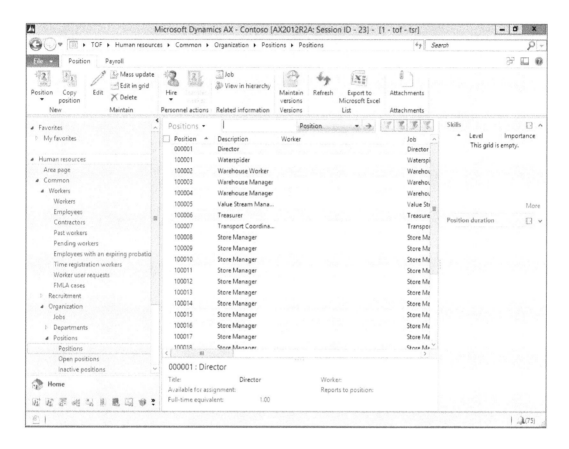

Now if you return back to the **Jobs** list page you will notice that there are a lot more jobs that you can assign your workers to.

© 2015 Blind Squirrel Publishing, LLC, All Rights Reserved
www.dynamicsaxcompanions.com

© 2015 Blind Squirrel Publishing, LLC, All Rights Reserved
www.dynamicsaxcompanions.com

Viewing Position Hierarchy Graphically

Earlier on we looked at the **Organizational Hierarchy** view and saw the position that we created, but now that we have more positions loaded, we will take another look at this feature and it will look a little more impressive.

Viewing Position Hierarchy Graphically

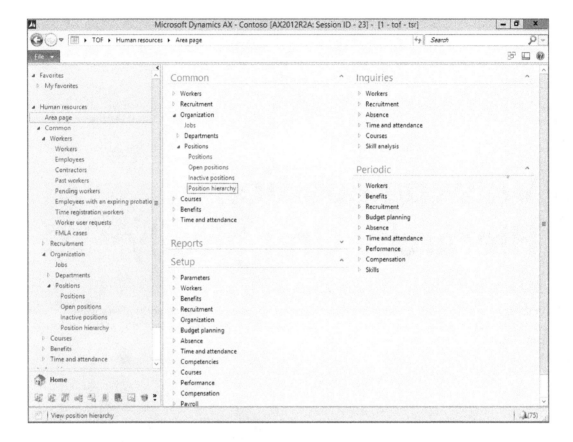

To do this click on the **Position Hierarchy** menu item within the **Positions** subfolder of the **Organization** folder within the **Common** group of the **Human Resources** area page.

© 2015 Blind Squirrel Publishing, LLC, All Rights Reserved
www.dynamicsaxcompanions.com

Viewing Position Hierarchy Graphically

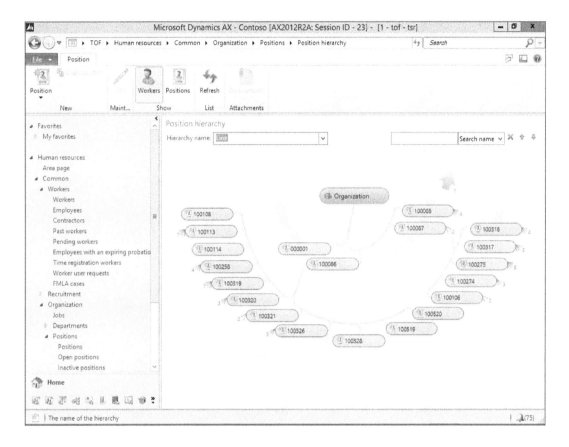

This will open up the full **Position Hierarchy** view showing the reporting structure and the multiple levels of positions.

© 2015 Blind Squirrel Publishing, LLC, All Rights Reserved
www.dynamicsaxcompanions.com

Viewing Position Hierarchy Graphically

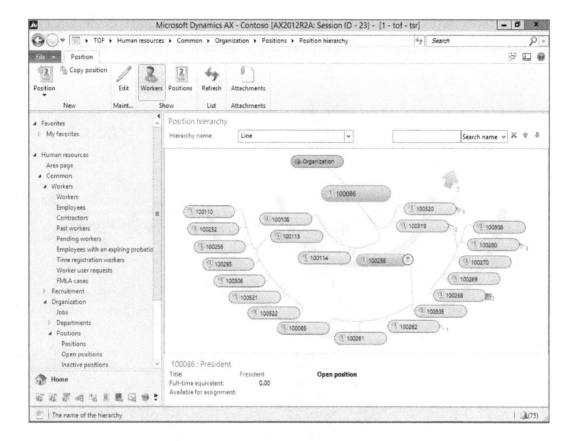

If you double click on any of the **Positions** then you will see the **Position** details, and also the hierarchy will drill down to show you even more detail.

How cool is that!

© 2015 Blind Squirrel Publishing, LLC, All Rights Reserved
www.dynamicsaxcompanions.com

© 2015 Blind Squirrel Publishing, LLC, All Rights Reserved
www.dynamicsaxcompanions.com

© 2015 Blind Squirrel Publishing, LLC, All Rights Reserved
www.dynamicsaxcompanions.com

Assigning Workers To Positions

Now we have our **Workers** configured and also our **Positions** designed within the
Organizational Position Hierarchy, let's link them together and start assigning our workers to
the positions. There are a couple of different ways that we can do this, and we will start with
an example of how you can assign **Positions** to **Workers**.

© 2015 Blind Squirrel Publishing, LLC, All Rights Reserved
www.dynamicsaxcompanions.com

Assigning Workers To Positions

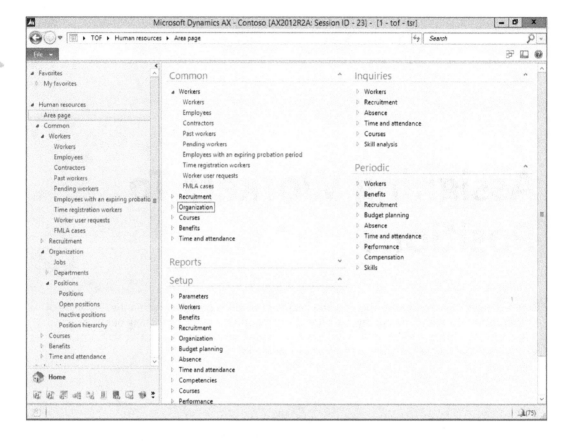

To do this, click on the **Employees** menu item within the **Workers** folder of the **Common** group within the **Human Resources** area page.

© 2015 Blind Squirrel Publishing, LLC, All Rights Reserved
www.dynamicsaxcompanions.com

Assigning Workers To Positions

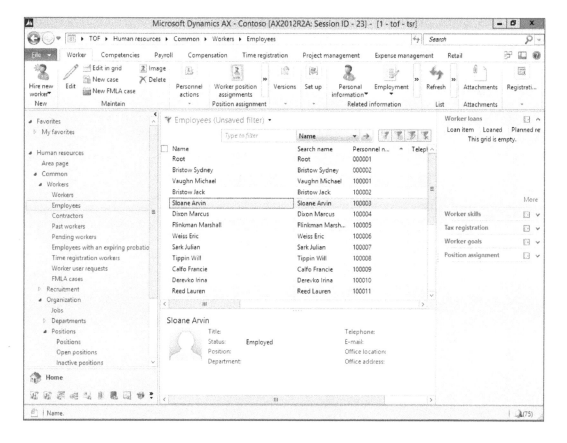

When the **Employees** list page is displayed, select an Employee that has not been assigned to any **Position**.

© 2015 Blind Squirrel Publishing, LLC, All Rights Reserved
www.dynamicsaxcompanions.com

Assigning Workers To Positions

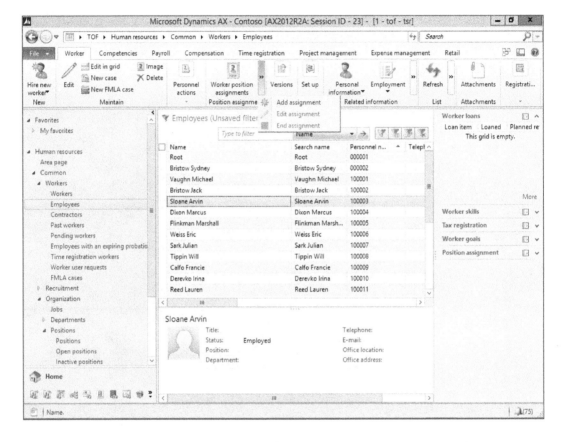

Then click on the **Add Assignment** button within the **Position Assignment** group of the **Worker** ribbon bar.

© 2015 Blind Squirrel Publishing, LLC, All Rights Reserved
www.dynamicsaxcompanions.com

Assigning Workers To Positions

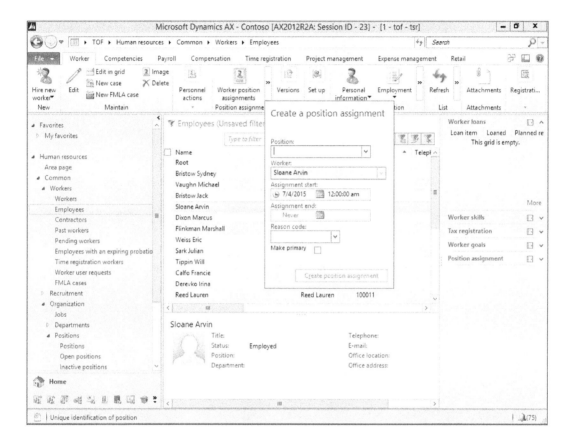

This will open up the **Create A Position Assignment** quick entry form.

© 2015 Blind Squirrel Publishing, LLC, All Rights Reserved
www.dynamicsaxcompanions.com

Assigning Workers To Positions

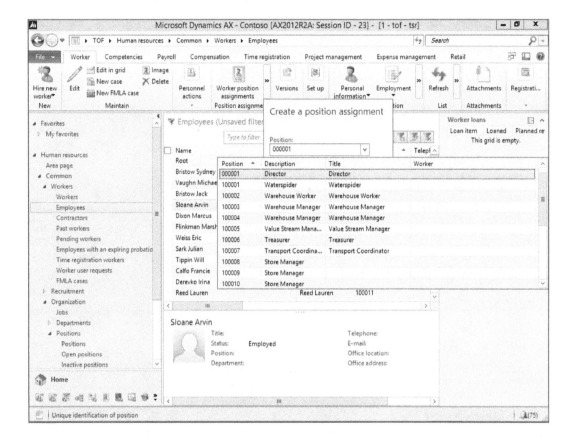

Click on the **Position** dropdown list and select the **Position** that you want to assign the **Employee** to. **Director** seems like a good position for **Arvin Sloane**.

© 2015 Blind Squirrel Publishing, LLC, All Rights Reserved
www.dynamicsaxcompanions.com

Assigning Workers To Positions

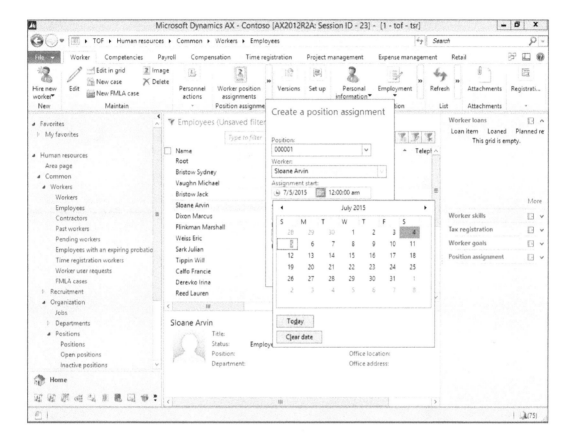

Next, click on the **Assignment Start** date picker and select the date that you want him to be assigned to the **Position**.

© 2015 Blind Squirrel Publishing, LLC, All Rights Reserved
www.dynamicsaxcompanions.com

Assigning Workers To Positions

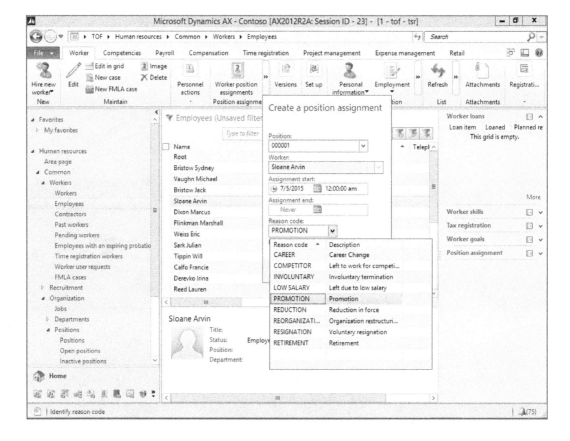

Now click on the **Reason Code** dropdown list and you will be able to assign a reason for the
Position assignment – for example **PROMOTION**.

© 2015 Blind Squirrel Publishing, LLC, All Rights Reserved
www.dynamicsaxcompanions.com

Assigning Workers To Positions

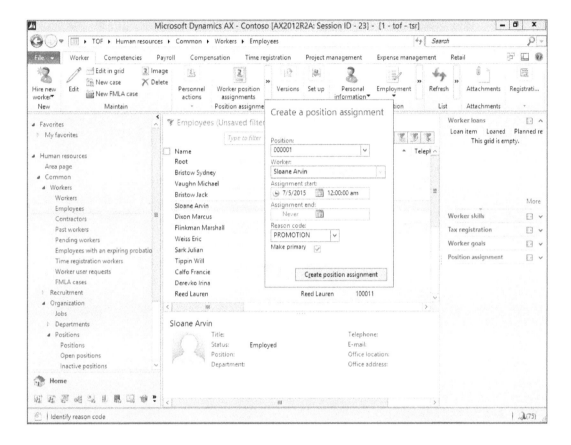

After you have done that, click on the **Create Position Assignment** button.

© 2015 Blind Squirrel Publishing, LLC, All Rights Reserved
www.dynamicsaxcompanions.com

Assigning Workers To Positions

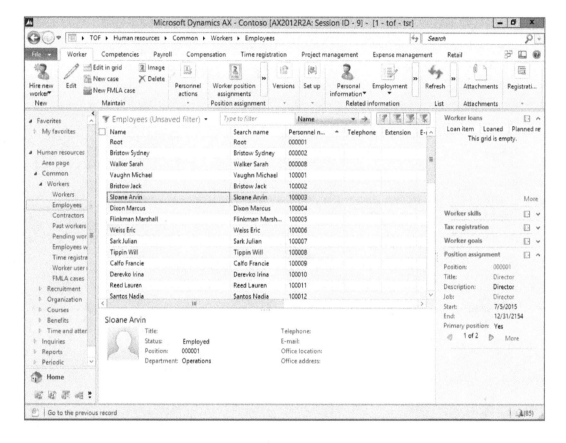

After you have done that, if you expand the **Position Assignment** fact box on the right hand side you will see that he has been assigned to the position.

© 2015 Blind Squirrel Publishing, LLC, All Rights Reserved
www.dynamicsaxcompanions.com

Assigning Workers To Positions

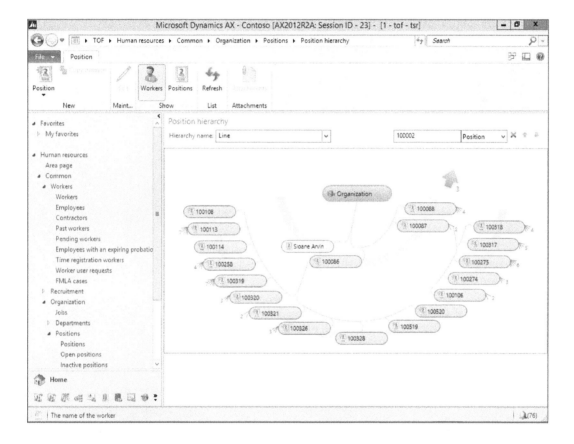

If you return back to the **Position Hierarchy** view then you will now see that **Arvin Sloane** is now associated with the **Director** position as well.

© 2015 Blind Squirrel Publishing, LLC, All Rights Reserved
www.dynamicsaxcompanions.com

© 2015 Blind Squirrel Publishing, LLC, All Rights Reserved
www.dynamicsaxcompanions.com

Assigning Positions To Workers

Another way that you can assign **Positions** to **Workers** is directly through the **Positions** or the **Position Hierarchy** view.

© 2015 Blind Squirrel Publishing, LLC, All Rights Reserved
www.dynamicsaxcompanions.com

Assigning Positions To Workers

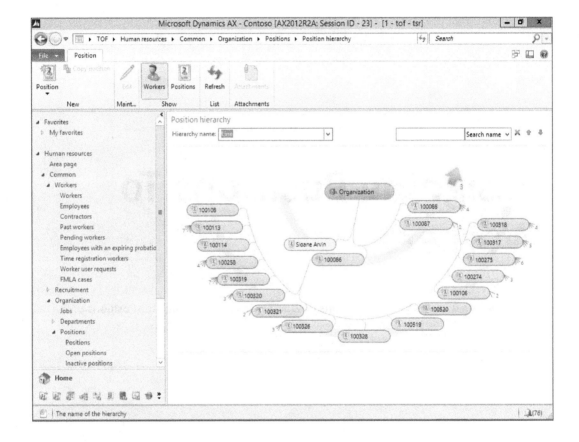

To do this open up the **Position Hierarchy** view.

© 2015 Blind Squirrel Publishing, LLC, All Rights Reserved
www.dynamicsaxcompanions.com

Assigning Positions To Workers

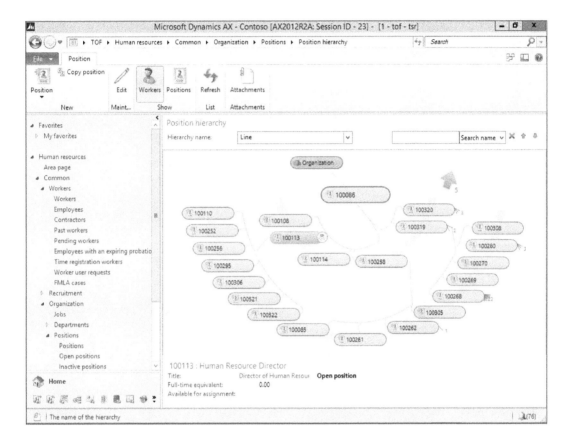

Then drill into the **Hierarchy** and double click on the **Position** that you want to assign the worker to.

© 2015 Blind Squirrel Publishing, LLC, All Rights Reserved
www.dynamicsaxcompanions.com

Assigning Positions To Workers

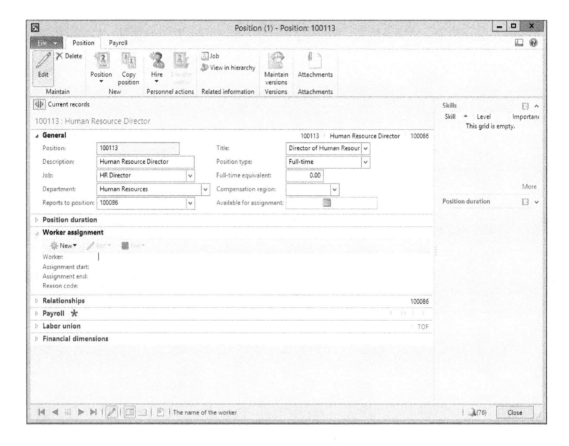

This will open up the **Position Detail** form, and you will need to expand out the **Worker Assignment** fast tab.

Then click on the **New** button within the menu bar for the **Worker Assignment** fast tab.

© 2015 Blind Squirrel Publishing, LLC, All Rights Reserved
www.dynamicsaxcompanions.com

Assigning Positions To Workers

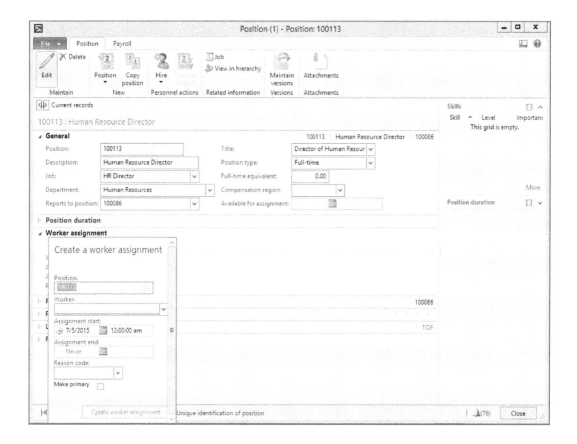

This will open up the **Create a Worker Assignment** quick entry form.

© 2015 Blind Squirrel Publishing, LLC, All Rights Reserved
www.dynamicsaxcompanions.com

Assigning Positions To Workers

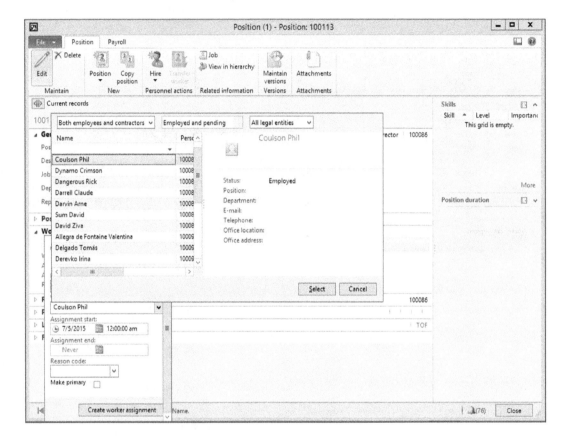

Click on the **Worker** field and select the **Worker** that you want to assign to the **Position**.

© 2015 Blind Squirrel Publishing, LLC, All Rights Reserved
www.dynamicsaxcompanions.com

Assigning Positions To Workers

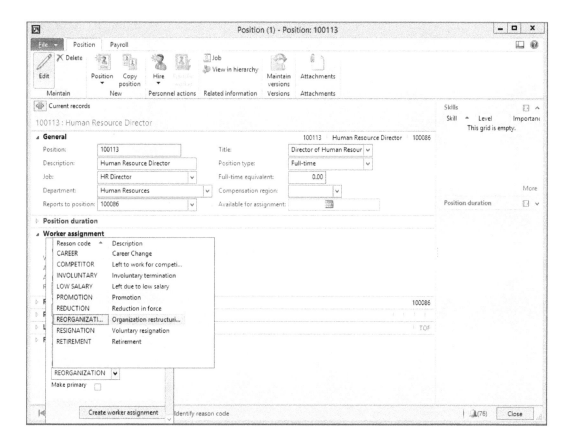

Now click on the **Reason Code** dropdown list and you will be able to assign a reason for the
Position assignment – for example **REORGANIZATION**.

© 2015 Blind Squirrel Publishing, LLC, All Rights Reserved
www.dynamicsaxcompanions.com

Assigning Positions To Workers

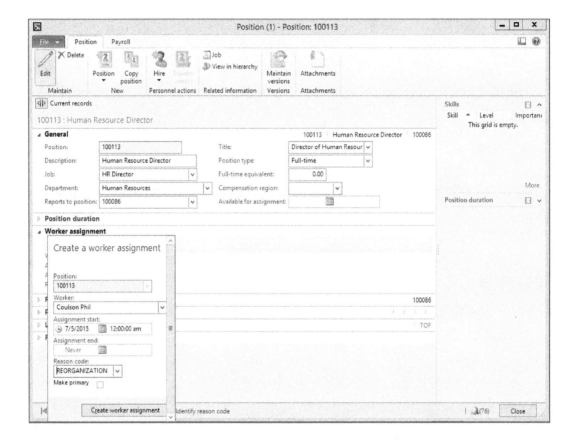

After you have done that just click on the **Create Worker Assignment** button.

© 2015 Blind Squirrel Publishing, LLC, All Rights Reserved
www.dynamicsaxcompanions.com

Assigning Positions To Workers

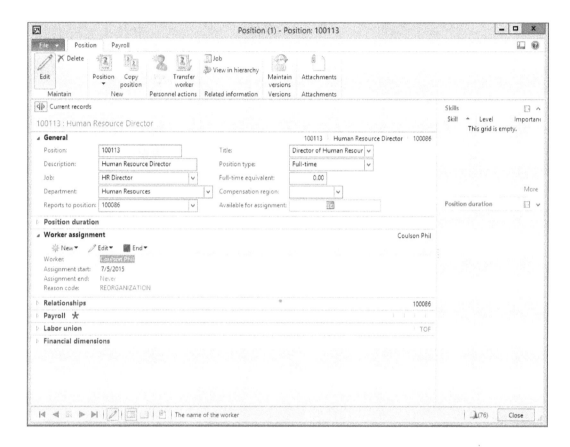

When you return to the **Positions** detail form you will see that the **Worker** has been assigned to the **Position** and you can click on the **Close** button to exit from the form.

© 2015 Blind Squirrel Publishing, LLC, All Rights Reserved
www.dynamicsaxcompanions.com

Assigning Positions To Workers

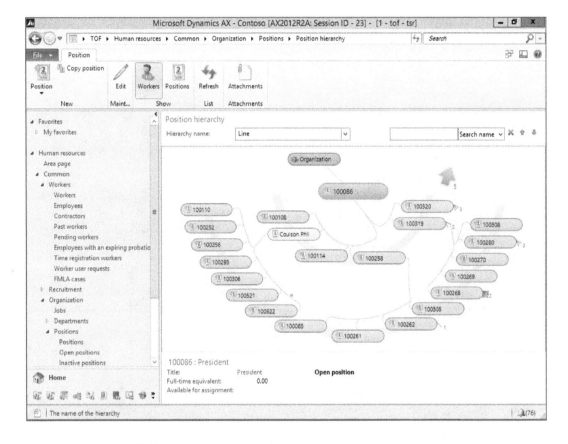

When you refresh the **Position Hierarchy** (**F5**) then you will see that the employee is now assigned to the **Position**.

© 2015 Blind Squirrel Publishing, LLC, All Rights Reserved
www.dynamicsaxcompanions.com

Assigning Positions To Workers

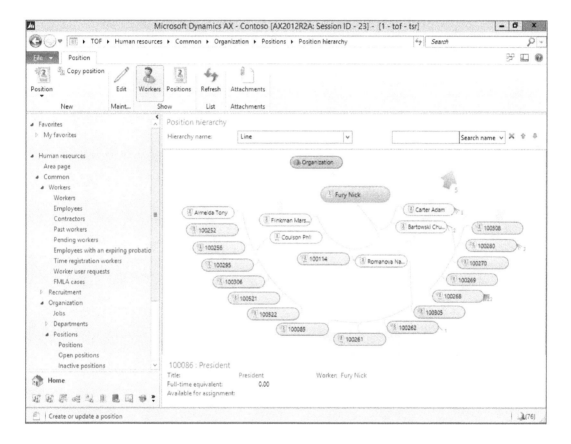

You can keep on fleshing out the organization **Positions** as much as you like.

Very cool.

© 2015 Blind Squirrel Publishing, LLC, All Rights Reserved
www.dynamicsaxcompanions.com

© 2015 Blind Squirrel Publishing, LLC, All Rights Reserved
www.dynamicsaxcompanions.com

CONFIGURING RECRUITING PROJECTS

Now that we have our workers in the right positions we can start getting even more efficient by taking advantage of the **Recruiting Projects** within Dynamics AX to create new positions, track applications & applicants and hire new workers.

© 2015 Blind Squirrel Publishing, LLC, All Rights Reserved
www.dynamicsaxcompanions.com

© 2015 Blind Squirrel Publishing, LLC, All Rights Reserved
www.dynamicsaxcompanions.com

Creating A New Position For Recruitment

Recruiting projects can be created to fill existing **Positions**, or you can create entirely new **Positions** that you are trying to fill – which is what we will do in this step.

© 2015 Blind Squirrel Publishing, LLC, All Rights Reserved
www.dynamicsaxcompanions.com

Creating A New Position For Recruitment

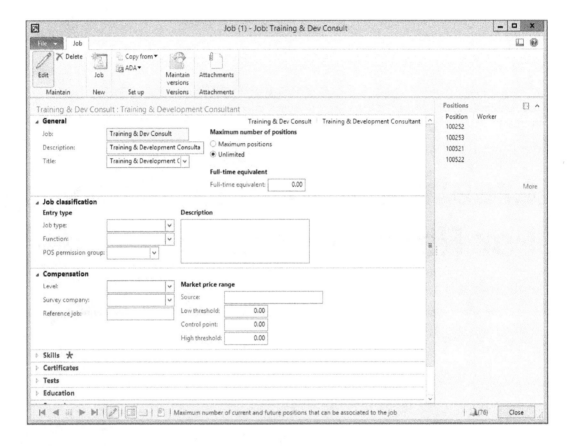

Before you start, make sure that you have a **Job** set up that you will be creating the new **Position** for. In this case we already have a **Training & Development Consultant** job, just no position.

© 2015 Blind Squirrel Publishing, LLC, All Rights Reserved
www.dynamicsaxcompanions.com

Creating A New Position For Recruitment

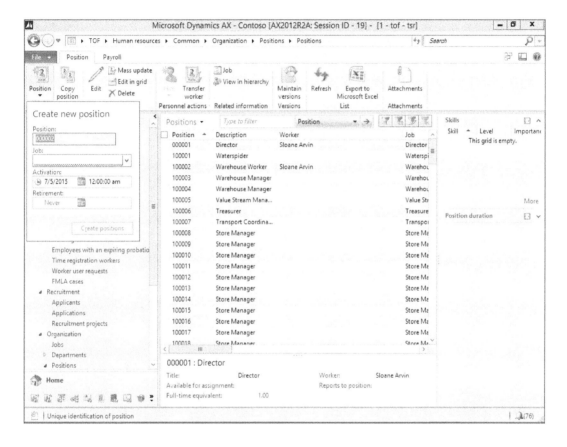

Open up the **Positions** list page and click on the **Position** button within the **New** group of the **Position** ribbon bar.

© 2015 Blind Squirrel Publishing, LLC, All Rights Reserved
www.dynamicsaxcompanions.com

Creating A New Position For Recruitment

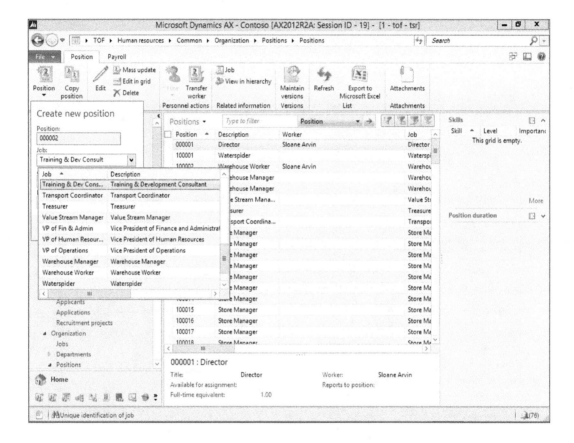

Click on the **Job** dropdown list and select the job that you want to recruit for.

© 2015 Blind Squirrel Publishing, LLC, All Rights Reserved
www.dynamicsaxcompanions.com

Creating A New Position For Recruitment

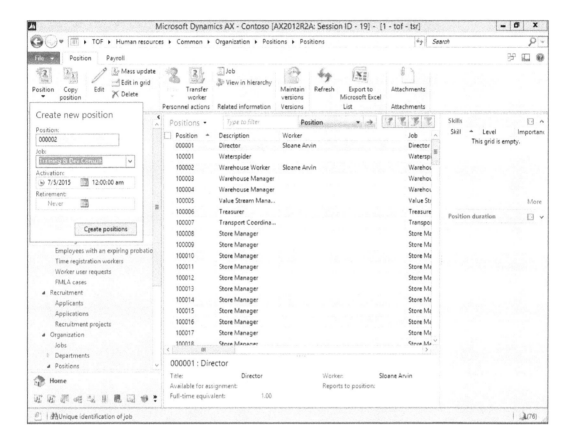

And then click the **Create Position** button.

© 2015 Blind Squirrel Publishing, LLC, All Rights Reserved
www.dynamicsaxcompanions.com

Creating A New Position For Recruitment

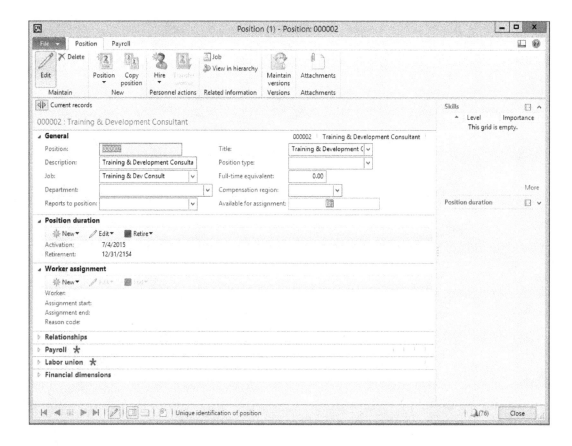

This will take you to the **Position** detail form.

© 2015 Blind Squirrel Publishing, LLC, All Rights Reserved
www.dynamicsaxcompanions.com

da<c

Creating A New Position For Recruitment

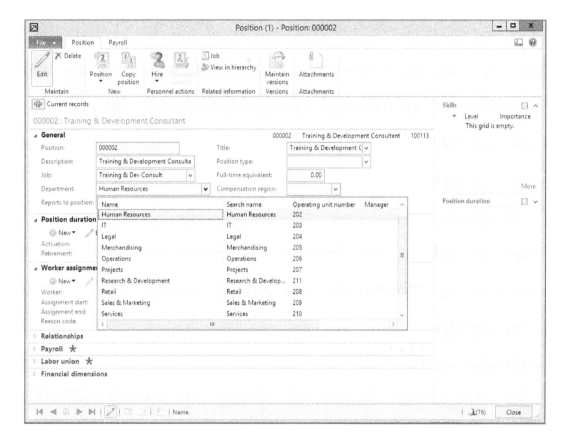

Now we will fill in some of the codes and classifications for the **Position**. Start off by click on the **Department** dropdown list and select the **Human Resources** department.

© 2015 Blind Squirrel Publishing, LLC, All Rights Reserved
www.dynamicsaxcompanions.com

Creating A New Position For Recruitment

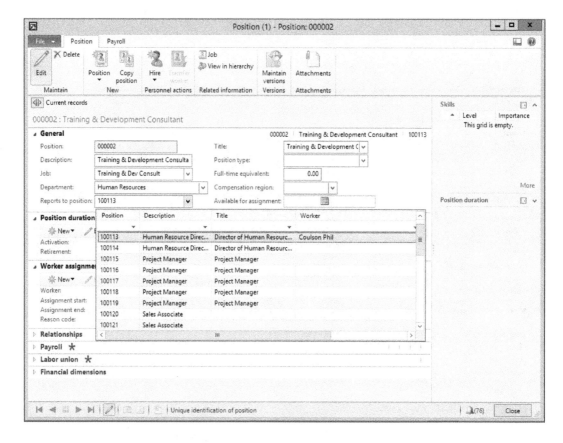

Then click on the **Reports To Position** dropdown list and select the superior position. **100113** is good since the employee will report to **Phil Coulson**.

© 2015 Blind Squirrel Publishing, LLC, All Rights Reserved
www.dynamicsaxcompanions.com

Creating A New Position For Recruitment

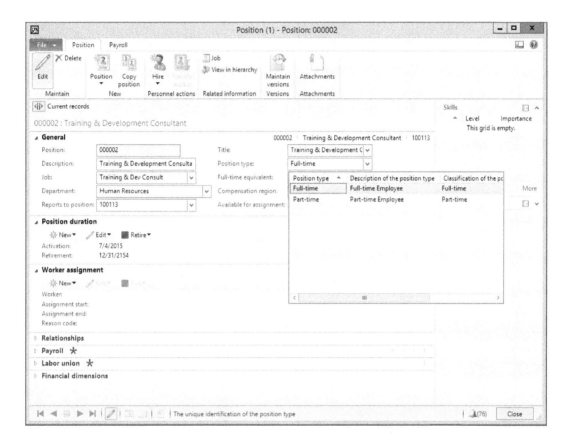

Then click on the **Position Type** dropdown list and select the **Full-Time** option.

© 2015 Blind Squirrel Publishing, LLC, All Rights Reserved
www.dynamicsaxcompanions.com

Creating A New Position For Recruitment

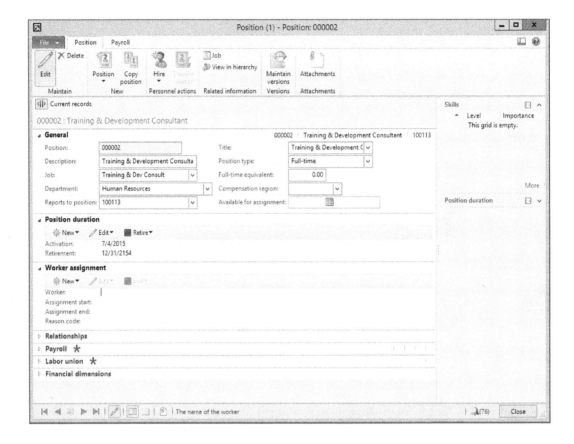

After you have done this, click on the **Close** button to exit from the form.

© 2015 Blind Squirrel Publishing, LLC, All Rights Reserved
www.dynamicsaxcompanions.com

© 2015 Blind Squirrel Publishing, LLC, All Rights Reserved
www.dynamicsaxcompanions.com

© 2015 Blind Squirrel Publishing, LLC, All Rights Reserved
www.dynamicsaxcompanions.com

Creating Recruitment Projects

Now that we have our new **Position** we can start creating a **Recruitment Project** to track all of the applications, applicants and assign the position.

© 2015 Blind Squirrel Publishing, LLC, All Rights Reserved
www.dynamicsaxcompanions.com

Creating Recruitment Projects

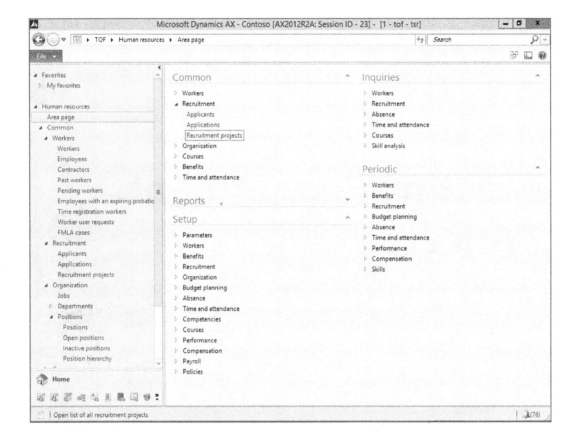

To do this, click on the **Recruitment Projects** menu item within the **Recruitment** folder of the **Common** group within the **Human Resources** area page.

© 2015 Blind Squirrel Publishing, LLC, All Rights Reserved
www.dynamicsaxcompanions.com

Creating Recruitment Projects

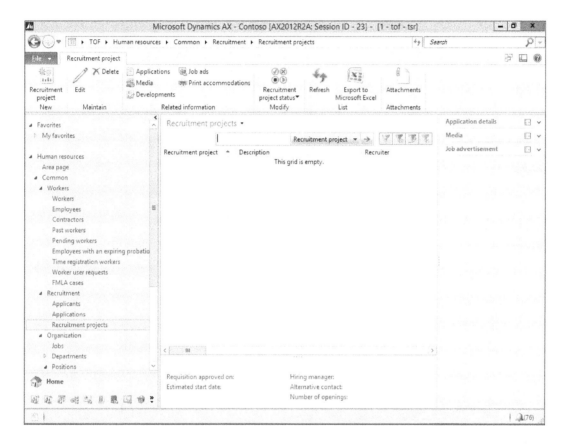

When the **Recruitment Projects** list page is displayed, click on the **Recruitment Project** button within the **New** button group of the **Recruitment Projects** ribbon bar.

© 2015 Blind Squirrel Publishing, LLC, All Rights Reserved
www.dynamicsaxcompanions.com

Creating Recruitment Projects

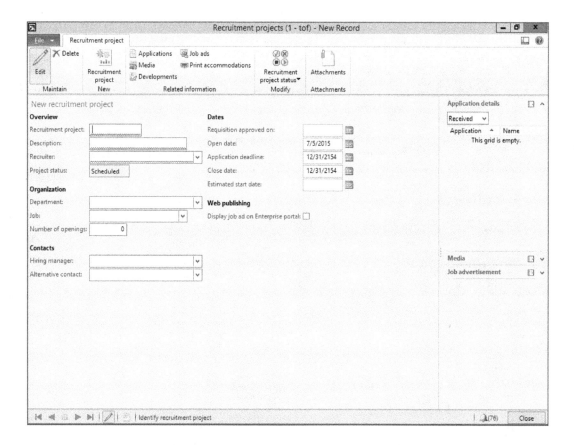

This will open up a new **Recruitment Projects** detail form.

© 2015 Blind Squirrel Publishing, LLC, All Rights Reserved
www.dynamicsaxcompanions.com

Creating Recruitment Projects

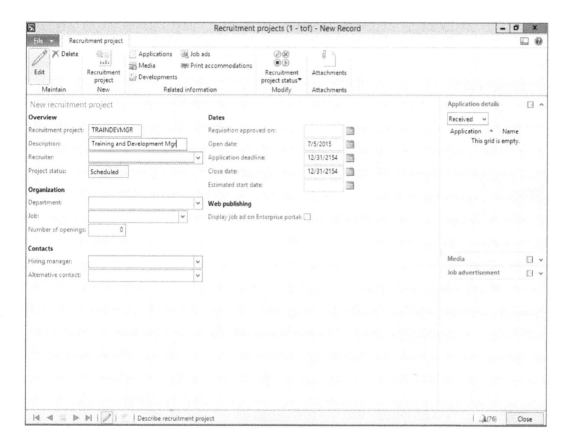

Set the **Recruitment Project** code to **TRAINDEVMGR** and the **Description** to **Training and Development Mgr.**

© 2015 Blind Squirrel Publishing, LLC, All Rights Reserved
www.dynamicsaxcompanions.com

Creating Recruitment Projects

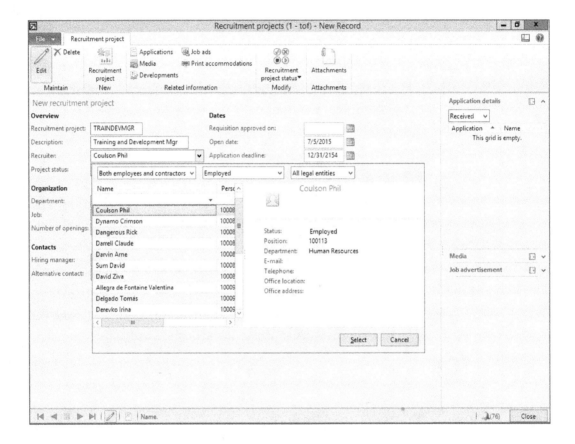

Click on the **Recruiter** dropdown list and select the **Worker** that will be managing the project.

© 2015 Blind Squirrel Publishing, LLC, All Rights Reserved
www.dynamicsaxcompanions.com

Creating Recruitment Projects

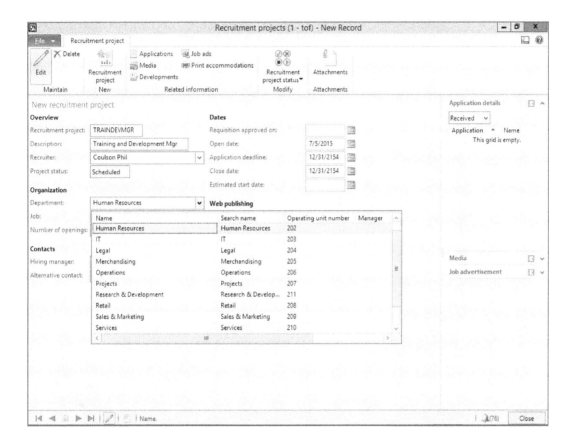

Then click on the **Department** dropdown list and select the department that you want to associate the project with – in this case we will choose **Human Resources**.

© 2015 Blind Squirrel Publishing, LLC, All Rights Reserved
www.dynamicsaxcompanions.com

Creating Recruitment Projects

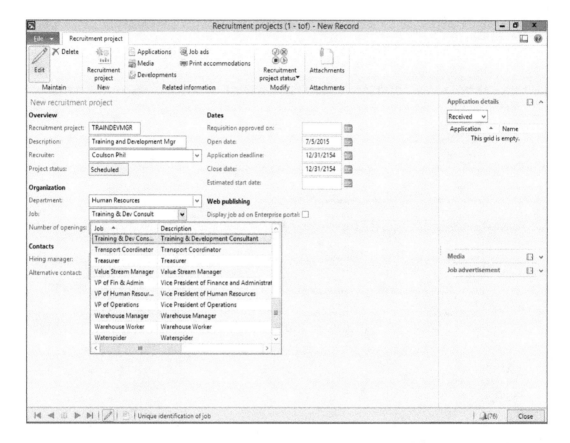

Next click on the **Job** dropdown list and select the **Job** that you want to recruit for. We will select the **Training & Dev Consultant** job.

Note: Notice that you don't select a Position here – because when we fill the Job, it will be assigned to the open position for that Job.

Creating Recruitment Projects

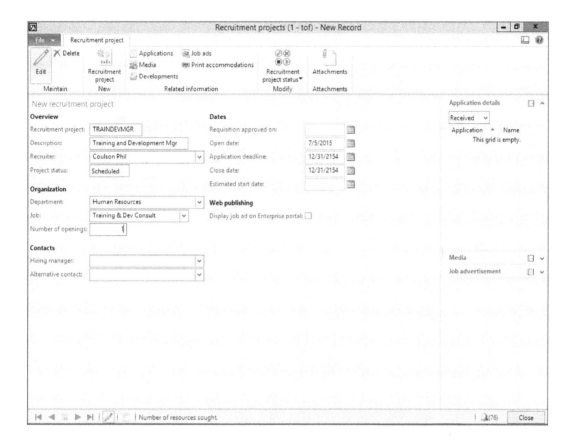

If you have multiple positions that you are trying to fill then you can change the **Number Of Openings** field – but for now we will keep this as **1**.

© 2015 Blind Squirrel Publishing, LLC, All Rights Reserved
www.dynamicsaxcompanions.com

Creating Recruitment Projects

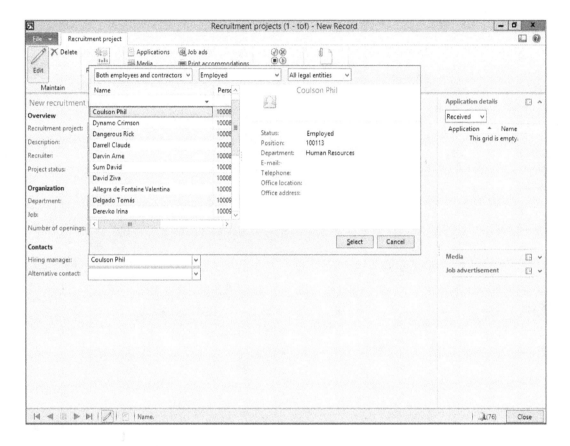

Next click on the **Hiring Manager** and select the worker that will be managing the hiring.

© 2015 Blind Squirrel Publishing, LLC, All Rights Reserved
www.dynamicsaxcompanions.com

Creating Recruitment Projects

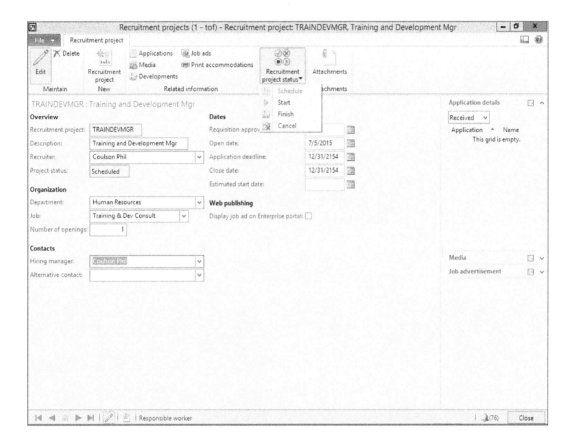

After everything is set up we can click on the **Recruitment Project Status** button within the **Modify** group of the **Recruitment Project** ribbon bar and select the **Start** option to indicate that the project is ready for applications.

© 2015 Blind Squirrel Publishing, LLC, All Rights Reserved
www.dynamicsaxcompanions.com

Creating Recruitment Projects

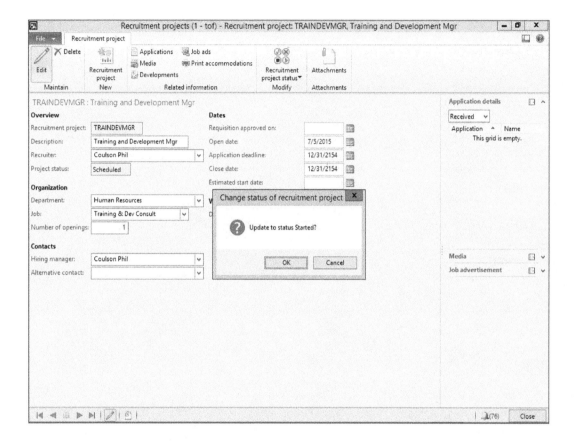

When the confirmation dialog box is displayed, click on the **OK** button.

© 2015 Blind Squirrel Publishing, LLC, All Rights Reserved
www.dynamicsaxcompanions.com

Creating Recruitment Projects

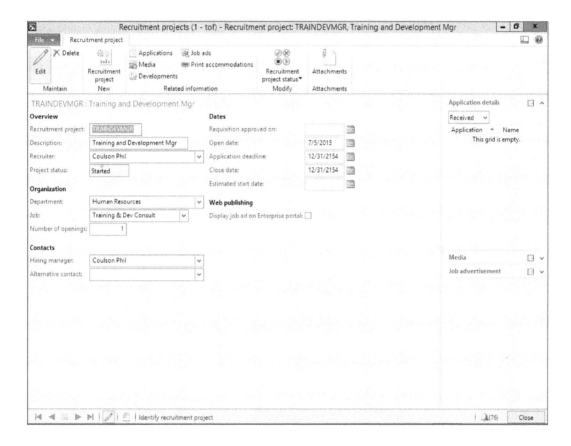

Now click on the **Close** button to exit from the form.

© 2015 Blind Squirrel Publishing, LLC, All Rights Reserved
www.dynamicsaxcompanions.com

Creating Recruitment Projects

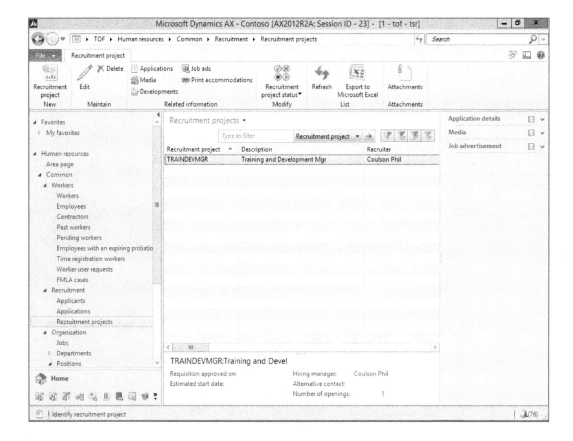

When you return to the **Recruitment Projects** list page you will see your new project is ready for you.

© 2015 Blind Squirrel Publishing, LLC, All Rights Reserved
www.dynamicsaxcompanions.com

© 2015 Blind Squirrel Publishing, LLC, All Rights Reserved
www.dynamicsaxcompanions.com

© 2015 Blind Squirrel Publishing, LLC, All Rights Reserved
www.dynamicsaxcompanions.com

Creating Applicant For Positions

Now that you have the **Recruitment Project** created you can start receiving **Applicants** and track all of their details.

© 2015 Blind Squirrel Publishing, LLC, All Rights Reserved
www.dynamicsaxcompanions.com

Creating Applicant For Positions

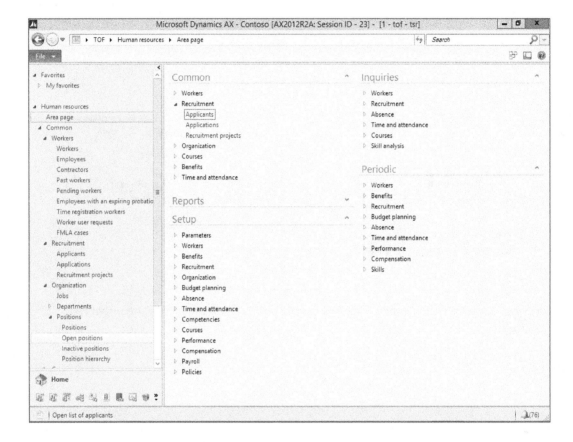

To do this click on the **Applicants** menu item within the **Recruitment** folder of the **Common** group within the **Human Resources** area page.

© 2015 Blind Squirrel Publishing, LLC, All Rights Reserved
www.dynamicsaxcompanions.com

Creating Applicant For Positions

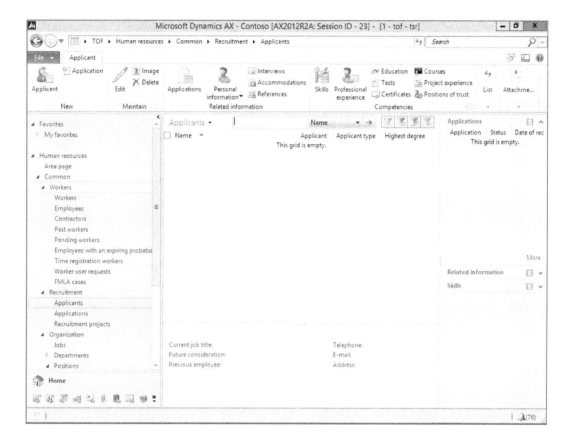

When the **Applicants** list page is displayed, click on the **Applicant** button within the **New** group of the **Applicant** ribbon bar.

© 2015 Blind Squirrel Publishing, LLC, All Rights Reserved
www.dynamicsaxcompanions.com

Creating Applicant For Positions

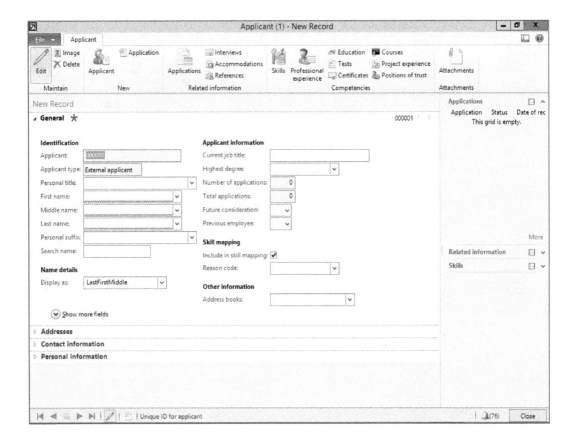

This will open up the **Applicant** details form.

© 2015 Blind Squirrel Publishing, LLC, All Rights Reserved
www.dynamicsaxcompanions.com

Creating Applicant For Positions

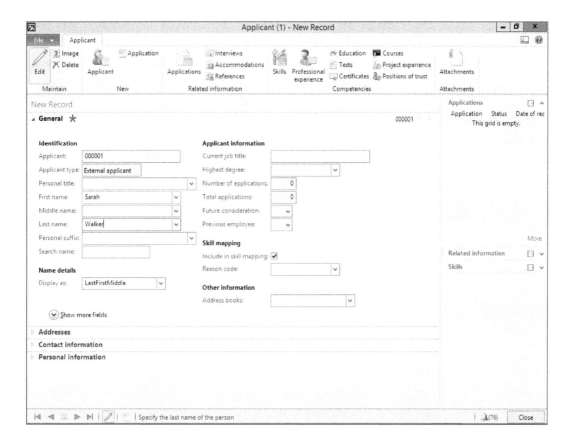

Enter in the **First Name** or **Sarah** and the **Last Name** of **Walker**.

© 2015 Blind Squirrel Publishing, LLC, All Rights Reserved
www.dynamicsaxcompanions.com

Creating Applicant For Positions

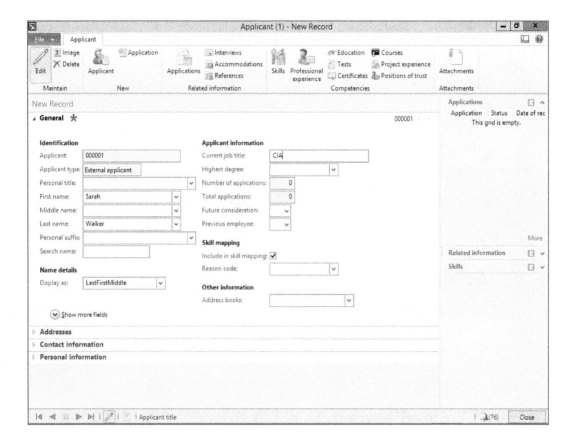

You can fill in more information about the **Applicant** such as the **Current Position**.

© 2015 Blind Squirrel Publishing, LLC, All Rights Reserved
www.dynamicsaxcompanions.com

Creating Applicant For Positions

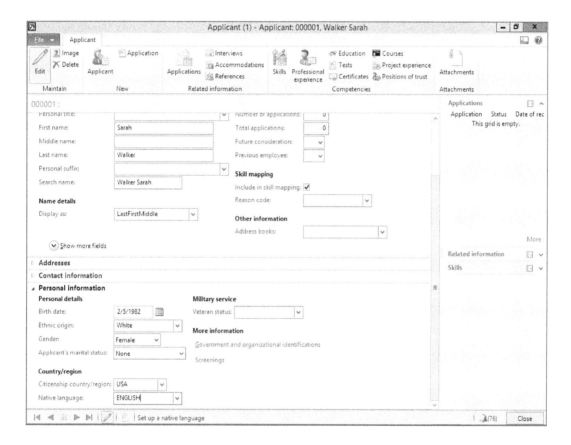

And also if you have access to the **Personal Details** then you can enter in the **Birth Date**, **Ethnic Origin**, **Gender**, **Citizenship Country/Region**, and even the **Native Language**.

Note: All of this information will copy over to the worker record if the applicant is hired.

© 2015 Blind Squirrel Publishing, LLC, All Rights Reserved
www.dynamicsaxcompanions.com

© 2015 Blind Squirrel Publishing, LLC, All Rights Reserved
www.dynamicsaxcompanions.com

Creating Applicant Applications For Positions

Now that you have an **Applicant** in the system you can create an **Application** for the **Recruitment Project** that you just created.

Creating Applicant Applications For Positions

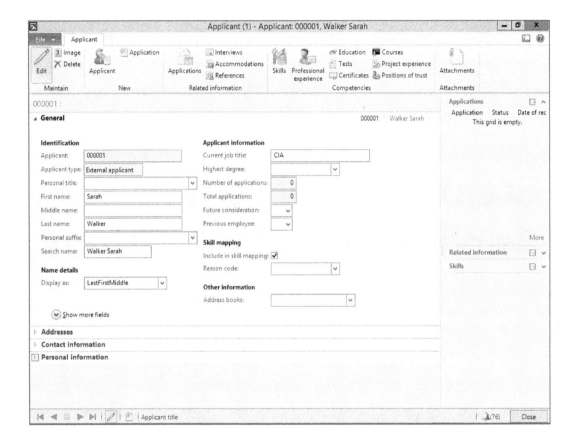

To do this return to your Applicant form and click on the **Application** button within the **New** group of the **Applicant** ribbon bar.

© 2015 Blind Squirrel Publishing, LLC, All Rights Reserved
www.dynamicsaxcompanions.com

Creating Applicant Applications For Positions

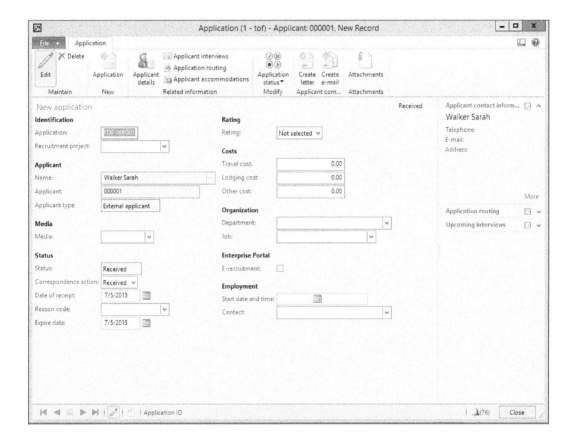

This will open up a new **Application** detail form.

© 2015 Blind Squirrel Publishing, LLC, All Rights Reserved
www.dynamicsaxcompanions.com

Creating Applicant Applications For Positions

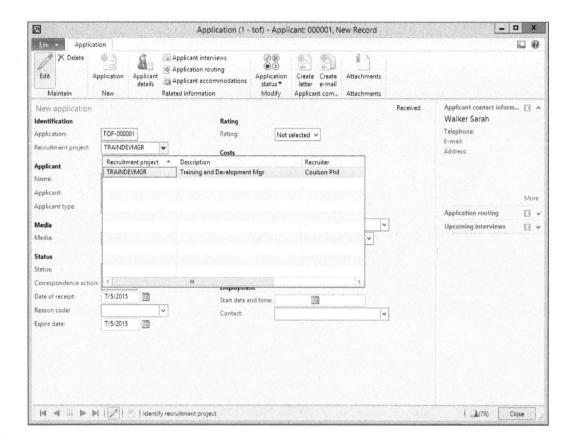

Click on the **Recruitment Project** dropdown list and select the **Recruitment Project** that the **Applicant** is applying for.

© 2015 Blind Squirrel Publishing, LLC, All Rights Reserved
www.dynamicsaxcompanions.com

Creating Applicant Applications For Positions

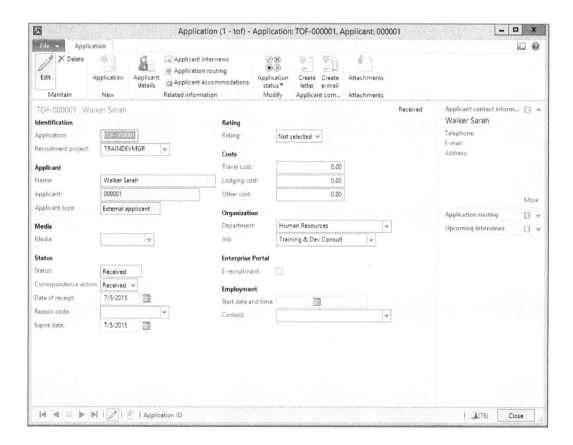

After you have done that you can click on the **Close** button to exit from the form.

© 2015 Blind Squirrel Publishing, LLC, All Rights Reserved
www.dynamicsaxcompanions.com

Creating Applicant Applications For Positions

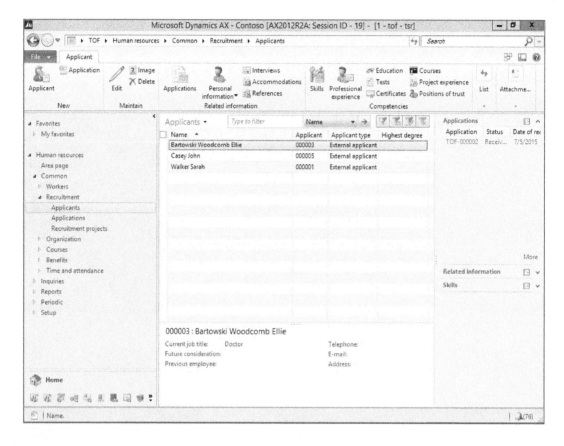

You can repeat the process and add more **Applicants** and **Applications** for the positions if you like.

© 2015 Blind Squirrel Publishing, LLC, All Rights Reserved
www.dynamicsaxcompanions.com

© 2015 Blind Squirrel Publishing, LLC, All Rights Reserved
www.dynamicsaxcompanions.com

© 2015 Blind Squirrel Publishing, LLC, All Rights Reserved
www.dynamicsaxcompanions.com

Creating Applications For Existing Employees

Applications do not have to be just for **External Applicants**, you can also track internal applications for positions by current **Workers** and **Employees**.

© 2015 Blind Squirrel Publishing, LLC, All Rights Reserved
www.dynamicsaxcompanions.com

Creating Applications For Existing Employees

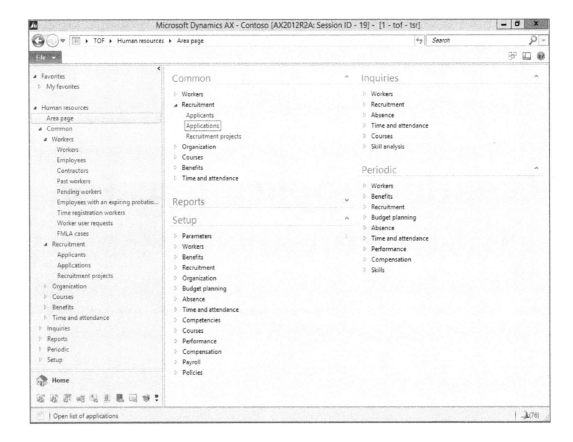

To do this, click on the **Applications** button within the **Recruitment** folder of the **Common** group of the **Human Resources** area page.

© 2015 Blind Squirrel Publishing, LLC, All Rights Reserved
www.dynamicsaxcompanions.com

Creating Applications For Existing Employees

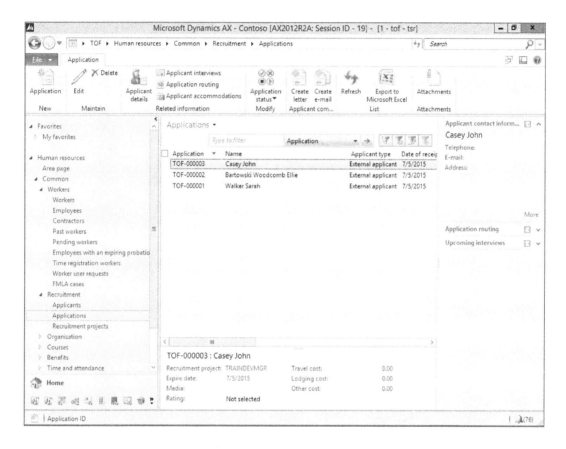

When the **Applications** list page is displayed, click on the **Application** button within the **New** group of the **Application** ribbon bar.

© 2015 Blind Squirrel Publishing, LLC, All Rights Reserved
www.dynamicsaxcompanions.com

Creating Applications For Existing Employees

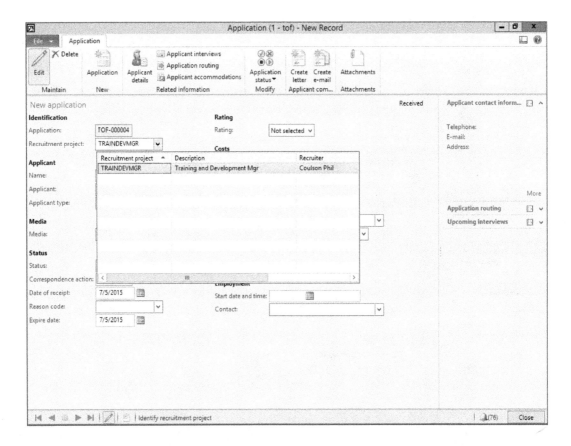

When the new **Application** record is displayed, click on the **Recruitment Project** dropdown list and select the **TRAINDEVMGR** project.

© 2015 Blind Squirrel Publishing, LLC, All Rights Reserved
www.dynamicsaxcompanions.com

Creating Applications For Existing Employees

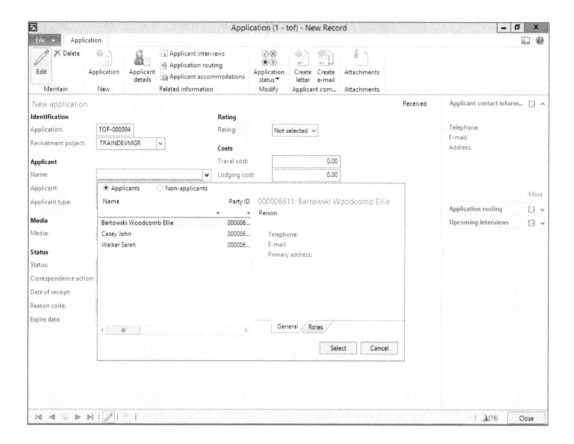

Then click on the **Name** dropdown list. Initially it will just show you the **Applicants** within the list.

© 2015 Blind Squirrel Publishing, LLC, All Rights Reserved
www.dynamicsaxcompanions.com

Creating Applications For Existing Employees

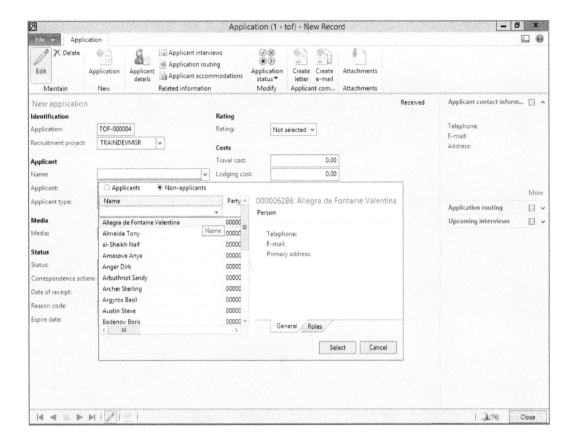

If you click on the **Non-Applicants** radio button though you will see all of the **workers** that you have loaded in the system.

© 2015 Blind Squirrel Publishing, LLC, All Rights Reserved
www.dynamicsaxcompanions.com

Creating Applications For Existing Employees

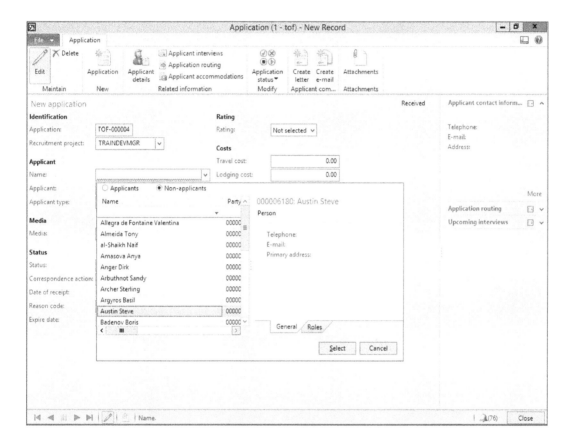

You can just select the **Worker** that you want to apply for the job – like **Steve Austin** - and then click on the **Select** button.

© 2015 Blind Squirrel Publishing, LLC, All Rights Reserved
www.dynamicsaxcompanions.com

Creating Applications For Existing Employees

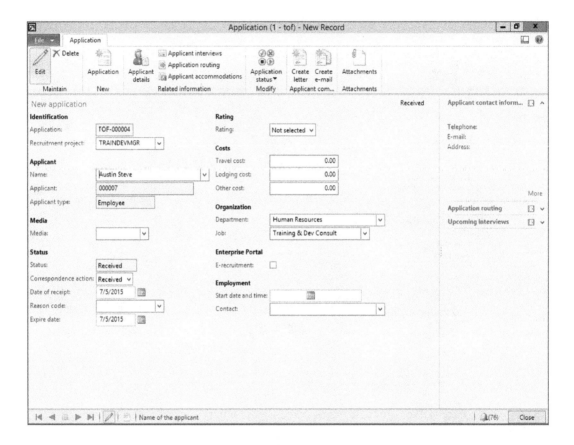

After you have done that, just click on the **Close** button to exit from the form.

© 2015 Blind Squirrel Publishing, LLC, All Rights Reserved
www.dynamicsaxcompanions.com

Creating Applications For Existing Employees

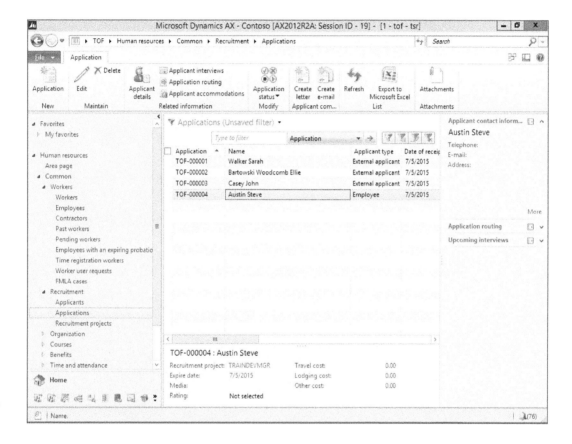

Now you have an **Employee** application in the mix.

How efficient is that!

© 2015 Blind Squirrel Publishing, LLC, All Rights Reserved
www.dynamicsaxcompanions.com

© 2015 Blind Squirrel Publishing, LLC, All Rights Reserved
www.dynamicsaxcompanions.com

Confirming Applications For Positions

As people apply for a **Position** you can start working them through the application process by updating their status. The first one of these changes is to move the **Application** to the **Confirmed** status.

Confirming Applications For Positions

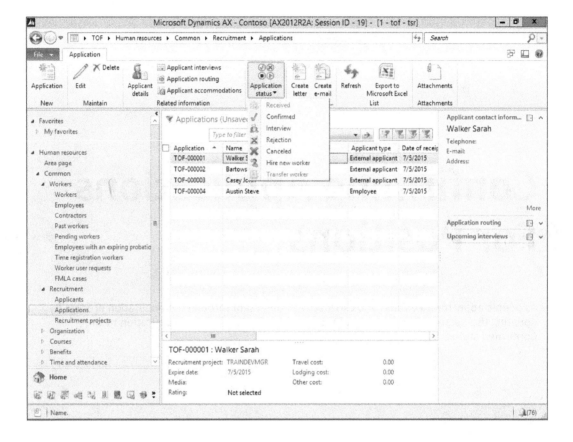

To do this open up the **Applications** list page, and select the **Application** that you want to confirm.

Then click on the **Application Status** button within the **Modify** group of the **Application** ribbon bar, and then select the **Confirmed** status.

© 2015 Blind Squirrel Publishing, LLC, All Rights Reserved
www.dynamicsaxcompanions.com

Confirming Applications For Positions

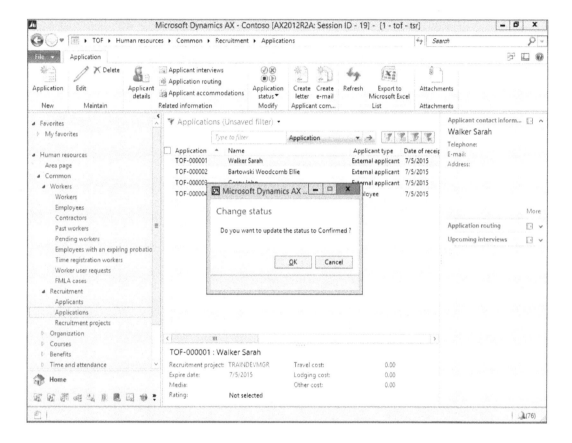

Then the status change confirmation dialog box is displayed, click on the **OK** button.

© 2015 Blind Squirrel Publishing, LLC, All Rights Reserved
www.dynamicsaxcompanions.com

© 2015 Blind Squirrel Publishing, LLC, All Rights Reserved
www.dynamicsaxcompanions.com

Scheduling Applicant Interviews

Once the **Application** is confirmed it's time to start scheduling your interviews. When that has been done we can update the status to reflect that.

© 2015 Blind Squirrel Publishing, LLC, All Rights Reserved
www.dynamicsaxcompanions.com

Scheduling Applicant Interviews

To do this open up the **Applications** list page, and select the **Application** that you want to confirm.

Then click on the **Application Status** button within the **Modify** group of the **Application** ribbon bar, and then select the **Interview** status.

© 2015 Blind Squirrel Publishing, LLC, All Rights Reserved
www.dynamicsaxcompanions.com

Scheduling Applicant Interviews

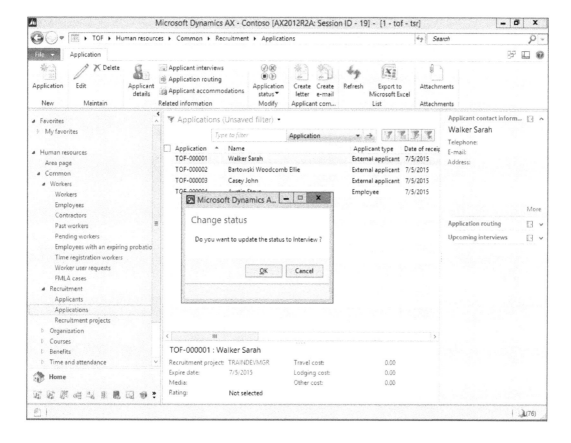

Then the status change confirmation dialog box is displayed, click on the **OK** button.

© 2015 Blind Squirrel Publishing, LLC, All Rights Reserved
www.dynamicsaxcompanions.com

Scheduling Applicant Interviews

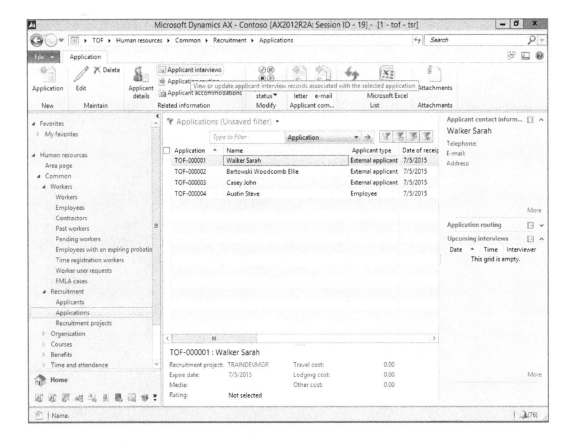

Now we will schedule the interview by clicking on the **Applicant Interview** button within the **Related Information** group of the **Application** ribbon bar.

daxc

© 2015 Blind Squirrel Publishing, LLC, All Rights Reserved
www.dynamicsaxcompanions.com

Scheduling Applicant Interviews

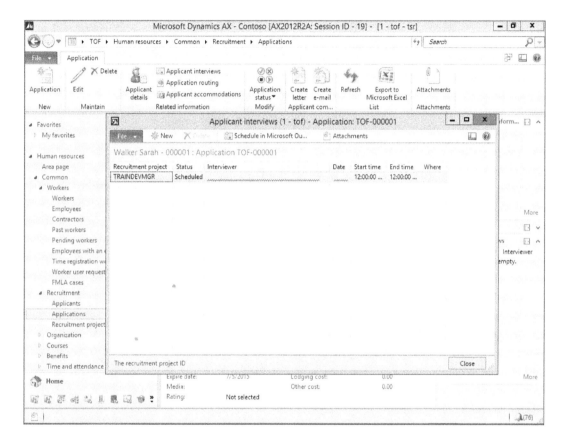

When the **Applicant Interview** list box is displayed, click on the **New** button in the menu bar to create a new record.

© 2015 Blind Squirrel Publishing, LLC, All Rights Reserved
www.dynamicsaxcompanions.com

Scheduling Applicant Interviews

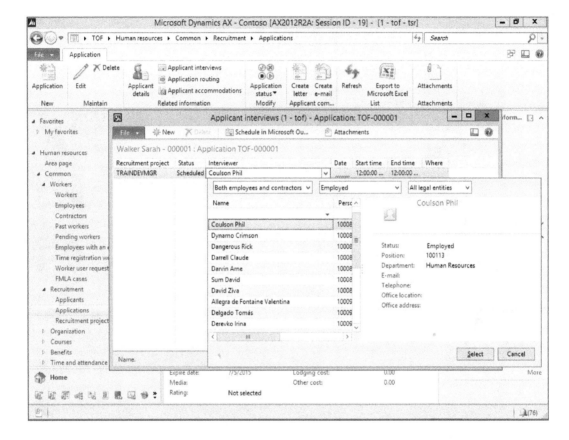

Click on the **Interviewer** and select the **Worker** that you want to perform the interview.

© 2015 Blind Squirrel Publishing, LLC, All Rights Reserved
www.dynamicsaxcompanions.com

Scheduling Applicant Interviews

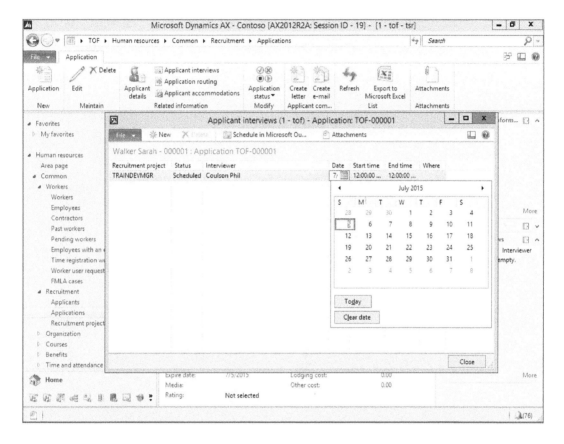

Then click on the **Date** dropdown list and select the date that you want to schedule the interview for.

© 2015 Blind Squirrel Publishing, LLC, All Rights Reserved
www.dynamicsaxcompanions.com

Scheduling Applicant Interviews

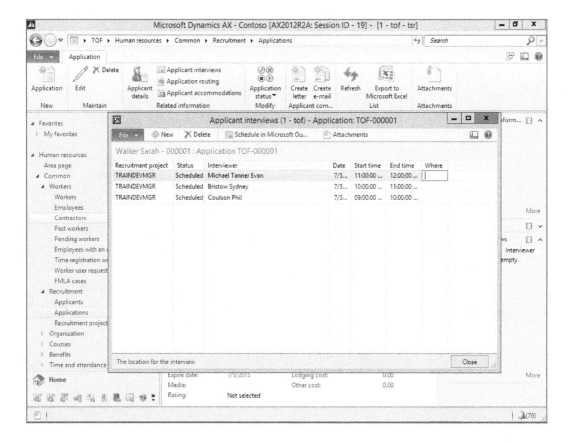

You can repeat the process and add as many interviewers that you want to and then click on the **Close** button to exit the form.

© 2015 Blind Squirrel Publishing, LLC, All Rights Reserved
www.dynamicsaxcompanions.com

© 2015 Blind Squirrel Publishing, LLC, All Rights Reserved
www.dynamicsaxcompanions.com

© 2015 Blind Squirrel Publishing, LLC, All Rights Reserved
www.dynamicsaxcompanions.com

Tracking Interview Statuses

As the **Interviews** are performed you will want to track their status to make sure no-one is missed.

© 2015 Blind Squirrel Publishing, LLC, All Rights Reserved
www.dynamicsaxcompanions.com

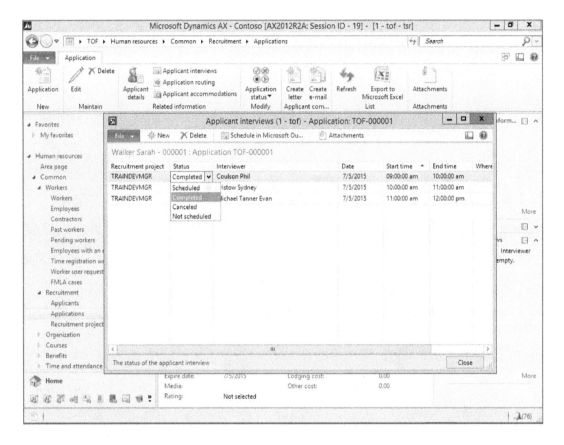

To do this select your **Applicant** and click on the **Applicant Interview** button within the **Related Information** group of the **Application** ribbon bar again.

When the **Applicant Interviews** are displayed, you can click on the **Status** dropdown for the **Interviewee** and select the **Completed** status to mark the **Interview** as done.

© 2015 Blind Squirrel Publishing, LLC, All Rights Reserved
www.dynamicsaxcompanions.com

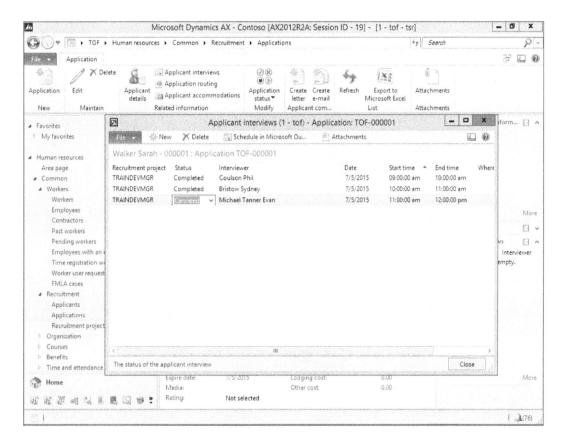

If any of the **Applicant Interviews** were cancelled then just click on the **Status** dropdown for the **Interviewee** and select the **Cancelled** status to mark the **Interview** as not done.

When you are done, click on the **Close** button to exit from the form.

© 2015 Blind Squirrel Publishing, LLC, All Rights Reserved
www.dynamicsaxcompanions.com

© 2015 Blind Squirrel Publishing, LLC, All Rights Reserved
www.dynamicsaxcompanions.com

Hiring Applicants

When you find the best **Applicant** for the **Recruiting Project** you will want to on-board them and convert them over to an **Employees.**

© 2015 Blind Squirrel Publishing, LLC, All Rights Reserved
www.dynamicsaxcompanions.com

Hiring Applicants

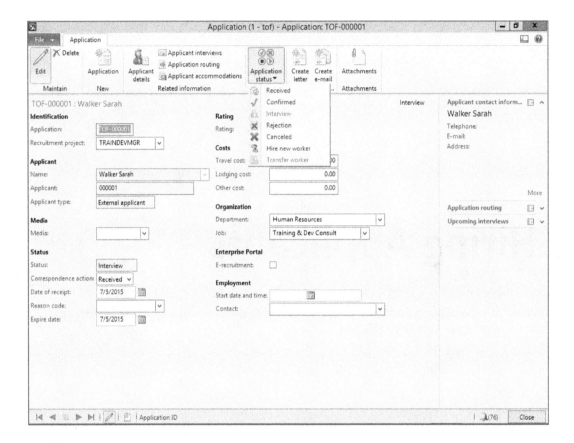

To do this, just open up the luck **Applicants Application** details, click on the **Application Status** button within the **Modify** group of the **Application** ribbon bar and select the **Hire New Worker** status option.

© 2015 Blind Squirrel Publishing, LLC, All Rights Reserved
www.dynamicsaxcompanions.com

Hiring Applicants

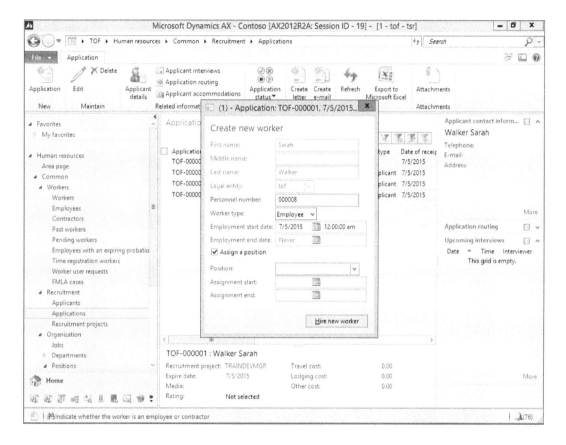

This will open up a **Create New Worker** dialog box which is already populated with the **Applicants** details.

© 2015 Blind Squirrel Publishing, LLC, All Rights Reserved
www.dynamicsaxcompanions.com

Hiring Applicants

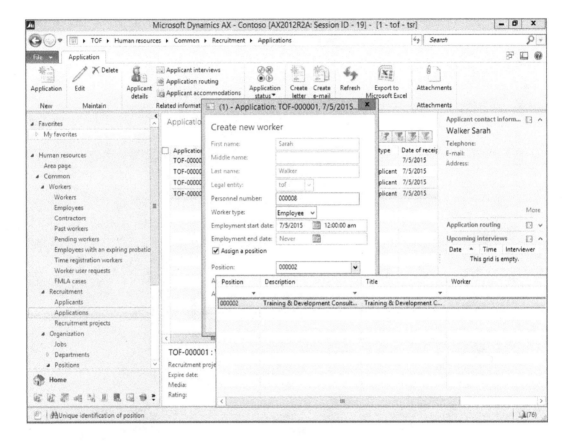

All you need to do is click on the **Position** dropdown list and select the open **Position** that you are assigning the **Applicant** to.

Note: Only the open **Positions** that match the **Job** that the **Recruitment Project** was created for will show up here.

© 2015 Blind Squirrel Publishing, LLC, All Rights Reserved
www.dynamicsaxcompanions.com

Hiring Applicants

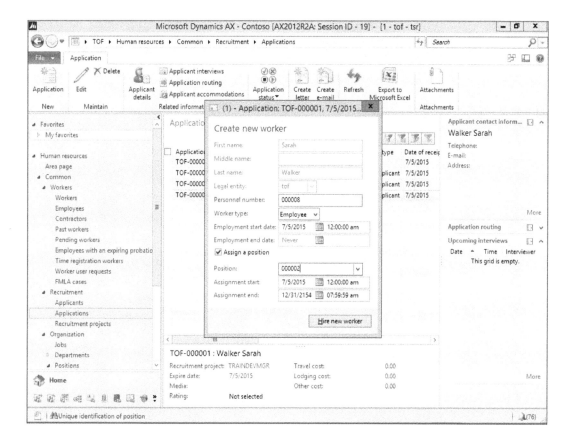

You can also set the **Assignment Start** date if you like and then click on the **Hire New Worker** button.

© 2015 Blind Squirrel Publishing, LLC, All Rights Reserved
www.dynamicsaxcompanions.com

Hiring Applicants

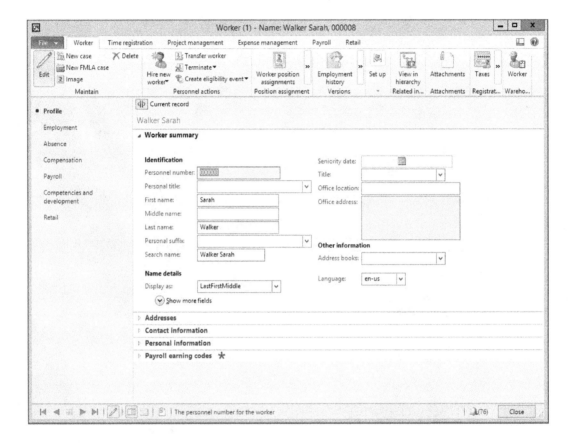

This will open up the new **Worker** details with all of the information from the **Applicant** record copied over.

If you want you can also click on the **View In Hierarchy** button in the **Related Information** group of the **Worker** ribbon bar.

© 2015 Blind Squirrel Publishing, LLC, All Rights Reserved
www.dynamicsaxcompanions.com

Hiring Applicants

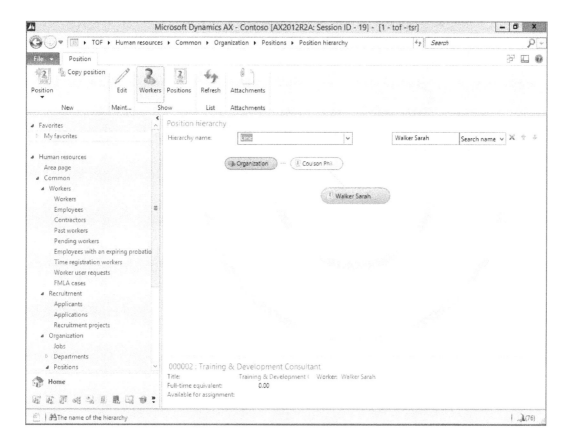

This will open up the **Worker** in the **Position Hierarchy** and you will also see the **Workers** direct superior.

© 2015 Blind Squirrel Publishing, LLC, All Rights Reserved
www.dynamicsaxcompanions.com

Hiring Applicants

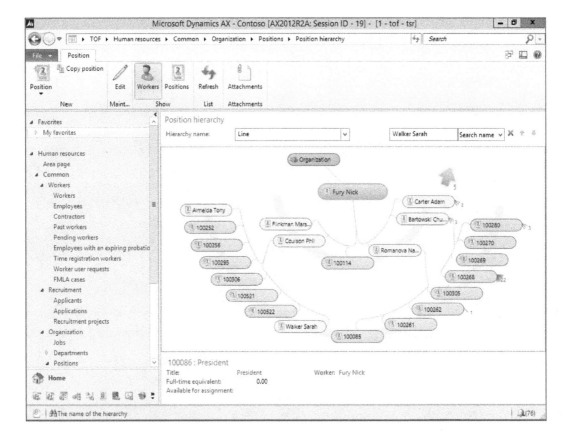

If you work your way up the **Position Hierarchy** then you will be able to see how the **Employee** fits in the business.

Now that wasn't too hard was it?

© 2015 Blind Squirrel Publishing, LLC, All Rights Reserved
www.dynamicsaxcompanions.com

© 2015 Blind Squirrel Publishing, LLC, All Rights Reserved
www.dynamicsaxcompanions.com

© 2015 Blind Squirrel Publishing, LLC, All Rights Reserved
www.dynamicsaxcompanions.com

SUMMARY

Hopefully this guide has given you a good foundation of knowledge of how the Human Resource Management area of Dynamics AX works, and also some of the key features that are available for you that allow you to configure and manage your **Workers**, **Employees**, **Jobs**, **Positions**, and the **Recruitment Projects**.

We are still just starting you off on your journey through the Human Resource Management module though. There is so much more that you can do including taking advantage of **Skill Tracking**, **Education & Certification Tracking**, **Training & Course Management** and much more. But unfortunately we have run out of space in this book so we will have to leave that for the next volume on **Human Resource Management**.

© 2015 Blind Squirrel Publishing, LLC, All Rights Reserved
www.dynamicsaxcompanions.com

© 2015 Blind Squirrel Publishing, LLC, All Rights Reserved
www.dynamicsaxcompanions.com

Want More Tips & Tricks For Dynamics AX?

The Tips & Tricks series is a compilation of all the cool things that I have found that you can do within Dynamics AX, and are also the basis for my Tips & Tricks presentations that I have been giving for the AXUG, and online. Unfortunately book page size restrictions mean that I can only fit 50 tips & tricks per book, but I will create new volumes every time I reach the 50 Tip mark.

To get all of the details on this series, then here is the link:

http://dynamicsaxcompanions.com/tipsandtricks

© 2015 Blind Squirrel Publishing, LLC, All Rights
www.dynamicsaxcompanions.com

© 2015 Blind Squirrel Publishing, LLC, All Rights
www.dynamicsaxcompanions.com

Need More Help With Dynamics AX?

LUKE SKYWALKER MAY HAVE HAD THE FORCE,
BUT HE STILL NEEDED R2D2 TO PLOT THE
COURSE FOR HIM.
WHO IS YOUR COMPANION THAT WILL HELP YOU
NAVIGATE DYNAMICS AX?

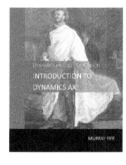

After creating a number of my walkthroughs on SlideShare showing how to configure the different areas within Dynamics AX, I had a lot of requests for the original documents so that people could get a better view of many of the screen shots and also have a easy reference as they worked through the same process within their own systems. To make them easier to access, I am in the process of moving all of the content to the Dynamics AX Companions website to easier access. If you are looking for details on how to configure and use Dynamics AX, then this is a great place for you to start.

Here is the link for the site:

http://dynamicsaxcompanions.com/

© 2015 Blind Squirrel Publishing, LLC, All Rights
www.dynamicsaxcompanions.com

© 2015 Blind Squirrel Publishing, LLC, All Rights
www.dynamicsaxcompanions.com

About Me

I am an author - I'm no Dan Brown but my books do contain a lot of secret codes and symbols that help guide you through the mysteries of Dynamics AX.

I am a curator - gathering all of the information that I can about Dynamics AX and filing it away within the Dynamics AX Companions archives.

I am a pitchman - I am forever extolling the virtues of Dynamics AX to the unwashed masses convincing them that it is the best ERP system in the world.

I am a Microsoft MVP - this is a big deal, there are less than 10 Dynamics AX MVP's in the US, and less than 30 worldwide.

I am a programmer - I know enough to get around within code, although I leave the hard stuff to the experts so save you all from my uncommented style.

WEB	www.murrayfife.me www.dynamicsaxcompanions.com www.blindsquirrelpublishing.com
EMAIL	murray@dynamicsaxcompanions.com
TWITTER	@murrayfife
SKYPE	murrayfife
AMAZON	www.amazon.com/author/murrayfife

© 2015 Blind Squirrel Publishing, LLC, All Rights
www.dynamicsaxcompanions.com

www.ingramcontent.com/pod-product-compliance
Lightning Source LLC
Chambersburg PA
CBHW080133060326
40689CB00018B/3774